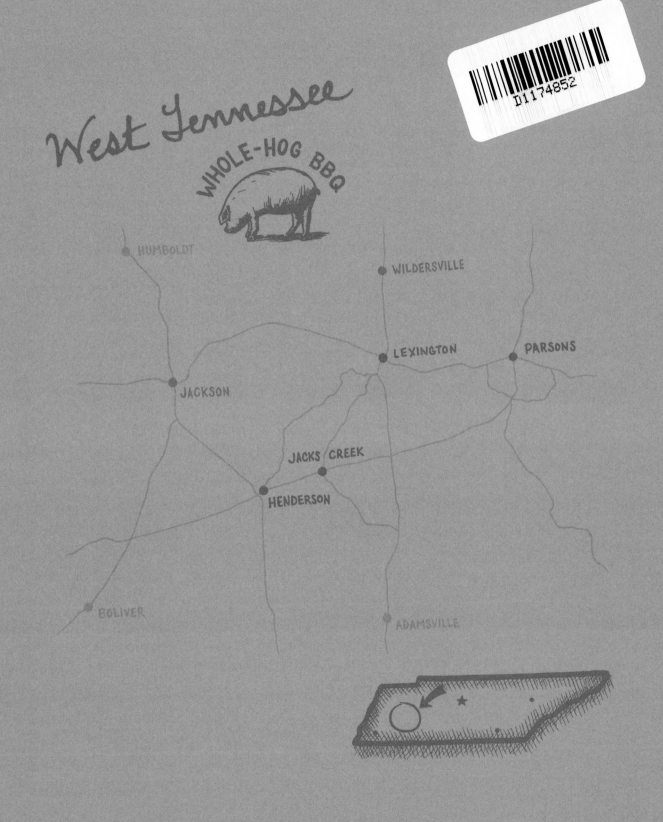

West Tennessee

WHOLE-HOG BBQ

HUMBOLDT

WILDERSVILLE

LEXINGTON   PARSONS

JACKSON

JACKS CREEK

HENDERSON

BOLIVER

ADAMSVILLE

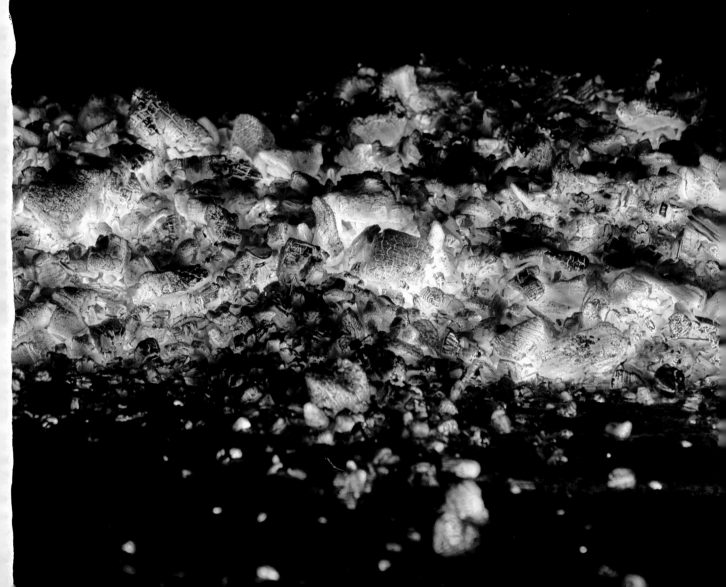

LIFE
OF FIRE

MASTERING THE ARTS OF PIT-COOKED
BARBECUE, THE GRILL, AND THE SMOKEHOUSE

LIFE
OF FIRE

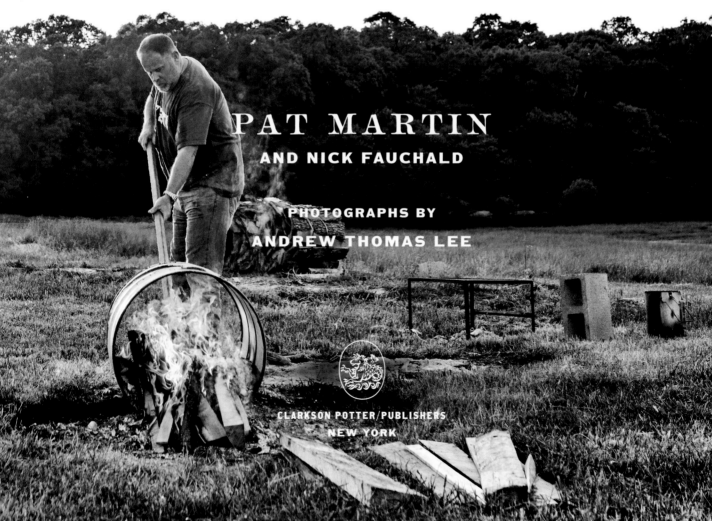

PAT MARTIN

AND NICK FAUCHALD

PHOTOGRAPHS BY

ANDREW THOMAS LEE

CLARKSON POTTER/PUBLISHERS
NEW YORK

FOR MARTHA, WYATT, DAISY, AND WALKER.
THANK YOU FOR ALL YOUR UNCONDITIONAL
LOVE AND SUPPORT.

INTRODUCTION

WHAT'S IN THIS BOOK

When I set out to write this book, I had two goals. First, I wanted to document West Tennessee whole-hog barbecue on paper. This had never been done before, so far as I know, and it needed to be done while this endangered species of regional barbecue style was still around. Second, I wanted to explore live-fire cooking at a level of detail I wish I'd been given in the barbecue and grilling books I read as I was learning how to cook. I'm no Julia Child, but her comprehensive, exhaustively detailed books taught a generation of home cooks how to make French food, and I wanted to do the same for live-fire cooking. Thankfully, I found an editor and publisher who agreed with me, and I'm thrilled to use these pages to teach you everything I know.

Understanding barbecue and other kinds of live-fire cooking—grilling, charring, ash-roasting, and cold-smoking—is mostly about mastering fire. We usually think of "fire" as a pile of wood set ablaze, but that's only one stage of a fire's lifespan, and this most primal source of heat has so much to offer beyond its hottest phase. So I've organized this book to follow each step in the life of a fire, and how to cook with it.

We begin with the basics of building a fire for cooking. Chapter 1 covers selecting and sourcing wood for live-fire cooking and how to build and maintain a "feeder fire" that will produce the fuel you need for various styles of grilling and barbecue.

Chapter 2 will teach you how to take the young coals produced by a fire and use them for high-heat grilling and charring. Most of the recipes in this chapter are vegetable-based, dishes that go great with barbecue or can stand on their own when you're not eating meat. I'll also show you how to use two grill-top tools—a grill basket and a cast-iron skillet—to cook fish and smaller ingredients.

Once the coals have cooled down a bit, they're ready to be used for open-pit barbecue. Chapter 3 will cover this technique and how to use it to smoke ribs, chicken, rabbit, and smaller whole pigs, as well as how to build a spit for cooking various cuts of pork.

While whole-hog barbecue is at the core of my story, I don't recommend jumping straight to pit-cooking a hog (Chapter 4) if you're new to barbecue. Whole-hog barbecue is a grueling (but immensely rewarding) marathon and requires a solid understanding of how to manage fire. But once you're ready, I'll take you through the entire process, guiding you every step of the way—including how to build a cinder block pit. (Don't worry, it's not as hard as it sounds: You can put one together in twenty minutes.) I'll also walk you through smaller cuts of pork that you can cook in a cinder block pit, as well as how to cook a hog in the most primitive way—in the ground.

Even once a fire has died down to ashes and embers, it still has lots to offer. Chapter 5 will teach you how to use the tail end of a fire to cook ash-roasted vegetables and various types of aluminum foil-pouch dishes.

One of fire's by-products, smoke, is in itself a tool for preserving and flavoring meat. Chapter 6 brings us to the smokehouse, where I cure and cold smoke everything from hog jowls to duck breasts, as well as my favorite DIY charcuterie, sock sausage. And if you like cured ham, I've included the ultimate guide to making Southern-style country ham, which, in my opinion, rivals the best hams that come out of Italy and Spain.

We end our live-fire journey on a sweet note, with a section that doesn't involve fire at all. Chapter 7 is a collection of my family's greatest dessert hits, with recipes from my mother, Pam, and my grandmothers. And I'll leave you with one last Martin family secret: how to make our old-fashioned, hand-cranked ice cream.

MY STORY

This book is a guide, pretty much everything I know, about the craft of barbecue and cooking with fire. Now, with barbecue, people are beyond opinionated. Folks love to talk about regional styles—the differences in vinegar versus tomato versus mustard based-sauces, the cuts and types of meat used in this corner of the world versus that one. The style I'm most connected to is the old, and dwindling, greatly overlooked but beautiful art of West Tennessee whole hog. I love cooking—and showing people how to cook—ribs, chicken, shoulders, hams, vegetables, sides, and more, but the art of pit cooking whole hog is not just the summit for me; it's my roots.

But I didn't learn all this from being born into some barbecue family, the stereotypical story of a boy knee-high to his daddy and following him around a pit house all of his life only to take the reins one day. Instead, I learned to cook barbecue through a few twists of fate, some epiphanies, a pitmaster mentor, a lot of experimentation and even more stubbornness, and more hours than I can count of staring at, listening to, smelling, feeling, and handling fire. This path started for me in high school, thirty-five years ago, and I'm still on it. And in my world, whether you want to go all-out and cook a whole hog (and I hope you do one day), or just grill up some supper, it's all about learning how to work with fire. I feel like it's my responsibility to share what I've learned about how to cook all through the life cycle of a fire—from what to char over a fresh, young fire; to open pit cooking with the powerful but controlled heat of a more mature fire; all the way to cold-smoking hams, bacon, and sausage with the fading embers of the winter fire. And in there, in the middle of that life of fire, is what I do with all my heart: barbecue.

My story begins as most do, with my family and its roots. You can't know me without knowing that backstory. Both sides of my family are from the same small town in northeast Mississippi: Corinth, sixty-five miles east of Memphis, Tennessee. I was born in Memphis, at the old Baptist hospital—the one Elvis was pronounced dead in.

My mom grew up in town. Her dad, my Pa-King, was a grocery rep for all of the little country stores in and around northeast Mississippi, and her mom, my Mi-Mi, worked for the railroad in Corinth. My dad had grown up dirt poor on a farm in Corinth, in a typical farming family growing or raising most of the food

my grandmother cooked. His dad, my Paw-Paw, was a small farmer his whole life and his mom, my Maw-Maw, worked as a bank teller at the old Bank of Mississippi. Dad attended Mississippi State on a basketball scholarship, majored in economics and business finance, and eventually moved us up north, becoming a legendary trader on The Street, which is what they all called Wall Street. He was literally the poor country boy who made it in the big city.

Early on, our move to Connecticut was great. There was a seemingly endless supply of woods and waters to swim in, with no cottonmouths to have to check the pond banks for before you jumped in like we'd have to do in Mississippi. Our church was a mainstay for our family, and most of the folks who went to church with us were also from the South, so it was both a place of worship and a cultural center. A lot of Sundays, Mom and several other women would preside over a table of fried chicken, cornbread, purple hull peas, creamed corn, and so on and so forth.

But as I started getting on up in school, life changed. Because of my ADHD, I was always making bad grades. And I started getting in trouble, a lot of trouble, and got suspended from—or kicked out of—one school after another. I remember, around fourth grade, being made fun of by some boys who were pretty big bastards for grade school. They came at me with all of the typical clichés about folks from the South: Can your parents read and write? Is there even running water in Mississippi or do you use outhouses? I'd get mad and fight back, end up getting roughed up, only to do it all again a few days later.

But then one day in fifth grade, something happened that left an impression far longer than an ass whipping from some overgrown kid on the bus. My teacher, Mrs. Pateraki, announced that we would have "Where Are You From?" days, where the kids in the class took turns sharing food, music, and culture from their families' heritage; we had Italian food, Puerto Rican food, Irish food, and so on. When it was my turn to present my family's story, I was pretty excited!

Mom got up early that morning and made a bunch of fried chicken tenders and biscuits for the class. I brought my tape recorder and a cassette of the Southern comedian Jerry Clower's greatest hits. I remember having my presentation ready. I was going to talk about my grandfather as a farmer, the battles of Shiloh and Corinth, William Faulkner and Hal Phillips . . . .

As my classmates were eating their chicken and biscuits and awkwardly laughing to Jerry's jokes, my teacher walked up visibly annoyed, hit the stop button on the tape player, and asked me, loud enough for the entire class to hear:

"Patrick, this is nice and all, your family's from Mississippi . . . but where are they really from?"

"From Mississippi," I answered, not really understanding her question at all.

"But what about before that?"

"I don't know what you mean. . . . There is no 'before that.'"

"Before your family came to America."

I didn't know how to answer that! I had never thought of that in my life, ever. I didn't know how to process what she was asking me. It confused me, but what it really did was embarrass the piss out of me. She basically communicated to me and the class that our family story and its roots didn't matter because I couldn't pinpoint some Celtic settlement over in Ireland or somewhere that is the origin of the Martin name. The class was silent and staring at me. It was a terrible feeling, and I can feel it now as I type this. I wanted to run out of the room. So she impatiently thanked me and asked me to sit down, not even allowing me to share the rest of my presentation except for Mom's fried chicken. Trying not to cry, I just sat there at my desk while the next kid was called up. I was so proud and excited to share of my roots, and instead was made to feel embarrassed. I was so hurt, and pissed.

Shortly after school would let out for the summer, my parents would send me down to Corinth to be with my grandparents for a while. When I would get there, they'd meet me at the gate at Memphis airport and we'd usually grab a barbecue sandwich before driving the sixty-five miles back to Corinth. Things would immediately start to feel normal. My Maw-Maw would get up in the morning, make us breakfast (always with fresh biscuits from scratch), and go to work at the bank. My Paw-Paw would be somewhere out across the highway 72 in the rows of soybeans, milo, or whatever. Families in that area don't leave, generations stay on or around—much like old villages in Europe my teacher wanted me to identify with. I started to become friends with a lot of kids there; almost all of these kids' parents went to school with my dad, or my aunt and uncles, and our friendships were very easy and fluid.

On weekends, our whole family would get together—uncles, aunts, cousins, the whole lot. On Saturdays, the

PHOTO COURTESY OF RANDI ANGLIN

men would fire up the grill. I was right there, watching in awe of them. Everything they did was with intent, and a lot of times the "hard way." They changed their own oil a certain way, shined their shoes a certain way, shaved a certain way, started fires a certain way. I'll never forget the first time Dad asked me to fill up the chimney starter with charcoal, stuff the bottom with newspaper, and light the grill. It was a big deal for me, like he invited me into the world of being a dadgum man.

We only really used the grill for burgers or steaks. That was fine by me, since I didn't know anything different and really, it was more about the feeling of being around the fire and family that mattered to me. When I was fourteen or fifteen, I saw a book in the book store called *Thrill of the Grill* by Chris Schlesinger and John Willoughby. I bought it, and it became my culinary bible for years. It was the first time my mind was open to cooking anything over fire, not just the red meat usual suspects. One part, in particular, grabbed me: a story that Chris wrote about cooking a whole hog with his dad when he was young. I thought that was cool and wanted to do that one day. Little did I know that an entire culture of whole-hog barbecue was just

forty-five minutes up the road from Corinth. And little did I know it would find me in just a few short years.

Fast forward a year later and we'd moved back from Connecticut for good because my Paw-Paw had a stroke and suddenly passed away, and Dad felt the need to get us back closer to home. After graduating high school, I moved forty miles north to Henderson, Tennessee, to attend Freed-Hardeman, a small private Christian university. I didn't get much of an academic education there—in fact, I failed out my first semester, but they gave me another shot—and because the school was so strict and conservative, I didn't have much of a traditional college type social life, either.

But I did find a subject I'd develop a passion for. The week I arrived at college, I searched around for the local barbecue joints. One of the first I came across was Thomas & Webb Barbecue. It was a small place, five or six tables. I walked up to the window and ordered a pork sandwich from Harold Thomas, a somewhat older man who was standing there smiling at me. He took just one step, leaning over to his right. He opened the cardboard lid of this huge box, and inside was a whole hog. My eyes were the size of a cast iron skillet when I

saw it. Mr. Harold pulled some meat from its shoulder, dropped it on a bun, and topped it with a scoop of coleslaw and asked me if I wanted it hot or mild. My whole world was blown apart. I remember thinking, *this guy cooked a whole frickin' hog and the son of a bitch is laying there in a box right in front of me.*

I ate it slow and easy, like it was my last meal and I was about to go on the electric chair. The smoke was there but not strong. The meat had a silkiness to it and was topped with a somewhat sweet vinegar sauce—not the thick, red-brownish sauce like I'd eaten my whole life in and around Memphis. That sandwich was unreal, and to this day it's still the best barbecue sandwich I've ever put in my mouth. As I was finishing my second one, I knew I had to learn how to do that, to cook a whole hog like that.

At the time, Henderson, a town of only a few thousand people, had six or seven barbecue joints, and all of them served whole-hog barbecue. That's literally all they served—no pork shoulders, no ribs, no chicken—just sandwiches and plates of soft, slightly smoky pork pulled from a pit-smoked hog. I had no idea that there was really any style of barbecue that

wasn't what I was accustomed to in Memphis, where heavily smoky ribs and shoulders rule . . . yet here in West Tennessee, there was this rich barbecue culture that was so different! And here I was, living in the middle of it. (Little did I know that it would only take two decades for this style to almost become extinct. As I sit here and type this, there are now only three of us in the state still doing it.)

I started eating at, or going by to hang out at, Thomas & Webb literally four or five times a week. Mr. Harold was a very gentle, kind man, and very generous with his time. He was humble and always had a smile. He loved playing the market, and would always ask me for stock tips (as if I had any to give) while I picked his brain about barbecue. I spent as much time there my freshman year as I did in class, and I would sneak out of my dorm at night—we had an 11 p.m. curfew, it being a strict school and all—and just go down to Mr. Harold's pit house to see what was going on.

By the beginning of my sophomore year in 1991, I was determined to cook my first whole hog and had a perfect opportunity to do so. Dad threw a fish fry every Columbus Day weekend, so I decided that would be my first attempt. Leading up to the cook, I started working on recipes for rubs, sauces, slaw, and baked beans in my dorm room—most of which are still the recipes I use today at Martin's Bar-B-Que Joint. Mr. Harold sourced my hog for me and told me how to build a pit. I remember vividly feeling him hit me on the right leg with his fingers to show me how high the grate should be positioned—on my upper thigh just below my hip. Then he walked me through the whole process.

I pulled my crew together. Brian Chandler was gonna stay up all night, John McCall was getting there the next morning, Shannon Sewell suggested we could "borrow" some masonry bricks from the building site for the new gymnasium on campus, and a few more buddies volunteered. I grabbed a big "road closed" sign from a bridge that was washed out, which we'd use as a giant spatula for flipping the hog midway through the cook and got some old tin roofing from a barn as a cover for the pit. (Don't worry, you won't need to steal any road signs when you do your hog.)

During the cook, I made my barbecue sauce in a cast iron pot, and set it inside the pit, where it slowly simmered for twenty-four hours, and we drank enough Busch ponies to float a battleship. We had a night of it! The next thing you know, we're done, and the hog was *good.* About mid-afternoon, the whole community

showed up. All the men were crowded around the fish fryers. The Hatchie Bottom Boys were playing bluegrass while some, especially my Aunt B, were out there buck-dancing to the tunes. Local and state politicians were there. Our cousin Theodore Smith, a longtime elected Democrat to the Mississippi state senate, was always there holding court, debating, or stumping for Bill Clinton over George Bush Senior. Everyone loved my hog, and I was so proud. Hooked, really; the moment tattooed barbecue on me emotionally. I couldn't wait to do it again.

But then, sometime later, Freed-Hardeman kicked me out of school for drinking beer. (The old school Church of Christ folks frowned upon partaking of alcohol. But going to a buffet after church and smashing five thousand calories of food was just fine because we're just not going to talk about gluttony—as if God didn't really mean that one!)

Anyway, instead of moving back in with my parents, my dad told me to pack a bag and to be ready to leave at 6 a.m. the next morning. All he said was to "be ready to go." Well, long story short, that morning he sent me down a path where I found an obsession with the pit . . . not the barbecue pit, but the trading pits in the pre-internet days of the stock market. I transferred to Lipscomb University in Nashville to finish up school and begin my career, leading to a stretch where I was making dang good money, but eventually found myself increasingly unhappy, unfulfilled at work, in a doomed marriage, drinking way too much, and with my faith in disarray. And when that career ended, it ended with me taking the Johnny Paychecks song "Take This Job and Shove It" to a whole new extreme. It was a spectacle. But depression was clouding all of my judgment back then.

I spent a few years in landscape construction, enjoying the fact that I was working for myself, but all the while, that marriage ended, things started spiraling, and I found myself living by myself in my house alone. Yet as dark as things were, and they were really dark, the light started to appear a little.

The bright side of fifteen-hour days of hard labor was that I had a few guys working for me, like Marteen García Pimentel, who were like family. I was coming home physically beat, but at least I remembered what it felt like to be proud of our crew and the work we were doing.

And the light really started to come because I had time to reflect . . . and time to cook again. My old buddy

Bryan, who was there with me on my very first whole hog cook in college, moved in with me, which made the house not so quiet. We'd light up a fire to cook something every weekend, and I picked up *The Thrill of the Grill* again. As I began to cook through that book as an adult, it made me realize I didn't really know anything about cooking at all, even a bare minimum of what my mom or my grandmothers knew. My curiosity started to overflow. I wanted to know *how* to cook, to heal and better my life.

I found Julia Child's *Mastering the Art of French Cooking*. I started at the beginning, almost nightly trying to learn the basic fundamentals of cooking—knife skills, making stocks. It was new, it was hard, but it was fun.

By this time, I was in a relationship with Martha, an old friend from college. She too had recently been divorced and was healing that part of her life up as well. She would come over on Saturday mornings, and we'd spend the day doing little things, odds and ends around my house or in the garden. She was my life preserver.

She taught me to think of time at home as something special, and she taught me to find a rhythm where we could find happiness again. She also encouraged me to keep cooking, telling me to get a job at a restaurant or go to culinary school. I was in my thirties and felt I was too old to change my career. But she wouldn't hear any of that. The fact is that Martha recognized my passion; over time, she started telling me "You love to cook, you love barbecue, you need to open a place." That sounded like so much fun, but I had zero restaurant experience and no money and all the reasons to say no.

And then one Monday morning in early April 2006, as my crew and I headed out on a job, one of my guys forgot to secure our equipment trailer to the truck. We made it about a mile up the highway when I felt a bump and looked in the rearview mirror just in time to watch the trailer roll up an embankment and flip over, crushing my mowers.

By late morning, the insurance adjuster gave me a check for $17,000. It was just getting to be time for lunch, and I decided to drive over to a little restaurant in Nolensville. A guy walked up from the shop and introduced himself as Vern. I asked him if he knew why the restaurant was closed.

"Because they owe me three months' rent," he said.

"What are you going to do with the space?" I asked.

He replied, "I guess we'll find another restaurant."

"I'll take it," I blurted out, before I ever really thought about what I was saying.

We talked details for a few minutes, and agreed on $1,500 a month in rent. I'll never forget how scary that sum

sounded to me, but we shook on it. As I was driving away in the truck, I immediately called Martha at work. "Whatever happens, everything is going to be okay," she said.

I met with a banker who gave me a small line of credit with my house as collateral. I left the bank and went to Home Depot, bought one of those orange *Home Improvement 1-2-3* books, and got to work building a restaurant with some generous friends who didn't mind getting paid in the form of Coors Light.

One night that summer, I went to hear my buddy Ward Boone play. After his set, he asked me how the restaurant was coming along, and I began telling him I needed a cook to help me man the kitchen. Ward pointed to the stage, and said, "The drummer up there is Bo Collier, he's a cook, and I think he just left his job today." I had a few beers in me at that point, so I stood up between songs and hollered, "BO COLLIER!" He stood up and looked out at the audience but couldn't see me because of the stage lights. "You're my new cook!" I yelled. Bo said, "Great, I just got a job." Then he sat down and counted the band into their next song, *one-two, one-two-three-four. . . .*

And like that, I had my first employee. Bo was and still is a walking enigma: Highly intelligent, an Eagle Scout, a redneck, and a practicing Rastafarian. Yes, you read that right, go ahead and marinate on that for a bit. It also turned out that Bo was a highly organized kitchen leader and an invaluable wingman.

As we neared opening, Bo I and wrote up our menu, which started with a deflating curveball. Despite my passion for old-style pit-cooked barbecue, it turned out that the building I'd rented couldn't be permitted for a real pit. So, in a smoker, we'd cook pork shoulders and Boston Butts because I could load them at the same time and they would come off exactly when I needed them to (the butts would be ready by lunch the next day, and shoulders by dinner the evening). I cooked these using the same dry rub and vinegar sauce I'd developed back in my college dorm room. My mom agreed to bake us a few cakes every weekend, and I figured having the best coconut cake in the world wouldn't hurt.

I had everything on the line and so kept adding to the menu. We committed to doing burgers, as well as some of the typical things such as chicken tenders. I also knee-jerked on sauce: Sweet, thick, tomato-based barbecue sauce has no roots in West Tennessee barbecue, but I knew folks would be asking for it, so I created one to avoid giving customers any reason *not* to return. And of course, it bothered me that we couldn't cook whole

hogs, but there was that pit problem. Plus, a whole hog serves around two hundred people—far more than we needed at our little joint, and I refused to serve day-old barbecue. Still, early compromises and all, we were on our way.

We opened Martin's at 11 a.m. on Monday, October 16, 2006. It was a cold, rainy, miserable day, and let's just say if you came in that evening, you would have seen my mom and Martha doing damage control in the dining room, apologizing to customers and handing them handwritten IOUs; my dad stooped over the sink washing dishes; and me trying to calm Bo down, who was losing his mind over not even knowing how many tickets behind we were.

And . . . I knew right then that I had found my new path. I was in love with the restaurant business and didn't know jack about it yet. The barely controlled chaos of that night was medicine for me after the years of pain and wandering, and I smiled from ear to ear. Soon, my crew grew: my old friend Marteen, who'd moved back to Mexico after the trailer accident, came back and we reunited. Roberto, Cho-Cho, Ward—who'd introduced me to Bo—joined us too and pretty soon, we had enough folks coming to eat with us in the summer months that I was able to rent a mobile cooker and start cooking whole hogs again on the weekend from time to time.

Four years later, by 2010, I had outgrown my little twelve-table spot. It was a blessing for the business to be doing well, but first and foremost, it allowed me to move across the street. . . which meant I could build a pit just outside the restaurant. I put it in front of a big garage door that opened into the dining room, so guests could see (and smell) their dinner slowly smoking away. That pit allowed me to turn my little barbecue joint into what I really wanted it to be: an homage to the barbecue that changed my life and to the old ways and heritage of West Tennessee whole hog.

We'd make a big deal of walking the hogs right through the dining room, and I sprayed the winch that lowered the pit cover with saltwater so it'd rust and creak every time we opened it. (A little showmanship never hurts.) It was like a bullhorn: Guests would come running up to watch the action, and line up to take pictures. People had the same jaw-dropped face as I did that day way back in September 1990, when I walked into Thomas & Webb BBQ and saw Mr. Harold reach over and take the lid off of that hog. West Tennessee whole hog barbecue was back, and I had been blessed enough to be the conduit in which it got here.

When I was an eighteen-year-old freshman, there were dozens of whole-hog joints all over the region. By the time I opened my first Martin's, our style of barbecue had almost become extinct. The economics of barbecue just made it harder and harder for folks to want to keep doing it. With all the fanfare barbecue has gotten over the past fifteen years, it's still regarded as the "peasant food" of the South. Because of that stupid mindset it's expected to be priced cheaply, which doesn't mix well with the hours it takes to cook it. An entire generation of old-school pitmasters passed away over the years without handing down their knowledge. Many of those who cooked whole hogs eventually gave in to the convenience and higher profit margins of Boston butts, and devasting pit fires destroyed the businesses of others. All that was left was a handful of folks who believed in the romance of cooking a whole hog, slowly and patiently, over a bed of coals.

I was lucky enough to have learned the art of West Tennessee whole hog, and stubborn enough that I wouldn't let it disappear on my watch. I also started to realize that barbecue was truly instrumental in helping me heal my life, to accept who I was regardless of the troubles I'd been through and the pain that I had caused. I learned to see that gray period of my life as a blessing in itself and, most of all, I realized that my roots and my ground are in Tennessee. I was born here, I've lived here for most of my life, and I found my path here, so I will do my best to honor this place and its barbecue forever.

CHAPTER 1

BIR

RTH

BUILDING A FIRE

FOR ME, FIRE IS THE HEART OF COOKING.
Which means that having the right kind of wood—and enough of it—is vital. Also essential is knowing how to turn that wood into a steady supply of coals, as is learning how to read and understand those coals while they burn, whether it's a short, hot fire for a quick grilling session, or if you're cooking low and slow for hours or days. This chapter will teach you what you need to know to get your fire going, and how to manage it while you're cooking.

SELECTING AND SOURCING WOOD

VARIETIES

The first thing to consider is the type of wood you're using. A lot of pitmasters have very strong preferences on their wood. I'm strict about certain guidelines but don't feel like there is one true wood to use. So here are the basics: When we're talking about barbecue as we know it in America, we use hardwood varieties (hickory, oak, maple, apple, etc.), which burn long and hot. Softwood comes from conifers (pine, cedar, spruce, etc.), and while I've got some chef buddies who burn softwoods to accent or finish their dishes, we use hardwood for most live-fire cooking, and save our pine for framing houses and building duck blinds.

The best wood for barbecue is usually the hardwood that grows closest to you. As with food, what grows together, goes together. In Tennessee—and other areas in the mid-South and upper Midwest—that's usually hickory. There are about a dozen varieties of hickory that grow in North America, and I haven't found one I don't like. (The old-timers in my area prefer pignut hickory, but I can't taste a difference between that and the other hickories I use.) Hickory smoke does impart a unique flavor profile, one that changes as the wood ages from freshly cut "green" wood to dried, or "seasoned," wood (more on this in a minute). Green hickory has a powerful aroma, while seasoned hickory is softer and sweeter on the nose with a very subtle flavor that sits in the background of whatever you're eating. That's especially nice with West Tennessee barbecue. It complements the flavor of the pork, instead of competing with it.

THE BEST WOOD FOR BARBECUE IS USUALLY THE HARDWOOD THAT GROWS CLOSEST TO YOU.

If I can't find hickory, my second-favorite variety is oak, which you can get pretty much anywhere. Oak also has a soft flavor; it doesn't have the nuanced sweetness of hickory, but it's not gonna do you wrong. For lack of a better term, I describe oak as "neutrally smoky." And in the rare case that I can't find oak, I'll look for apple or peach. Cherry trees and nut woods, like pecan, are good as well, but the smoke they produce will make your meat a little darker (which doesn't bother me because it's still gonna taste great).

Which brings me to a couple of important points when you're considering wood for any style of barbecue. First, the larger the piece of meat you're cooking, the less smoke you're going to taste in the final product. Think about it: The smaller the meat, the more relative surface area it has outside to absorb the smoke flavor, and vice versa. That means you'll taste a good amount of smoke in smaller cuts like ribs, and a bit less in shoulders and hams. With whole-hog barbecue, the flavor of the smoke is even more subtle.

Most important, I want you to understand the difference between barbecue cooked in a smoker and barbecue cooked in a pit, and how they interact with your wood and your smoke. With most styles of smokers, the fire is burning next to (or directly below) the chamber holding the meat, and as you feed fresh wood into the fire, the meat absorbs all of the flavors (good and bad) that the fresh wood produces. I've met a lot of people who say they don't like the flavor of hickory-smoked barbecue. Usually this is because they've tasted barbecue from a smoker that was fueled with unseasoned hickory. In this case, I can't blame 'em: The smoke from unseasoned hickory imparts a bitter, acrid flavor when used to cook in a smoker.

But when cooking in an open or closed pit, you make a "feeder fire" off to the side where you burn the wood down to coals, then you move those coals to your pit for the actual cooking. By the time the "mature" coals are ready for the pit, a lot of smoke has been burned out of the wood, along with the excess water and impurities that can make hickory smoke taste off-putting. The result is smoke that produces a softer, more subtle flavor that's distinctive to pit barbecue. Since most of my cooking is done in a pit, I don't get too crazy about the variety of wood I use—the differences are really pretty subtle with this method.

SEASONED WOOD VS GREEN WOOD

The best firewood for barbecue and grilling has been seasoned, which means that after being cut it's dried for at least three months (preferably six) and stored in a well-ventilated area, covered to protect it from the elements. Seasoned wood will look grayish, and the ends of the logs will have started to split a little. A log of seasoned wood is noticeably lighter in weight than one from a freshly cut tree, as it contains less moisture. As it's burning, seasoned wood drops big, pretty coals, ranging from the size of a Ping-Pong ball (the perfect size for pit barbecue and grilling) to coals about the size of your fist. The smoke from seasoned wood also tastes better, as the aging process mellows out some of the harsher flavors, and it produces a really pleasant, almost sweet-tasting smoke.

You might be able to find some seasoned firewood in your area. Call a local firewood company a few months before you plan on cooking and tell them you need some properly seasoned wood in time for your cook. They might tell you that their wood is seasoned, but you should check—often it's just been sitting for a month, which is why I recommend calling ahead by a few months.

If you can't find seasoned wood, with some patience and planning, you can season green wood at home. Start by splitting each log lengthwise to help it dry more quickly. Then stack the split logs in a shed or in the yard with the top third of the pile covered with a tarp (be sure to keep the rest of the stack exposed to air, so it can dry out). It should take three to six months to season, depending on how humid or dry your part of the country is (it's humid here in the South, so it takes a bit for us).

It's possible to have wood that's *too* dry—like logs that have probably been sitting in someone's yard for years and don't have a drop of moisture left in them. You'll know it when you see it: The wood will be shockingly lightweight when you pick it up. You can certainly use this stuff for barbecue, but it burns very quickly and shatters into tiny pebbles of coal as it does, as well as releases loads of ash. This means you'll need quite a bit of extra wood—double the amount, to be safe—and you'll work harder to maintain your feeder fire. It'll work, but in short, I'd avoid super-dry wood.

If you don't have the time or space to season wood, more often than not, you're going to find yourself cooking with green wood. Most wood-supply outfits specialize in firewood, and most firewood is green. It's tough to find a wood company that has the space to lay out and season a bunch of cut wood; they're more likely to try and move their product as quickly as possible.

The drawbacks to using green wood are that it takes longer to burn down to coals, because there's so much moisture inside, and it produces a lot of ash. Now, ash is a great insulator for a coal bed because it's light and airy enough to allow coals to burn but dense enough to still hold and conduct heat throughout the bed. However, if you build up too much ash, it will start to weigh down on itself and choke out your coals—this is why you should always clean out your burn barrel or other feeder fire between cooks. This also means that you're going to burn through more green wood to produce enough coals for your cook. It's not as big of a deal when you're using a smaller amount of wood for grilling, or smoking ribs or chickens, because your cook time will only be a few hours at most. But when you get into larger cuts such as shoulders—and whole pigs or hogs—you'll notice it, along with the extra cost of buying more wood. What's more, not all green wood is created equal. Some logs are slap-full of water, while others arrive half seasoned. The best way to gauge the water content of green wood is to pick up a few logs of the same size: The heavier ones contain more water, and you'll know to select drier wood for the fire if you need coals sooner rather than later, or vice versa.

The reality for my restaurants is that I can't source enough seasoned wood for the quantity of barbecue we produce, so we mostly use green wood and just deal with all of the dadgum ash. But I supplement my wood with an insurance policy: lump hardwood charcoal. If we're using a lot of green wood in our feeder fire and falling behind on coal production for our pits, we'll dump half a bag of lump charcoal directly into the feeder fire. This is especially important on the front end of a long cook, when you'll make the biggest dent in your wood pile. At my restaurants, we'll often refresh our fire with a bag of lump coals first thing in the morning after the fire has burned, unattended, through the night. This way, the cook continues with new coals while we get caught up with our feeder fire. If all you can find is green wood, and you're doing a long cook, that's a way to get around it.

SOURCING WOOD

I know I mentioned firewood suppliers before, but my personal go-to sources of wood for barbecue are the sawmills in my area, which process logs into slats used to manufacture shovel handles and similar products. The by-products of cutting logs into handles are slats about 3 inches thick (sometimes larger) and 42 inches long. These long "blanks" make it easy to keep your feeder fire burning at a steady pace, as their relative thinness means they burn pretty quickly, at a consistent pace, and you can push the blanks farther into the fire as they burn down.

My favorite wood for barbecue, though less easily sourced, are the 2 × 2 × 18-inch hickory blanks that come from local drumstick mills. (This is Nashville, after all.) Hickory is the favorite wood of drummers because of its density. Drumstick blanks will quickly burn down into coals, so you don't have to run through a lot of fuel to maintain your coal bed, which eliminates the waste of burning down larger pieces. The manufacturing process produces enough rejected blanks that I can usually buy enough for an entire 24-hour whole-hog cook.

You probably don't have a drumstick manufacturer in your area, but if you look around you'll probably find a local mill that uses hickory or other hardwoods, and their rejects will be an excellent (and cheap) source of wood.

Can't find a mill? You should have no problem sourcing firewood, even if you live in a city. A quick Internet or Craigslist search will direct you to local wood suppliers who'll deliver it to you and, in most cases, stack it for you as well. What you should NOT do is roll down to Home Depot or Lowe's and buy construction lumber for your cook. Most generic lumber is made from softwoods, like pine, that are unfit for barbecue. And most hardwood lumber has been chemically treated with a preservative that's unsafe for you when burned. Don't use it.

QUANTITY

The most common—and avoidable—mistake I see committed by folks new to barbecue is they don't buy enough wood to get them through a whole cook—especially with whole hogs, shoulders, and other longer cooks. When you've got a feeder fire going and are sitting around all day looking at it, it's hard to resist throwing wood into that fire. So more than likely, you're going to be producing coals faster than you can use them, which wastes a lot of your stack. That's a better problem to have than running out of coals, of course, but it still means you might be going through your wood too quickly. You want to err on the side of having too much fuel for your fire. This is another reason why the slats used to make drumsticks and shovel handles are so great. They burn quickly, so you can keep a good bed of coals going without wasting a lot of the wood. No matter what type of barbecue or grilling I'm doing, I try to always have 3 to 4 shovelfuls of coals ready to go in my feeder fire.

For a whole hog, I advise buying a full cord of wood, which is a stack measuring 4 × 4 × 8 feet, or 128 cubic feet. The standard length of firewood logs is 16 inches long. Even if the wood is green or super dry, that will get you through a whole cook. Just make sure you're ordering a "full cord" and not a "face cord," which is about one-third as much. If you're buying slats from a sawmill, they'll usually come in 4-foot bundles—two of these bundles will get you where you need to go. If they're not bundled, a pickup truck bed filled to the brim is about the same amount.

NO MATTER WHAT
TYPE OF BARBECUE OR
GRILLING I'M DOING, I TRY
TO ALWAYS HAVE 3 TO 4
SHOVELFULS OF COALS
READY TO GO IN MY
FEEDER FIRE.

THE FIRE

What we'll focus on in this section is building feeder fires for pit barbecue, or for longer grilling or open-pit barbecue.

CHIMNEY STARTERS

Whether I'm starting a fire for grilling or a feeder fire for pit barbecue, I always like to start by using charcoal. If you use a charcoal grill, you probably own a chimney starter. If not, go buy yourself one, and don't cheap out: A good chimney starter (like the ones Weber makes) has ventilation holes around the perimeter to increase airflow and help the coals ignite more quickly, while cheap starters are solid metal all the way around, and you'll find that the coals on the bottom half of the chimney are worthless lumps of ash by the time the coals on top are ready. (If you've already got one of these crappy chimney starters, take a Phillips-head screwdriver and bust about 15 or so holes in two or three evenly spaced rows around the perimeter, to give the coals better airflow.)

A chimney or two of coals is probably enough for you to cook a quick dinner, and is pretty self-explanatory—you get the coals burning in the starter, then dump them in your grill.

FEEDER FIRES FOR PIT BARBECUE

A feeder fire is the lifeblood of pit-cooked barbecue, which is the focus of this book. (If you have a big offset or pellet smoker and are comfortable using it, great! That's not how I make barbecue, though any of my barbecue recipes, minus the whole hog, can be cooked in your smoker of choice.) A feeder fire is basically a factory for the hot coals you'll be shoveling into the pit throughout the cook. Since you'll be shoveling those coals from the fire to your pit for up to 24 hours, you want to place your feeder fire within a few steps of the pit, making sure it's not facing downwind. Likewise, you'll want to stack your wood close enough to the fire so you can feed it frequently without having to take a stroll every time you need to add wood, especially if it's raining.

You can build a feeder fire however you want to do it, so long as you keep the fire going to produce the coals you need for cooking.

If you're just getting ready for a shorter cook (say, a couple of hours), you can burn your wood in a charcoal grill, such as a kettle grill, while you cook on a larger grill, like the custom grate setup I recommend (page 42). Build your wood fire on top of the coals, replenishing as necessary.

THE **BURN BARREL**

In my opinion, the best feeder fire for longer barbecue cooks is a "burn barrel," a 55-gallon metal drum with both ends cut off that you lay on its side. You can buy these from building supply stores or industrial supply companies such as W. W. Grainger. (Just make sure you're NOT cutting one that previously held flammable substances; they've been known to go off like a bomb.) This style of barrel is perfect for the slat wood we use, but it's great for burning firewood as well. When you build a fire inside, the cylinder allows air to flow straight through, which helps your fire burn hot and fast. The top of the barrel also radiates heat down back onto the wood from the top, which will produce better coals more quickly than an open-air fire. A new burn barrel will be perfectly round, but after getting pounded with fire for a while, the metal will start to weaken and the top of the barrel will start to bow and collapse a little. This is actually a good thing, as it will radiate heat even more efficiently, like the broiler in your oven. If I'm about to use a new barrel, I'll

even sit my big ass down on top of it to try to bend the barrel a bit before I start my fire.

An upright burn barrel is also a great way to build a feeder fire, but they take a bit more work to make. To build one, start with two 55-gallon drums. Cut a third off the top of one barrel and weld it over the second barrel, then cut a door out of the bottom of the stacked barrels for shoveling out the coals. Drill holes in the side for adding rebar, which you'll crisscross to hold logs as they burn (you can find a diagram for this below). I like these and they work really well, but if you're sloppy about loading it with wood, you can actually tip the thing over. All things considered, I still prefer a single barrel laid on its side.

CINDER BLOCK WALL

If you don't have a barrel or two handy, you can make an L-shaped wall out of cinder blocks, a few blocks high. Build your fire where the two walls intersect, and feed the fire by leaning fresh wood, almost vertically, against the wall. Try to burn this fire on Mother Earth herself. Building a fire on top of concrete is fine, but you'll want to lay out a couple inches of sand first to protect it. (Concrete retains moisture, and when a really hot fire sits on it for a while, that moisture can cause the concrete to crack, or worse, explode.) Also, please don't build your fire

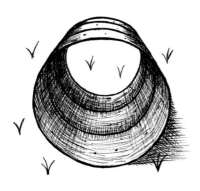

BURN BARREL

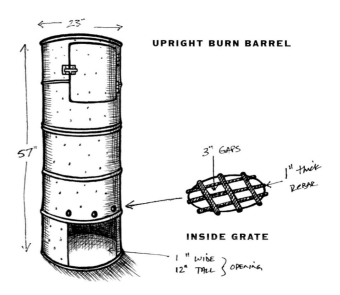

UPRIGHT BURN BARREL

23"

57"

3" GAPS

1" THICK REBAR

INSIDE GRATE

1" WIDE 12" TALL } OPENING

(or your pit) on asphalt or anything tar-based. If it doesn't catch on fire, it will melt, and guess what your barbecue will taste like? I learned this lesson firsthand back in 1993, when I was cooking a hog for a college event. It was a disaster.

STARTING
THE FIRE

Build your feeder fire within 10 to 15 feet of where you're cooking, to keep the trip from the fire to your grill or pit (while carrying shovelfuls of coals) short.

If I'm using my preferred method of a 55-gallon drum on its side, I'll light up a full charcoal chimney (preferably two). When the coals are ready, I'll pour them into the middle of the barrel and dump a bag of lump charcoal on top. Briquettes will work as well, but they burn down to ash more quickly, and over the course of a long cook all that dense ash can make it harder for your coals to breathe, and therefore burn properly.

To start a fire in an upright burn barrel, lay 3 logs across the crisscrossed bars, then dump two chimneys of lit charcoal on top. Add a few more logs, in a teepee shape, on top of the charcoal. Once those are lit, keep feeding the fire with fresh wood until the barrel is full of burning logs.

If you're using a cinder block wall for the feeder fire, dump two chimneys of lit charcoal at the intersection of the walls, then crisscross 6 logs, 2 at a time, on top of that. Once those logs are burning, you can keep feeding the fire.

Let me stop right here and get this out of the way: Don't be tempted to use "impregnated" charcoal briquettes (aka match-light charcoal, which has been soaked with lighter fluid) to get your fire going. A small bag of the stuff probably won't affect the flavor of what you're cooking, but a big bag can make it taste like someone sprayed it down with diesel fuel. If you're gonna insist on using match-light charcoal, then let's agree to part ways right now, and you just use this book to start your fire.

Once the lump has burned down to glowing coals, I'm ready to start feeding wood into the fire.

If I only have a small amount of charcoal on hand, I'll fill a chimney starter with charcoal and light it, then fill the barrel with logs or wood slats (whatever fuel I've been able to source at the time) as the chimney starter does its work. When the coals at the top of the starter begin to turn gray and ashy, I'll dump them over the wood inside the barrel.

And when I don't have any charcoal to kick-start my feeder fire, I'll use kindling, leaning it together in a teepee shape, and lighting it to make a small fire just inside the burn barrel (or at the juncture of the cinder block walls). Once that's raging, I'll feed it with wood logs or slats.

MAINTAINING
THE FIRE

Maintaining the fire is as simple as adding fresh wood on top of it as it burns, but the key to keeping a raging fire is to add enough wood. Plan on adding a couple logs about every 15 minutes or so, or even more during the front end of a long cook.

Including the fuel you'll use to prepare the pit for cooking, you'll burn dang near half of your wood supply during the first 6 to 8 hours of a whole-hog cook, as the pit will need fewer and fewer coals to maintain its temperature during the back end. Over time, you'll learn to get a sense of how much fuel and fire produces the amount of coals you'll need, but especially in the beginning (both of the cook and of your barbecue training), it's better to err on the side of burning too much wood rather than too little. You don't want to be caught without coals to fire the pit when you need them. So don't be stingy with fuel before your cook and during the first, crucial few hours of it; you'll use up all those coals the feeder fire produces pretty quickly. As the cook progresses, you'll find yourself feeding the fire less and less, just enough to keep a healthy bed of glowing coals at the ready.

You can also get double-duty out of that feeder fire by using extra coals for grilling, and the abundance of ashes your fire will be producing are great for making ash-roasted vegetables (see Chapter 5). When I'm doing a whole-hog cook, I'll often have a grill set up nearby where I cook our meals during the 24-hour marathon.

FEEDER FIRES FOR GRILLING AND OPEN-PIT BARBECUE

When I grill (see Chapter 2, page 38), I usually do so on a custom-fabricated open-pit grill grate that sits on the ground (this sounds fancier than it is; see My Custom-Fabricated Grill, page 42). To create a steady supply of coals, I'll skip the burn barrel and build a feeder fire directly behind the grate so I can pull hot coals under the grill with my shovel as needed. To do so, I start the fire with a chimney or two full of hot coals, then dump them in a long pile on the ground behind the grate. As the wood burns down, I add fresh wood toward the back of the fire, away from the grill. When I don't have charcoal to kick it off, I'll build a small log cabin-style fire with kindling behind the grill, then spread out the coals once I have enough to ignite larger pieces of wood.

If you're planning to use another style of grill, such as a kettle or kamado, you'll want to keep your feeder fire separate, either in a burn barrel, fire pit, or a simple campfire, so you can transfer coals as needed to your grilling vessel.

OVER TIME, YOU'LL LEARN TO GET A SENSE OF HOW MUCH FUEL AND FIRE PRODUCES THE AMOUNT OF COALS YOU'LL NEED, BUT ESPECIALLY IN THE BEGINNING (BOTH OF THE COOK AND OF YOUR BARBECUE TRAINING), IT'S BETTER TO ERR ON THE SIDE OF BURNING TOO MUCH WOOD RATHER THAN TOO LITTLE.

I use the same custom grill grates for open-pit barbecue (see Chapter 4), but the process is a little different. While grilling involves cooking directly over coals for the duration of the cook, open-pit barbecue is similar to indirect grilling, where the heat source mostly radiates from around the perimeter of the food. Because open-pit barbecue requires a longer cook (and more coals), I build the same style of feeder fire that I use for closed-pit barbecue, either in a burn barrel or in the corner of two cinder block walls.

CHAPTER 2

YOU

JTH

THE HOT, TEMPERAMENTAL FIRE

ONCE YOUR FEEDER FIRE IS PRODUCING HOT, RED COALS, you're ready to start grilling. The heat of young coals is intense and fleeting; this is the kind of heat you want to use for fast charring and searing. I especially love vegetables this way, which is why they're featured in most of the recipes in this chapter. You can get your vegetables cooked while you wait for more temperate coals to cook the rest of the meal, or grab a cast-iron skillet and use that to harness the wild heat of young coals.

A GOOD GRILL IS STURDY ENOUGH TO LAST A LIFETIME AND, LIKE A GOOD TRUCK, HAS PLENTY OF ROOM FOR YOUR STUFF. I DON'T THINK OF A GRILL AS AN EXTENSION OF MY KITCHEN, BUT AS THE KITCHEN ITSELF.

STYLES OF OPEN-PIT GRILLS

Grills are a lot like trucks. There are trucks that are fashion statements, and there are trucks that are durable and functional, and ready for the job. Likewise, there are grills that are flash and flair, but a good grill isn't flashy—in fact, it's probably ugly. A good grill is sturdy enough to last a lifetime and, like a good truck, has plenty of room for your stuff. I don't think of a grill as an extension of my kitchen, but as the kitchen itself. So I need a grill large enough to cook an entire meal on.

There are lots of great home grills out there, but in my opinion the reigning champ is still the classic 22-inch Weber kettle grill. I use mine pretty often, especially when I just need to quickly cook some meat or fish for supper. But when I'm cooking for my family on the weekend or want to grill up a meal for my buddies during a long whole-hog cook, I use a custom-fabricated steel grill that sits on the ground. Yes, on the ground, which means the coals below are going to burn a hole in your yard. But that shouldn't be a problem or you wouldn't be using this book, right? The added upside is that once you've burned that hole in the yard, it ain't going anywhere, so you might as well keep cooking on it.

With a kettle-style grill, it's hard to create more than two temperature zones, and even then you're not left with much surface area to work with. Plus, it's hard to feed and maintain your coals when you have a metal grate (and probably some food) sitting on top of it. Ceramic cookers such as Big Green Eggs and similar kamado-style grills are incredibly efficient, burn hot, and maintain their heat well. I love using them to cook pizzas, but they only give you one temperature zone to work with, and for me, grilling is all about having multiple heat zones and being in control of the fire.

So I strongly suggest you have a metal shop fabricate a custom grill grate like the one I use, especially if you're going to do any open-pit barbecue. One will run you around $300 to $400, including parts and labor, which is an investment, but I doubt you bought this

book to sit on a shelf forever, and that grill will last you a lifetime and the lifetime of your kids, too. You can show the diagram of my grill on page 42 to your local metal shop and ask them to build it for you. If you don't want to have a custom grate built, get a large, sturdy (heavy steel or cast-iron) grill grate and prop it over a fire on cinder blocks.

MY CUSTOM·FABRICATED GRILL

My grill is basically a low, grated table. It's a grilling surface of 24 × 36 inches mounted on four 12-inch legs. I like this distance between fire and cooking surface, because I find I can manage my heat better than on a taller grill, which would take substantially more coals to deliver the heat I want. My grill is open on all sides, which makes it easy to move the coals around below to create multiple heat zones. Its grate is made from thick steel bars that can take any amount of heat you throw at it without warping, and they're strong enough to support a 50-pound pig. This grill is a beast (luckily I have a truck!), but it's the same piece of equipment I use for open-pit barbecue (see Chapter 3, page 82), so I get a lot of use out of it.

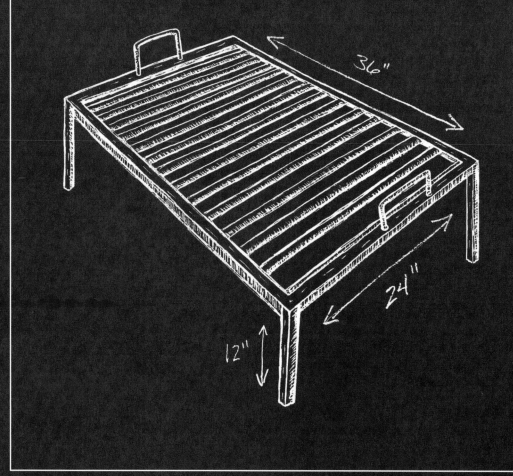

FUEL

While my intention is to set you up for my style of open-pit, wood-fired grilling and barbecue, all of the recipes in this chapter can be cooked on a kettle grill or whatever style of grill you have, with whatever fuel you have. That said, you're going to get tastier results—no matter the style of grill you use—if you cook with coals from a hardwood fire rather than bagged charcoal—the amount of wood smoke flavor you get from wood can't be matched by charcoal. But if you must use charcoal only, buy the lump hardwood variety, which will give you a bit more wood-grilled flavor than the briquettes, and if possible, lay some fist-size chunks of hardwood on top of the burning coals. And for God's sake, whatever you do, please promise me you will never use chemically impregnated (match-light) briquettes when grilling, as you'll certainly taste the lighter fluid in whatever you cook.

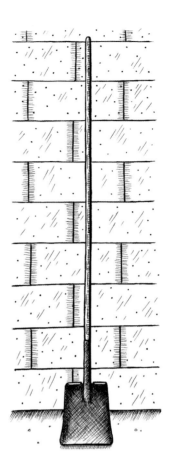

YOU'RE GOING TO GET TASTIER RESULTS—NO MATTER THE STYLE OF GRILL YOU USE—IF YOU COOK WITH COALS FROM A HARDWOOD FIRE RATHER THAN BAGGED CHARCOAL—THE AMOUNT OF WOOD SMOKE FLAVOR YOU GET FROM WOOD CAN'T BE MATCHED BY CHARCOAL.

TOOLS

In addition to a grill, you'll need a **CHIMNEY STARTER** (see Chimney Starters, page 32) for igniting your feeder fire, a **FLAT-HEAD SHOVEL** (preferably a pit shovel with a custom long wood handle) for pushing logs and coals around, a **WIRE GRILL BRUSH** to clean your grates, and a pair or two of **STURDY TONGS** for moving food around the grill top. If you'll be grilling beans and smaller vegetables, a **GRILL BASKET** (see Using Grill Baskets, page 65) will keep everything from falling into the fire. If you're cooking fish or hoecakes, have a **CAST-IRON SKILLET** (see Cast Iron Cooking on the Grill, page 73) and a **SPATULA** around. And if you're cooking at night, a **HEADLAMP OR FLASHLIGHT** is handy as well.

GETTING READY TO GRILL

As I said before, if you just want to grill a couple burgers or hot dogs, or any of the recipes in this chapter, you can simply fire up your charcoal grill with a chimney of lump hardwood charcoal and you're on your way.

But when I cook over a live fire, it's a dadgum commitment. If I'm gonna grill, then I'm gonna *grill*. That means I'll be in my backyard for at least a couple of hours: music blasting, kids playing nearby, and drinking some great wine with my friends. I'll cook our entire meal out there, and once these young, hot coals have done their job, I can hold the vegetables or whatever else I've cooked off to the side for a bit, and I'll get ready to work with the more moderate coals to cook the next course of supper. Then maybe roast some potatoes or other vegetables in the ashes and embers (see Chapter 5, page 222) to be eaten later.

I included the basic setup for building a feeder fire for grilling in the previous chapter (see Feeder Fires for Grilling and Open-Pit Barbecue, page 37), but here I'll go into more detail for a fire for a shorter cook. If you're using a grill grate like I described above, find a spot in your yard (or in a field) where you don't mind burning out a piece of ground about 4 feet square. If it's a grassy spot, you'll want to burn off that grass before you start to cook.

If you are in it for a short-to-moderate grilling session—as opposed to getting ready to do a serious, multihour open-pit barbecue cook—you can build your feeder fire right behind your grill, no burn barrel necessary. An hour or so before I'm ready to cook, I'll start building my feeder fire directly on the ground near the grill. I use a couple chimneys full of lump charcoal or briquettes (it doesn't really matter for this purpose), laying down a mound of burning coals just behind the back of my grill. Then I'll lay 2 or 3 logs right on top of the charcoal to get them burning. Once those logs are charred all over and starting to break apart into large coals (around the size of a baseball), I'll pull some of those coals away from the feeder fire with a shovel and spread them out below the grill. At this point, I can use this bed of coals to burn a few more logs, laying them around the outside edge of the bed. As these logs burn

WHEN I COOK OVER A LIVE FIRE, IT'S A DADGUM COMMITMENT. IF I'M GONNA GRILL, THEN I'M GONNA *GRILL*. THAT MEANS I'LL BE IN MY BACKYARD FOR AT LEAST A COUPLE OF HOURS: MUSIC BLASTING, KIDS PLAYING NEARBY, AND DRINKING SOME GREAT WINE WITH MY FRIENDS.

down, I can now pull those fresh coals in from all four sides of the grill, and replenish the logs as needed to produce more coals.

Now, I'm about to say something that may seem obvious to folks who've cooked over live fire before, but just in case—I only cook over *coals*, not over a bed of flames. Cooking over flaming wood is a recipe for burnt, nasty food. Coals are what give you controllable heat and smoke flavor.

I know I'm ready to grill once I have a bed of hot coals that's about 2 inches deep and covers the entire surface area below my grill. The coals should be burned hot and covered in a light gray ash. To determine the coals' temperature, I use the Hand Test (see page 46).

Before throwing any food onto the grill, I'll give the grates a good cleaning with a wire brush, then wipe them down a few times with a vegetable oil-soaked towel. Grapeseed is my favorite oil to use, as it has a high smoke point and neutral flavor. Make sure not to use oils with lower smoke points, such as olive oil, as they will burn and give your food an acrid taste. If you don't have a wire brush, roll up a ball of aluminum foil about the size of a softball and use it to give the grates a good scrub.

So that's the basics. Let the grates get hot, and you're ready to grill.

THE HAND TEST

To gauge the temperature of the grill, I hold my hand about four inches above the grate. The grill is ready for high-heat grilling when I can only hold my hand there for 2 to 3 seconds. (This isn't a contest, so don't be the douche who tries to see how long you can hold it there before going to the Vanderbilt burn unit. Just hold it till it starts to sting a little.) Most of the recipes in this chapter call for high-heat grilling, so this is your target. When you can keep your hand there longer, for 4 to 5 seconds, your fire is medium-high and perfect for grilling steak, chops, and burgers, as well as larger vegetables like Charred Butternut Squash (page 58). The hand test is also useful in open-pit, spit barbecue, and ash cooking, so you'll see me frequently referencing it throughout the book.

COOKING OVER
FLAMING WOOD IS A
RECIPE FOR BURNT,
NASTY FOOD. COALS
ARE WHAT GIVE YOU
CONTROLLABLE HEAT
AND SMOKE FLAVOR.

GRILLED
SUMMER SQUASH

Summer squash is one of the easiest vegetables to grow at home. They're also usually the first vegetables of the late spring. You only need one plant, which will start producing a couple of squash per week beginning in the early summer. I'm always excited when my first squash starts to produce. I'll make this recipe once or twice a week until the rest of the garden catches up; to be honest, by then I've grown bored of summer squash and am ready to move on.

Still, the great thing about grilling summer squash is you can really beat the piss out of them on the grill—I know these are done when they're soft enough to pierce with a fork but haven't collapsed and turned to mush. If you pull them at the right moment, they'll keep just enough of their firmness. Summer squash contain so much moisture that they won't char as deeply as a winter squash, but they'll take on enough char to turn the almost-flavorless vegetable into something that can stand up to barbecue and grilled meat, or diced and tossed with pasta or a salad. And with the proper char and a light dusting of Memphis-Style Seasoning for flavor, these are so great that even the little chicken finger-loving kids will smash them.

4 servings

4 medium summer squash, cut lengthwise into ½-inch-thick slices

2 tablespoons olive oil

2 teaspoons Diamond Crystal kosher salt

1 teaspoon Memphis-Style Seasoning (page 66)

Prepare a hot grill (2 to 3 seconds using the Hand Test, page 46). Clean and oil the grill grates well.

In a large bowl, toss the squash with the olive oil until coated, then season with the salt. Place the squash on the grill and cook until charred on the bottom and the squash releases easily from the grates, about 5 minutes. Flip the squash over and cook on the other side until very tender but not falling apart, another 3 to 4 minutes.

Return the squash to the bowl, add the Memphis-Style Seasoning and toss to coat. Serve warm.

MARTHA'S OPEN-FACED
GRILLED TOMATO SANDWICHES

Makes 2 open-faced sandwiches

1 large heirloom tomato (use
    a meaty, sweet variety,
    like Cherokee Purple or
    Brandywine)

2 tablespoons hemp hearts or
    pumpkin seeds

2 teaspoons olive oil

Fleur de sel or other flaky salt

2 thick slices sourdough or
    country white bread

Mayonnaise (Duke's brand
    strongly preferred), to taste

I first made this sandwich for my wife, Martha, years ago, and she frequently asks for it whenever our tomato plants come into season. I can't blame her: Tomatoes on toast with Duke's mayonnaise (and please use Duke's, even if you have to order it from Amazon . . . it's just the best). Over a hot grill, tomatoes will quickly take on a lot of char and smoky flavor before they start to get mushy. This extra step turns this Southern staple into something really savory, really special. Just be sure to use ripe, in-season local tomatoes (preferably heirloom varieties). Those grainy-ass, rock-hard tomatoes they pick green on the other side of the country and spray with nitrogen or whatever are an absolute sin. Tomatoes should only be eaten fresh when they're in season—3 to 4 months out of the year for us—and that's it!

For a bit of nutty crunch, I top the sandwich with a sprinkle of toasted hemp hearts, which are the hulled seeds of the hemp plant. If you can't find them, you can substitute toasted barley, pumpkin seeds, or another crunchy topping—the texture is the most important thing.

Do me a favor too and eat this sandwich with your significant other over a bottle of nice Champagne. I don't care how big and tough you think you are, your ass will thank me later. So pop the Champagne and eat!

Cut the tomato into ¾-inch-thick slices. Refrigerate until well chilled, at least 30 minutes.

In a small skillet, heat the hemp hearts over medium heat, tossing constantly, until the hearts start to turn brown and smell nutty, 2 to 3 minutes, but trust your eyes and nose more than a timer. Remove from the heat and toss the hearts for another 30 seconds, then transfer to a bowl and set aside.

Prepare a medium-high grill (4 to 5 seconds using the Hand Test, page 46). Clean and oil the grill grates well.

Brush both sides of each tomato slice with the olive oil and season with fleur de sel. Grill the tomatoes until lightly charred on one side, about 3 minutes, then flip and grill until the other side is lightly charred, about 3 minutes longer. Meanwhile, brush both sides of the bread with mayonnaise and grill until toasted, 1 to 2 minutes per side.

To assemble, spread more mayonnaise on one side of each piece of toast. Top with a tomato slice and sprinkle with toasted hemp seeds and fleur de sel. Serve.

SOME THOUGHTS ON CHAR

If there's one lesson you take away from this chapter, let it be this: Don't be afraid of char. The deep caramelization that a hot fire can give your food is, for me, the payoff for doing all the work to prepare the grill in the first place. And it's a lot harder to take the char too far than you think. Now, there's a difference between charring something and burning something, just as there's a difference between caramel and sugar that's been burnt to all hell and back. Color wise, I'm looking for a really dark mahogany color. But the more important distinction between charred and burnt is flavor: Once something is burned, it will be unpleasantly bitter, and that's all you will taste. If the food looks burned but still tastes deliciously savory, that's some good char. You'll know it when you've burned something, and everything up to that is simply a degree of char.

That said, not everything you put on the grill should get deeply charred. Too much char flavor can overpower small spring and summer vegetables, but once you get into larger, denser fall and winter vegetables, bring it on. Likewise, with meat: Although the meats in this book are mostly smoked or grilled over a cooler fire, when I'm grilling meat over a hot fire, I'll aim to get more char on thicker, fattier cuts of meat rather than thinner, leaner cuts.

CHARRED CARROTS
WITH SORGHUM AND BUTTERMILK

As a kid, I thought buttermilk was so disgusting, but here I am as an adult and I love it. In the summer, when my parents would ship me home to the farm in Mississippi, my Paw-Paw would drink it all the time. After mornings of him working the farm and me playing around, we'd come into the house for lunch and Paw-Paw would fill a glass about two-thirds full with buttermilk, add a big piece of leftover corn bread, and smush it up. This was what folks around there ate when they didn't have a lot of money but needed calories. My grandparents were neither poor nor rich, but Paw-Paw loved it anyway. In his honor, I put his buttermilk/corn bread concoction on the original menu at my first Martin's joint, but I can't recall anyone ever ordering it.

I created this side dish to showcase my love of buttermilk, whose combination of creaminess and slight sourness can add balance to so many foods besides corn bread. In this case, it goes with two other favorite ingredients: carrots and sorghum syrup. I love what a hot grill does to dense vegetables like carrots, but it takes longer than you'd expect to turn them into soft, caramelized spears. I'll throw the carrots on the grill as I go about my business (or grill something else), rotating them a quarter-turn every few minutes. This will take a bit because I want you to char them pretty good! The carrots will get extra sweet and caramelized thanks to golden-brown sorghum syrup, the maple syrup of the South. It should be a light to medium caramel color. Don't use blackstrap molasses, as it's too bitter. If you can't find sorghum molasses where you live, use a dark honey or maple syrup—or a dark cane syrup. You add tangy, rich buttermilk to all that sweetness, and you have a winner.

As with the Hoecakes (page 78), you'll want to use whole (full-fat) buttermilk here, which will thicken into a heavy cream-like texture when you whip it.

Measure out the buttermilk and let it sit at room temperature while you prepare a hot grill (2 to 3 seconds using the Hand Test, page 46). Clean and oil the grill grates well.

In a large bowl, combine the carrots, olive oil, sorghum, and fleur de sel and toss until the carrots are well coated.

Place the carrots on the grill and cook, rotating them a quarter-turn every couple of minutes, until tender and well charred all over; this will take anywhere from 10 to 30 minutes, depending on the size of the carrots. Transfer to a platter.

As soon as the carrots are finished, pour the buttermilk into a bowl and use a whisk or electric mixer to beat the buttermilk until it's thickened to the texture of soft whipped cream. Drizzle the carrots with the whipped buttermilk and serve warm.

2 to 4 servings

½ cup whole buttermilk (see Note)

1 pound carrots, peeled and left whole

2 tablespoons olive oil

3 tablespoons golden sorghum syrup

2 teaspoons fleur de sel or other flaky salt

NOTE If you can't find whole buttermilk, add a splash of heavy cream to low-fat (1%) or light (1.5%) buttermilk, or use whole milk yogurt as a substitute.

YOU'LL KNOW IT WHEN YOU'VE BURNED SOMETHING, AND EVERYTHING UP TO THAT IS SIMPLY A DEGREE OF CHAR.

GRILLED
COLLARD GREENS

4 to 6 servings

2 pounds collard greens leaves, rinsed

3 tablespoons olive oil

Fleur de sel or other flaky salt

1 lemon, for zesting

As ubiquitous as collard greens are in Southern cooking, they rarely get their turn on the grill, which is a shame. I throw them over hot coals and cook them until their edges start to look like kale chips, then I stack them into a pile and let them steam for a few minutes to help tenderize them. It's unexpected and delicious, a totally different texture than braising them until soft or sautéing them, and the grill gives them a roast-y, broccoli-like flavor.

I like to serve these as a side for meat or fish, or with some ash-roasted potatoes (see "Arsh" Potatoes, page 227). But my favorite way to eat these, and I'm not ashamed to say it, is to grab a leaf off the grill and dip it in ranch dressing.

Prepare a medium-high grill (4 to 5 seconds using the Hand Test, page 46). Clean and oil the grill grates well.

Place the collards and olive oil in a large bowl and toss well to evenly coat; don't be afraid to get in there with your hands and rub the oil on the leaves. Season generously with salt. Working in batches, spread the leaves over the grill in one layer and cook, turning frequently, until charred in places, crispy around the edges, and slightly wilted, 8 to 10 minutes. While still hot, transfer the leaves to a cutting board or bowl, stack them, and let them sit for a few minutes.

Cut any super-tough parts of the stems from the collards and discard, then cut the leaves into bite-size pieces and season again with salt if needed. Grate some lemon zest over the greens and serve warm.

CREAMED
CHARRED CORN

This recipe is about adding the flavor of the grill to a dish I loved growing up. Back then, I was as picky as most kids are, but I loved my Maw-Maw's creamed corn because it was sweet. She would always use Silver Queen corn, but you could use Peaches and Cream or another local variety that's in season, preferably a white corn (which, on a side note, makes by far the best corn "likker"). Here, I take her recipe and add charred corn and jalapeños for some smoky heat. Feel free to keep the jalapeños out if you're feeding little ones (which can mean the kids or adults who can't stand the heat).

4 servings

4 ears corn, shucked

2 jalapeño peppers

2 teaspoons canola oil

2 cups canned cream-style corn

2 tablespoons sugar

1 tablespoon butter

1½ teaspoons Diamond Crystal kosher salt

Prepare a hot grill (2 to 3 seconds using the Hand Test, page 46). Clean and oil the grill grates well.

Rub the corn and jalapeños with oil and grill, turning frequently, until well charred all over, about 10 to 15 minutes. Remove from the heat and set aside until cool enough to handle.

Meanwhile, in a medium cast-iron skillet, combine the canned corn, sugar, butter, salt, and 2 tablespoons water and set over medium-high heat. Cook, stirring occasionally, until the sugar has dissolved, the water has been absorbed, and the mixture is heated through, about 7 minutes.

To cut the corn from the cob, stand the ear up vertically and with your chef's knife, slice downward to the cutting board, making sure you are only removing the kernels from the cob. (Even better, cut the corn over a pie dish, as this will catch all the kernels for you.) Remove the stems and seeds from the jalapeños and finely dice.

Add the corn and jalapeños to the creamed corn and stir to combine and heat through. Serve.

CHARRED
BUTTERNUT SQUASH

6 to 8 servings

FOR THE CHILE OIL

1 cup grapeseed oil

3 tablespoons red pepper flakes

½ teaspoon Diamond Crystal
kosher salt

1 garlic clove, smashed

FOR THE SQUASH

2 medium butternut squash
(2 to 3 pounds each)

Olive oil

Fleur de sel or other flaky salt

Grilled winter squash is a great place to start your own education in live-fire cookery. If you are one of those people who think you've always got to have meat for every meal, then this will change your head around. It'll give you a lesson in how a higher heat intensifies the flavors and sweetness of vegetables, and how the flavor of wood smoke can deeply impregnate larger vegetables—something you absolutely cannot achieve with gas or charcoal briquettes. I grill butternut squash in halves over a medium-high fire, once the hottest coals have started to die off, but no matter how hot your fire is, it's hard to burn squash as long as you move it around and turn it a couple of extra times. I serve this deeply caramelized squash family-style, placing them in front of guests and giving everyone a spoon to dig in.

MAKE THE CHILE OIL: In a small saucepan, heat the grapeseed oil over medium-high heat for 2 to 3 minutes. Add the pepper flakes, salt, and garlic and stir. Reduce the heat to low and let infuse for 30 minutes. Remove from the heat the let the oil cool to room temperature. Transfer to a jar and refrigerate until ready to use; the oil will last for about 3 months.

GRILL THE SQUASH: Prepare a medium-high grill (4 to 5 seconds using the Hand Test, page 46). Clean and oil the grill grates well.

Cut the squash in half lengthwise and scoop out the seeds. Brush the cut side with olive oil and season generously with salt. Place the squash halves over the heat, flesh-side down, and grill. Begin checking the squash after about 10 minutes: Gently nudge it to see if it's no longer sticking to the grill. Once it moves easily, continue cooking, flipping it and moving it around the grill to cook it evenly all over. Cook until the cut side is well charred all over and the thickest part of the squash is tender when pierced with a knife, 30 to 40 minutes total. If the squash picks up too much char on one side before it's tender, flip it over and continue grilling until tender.

Drizzle with the chile oil, season with more salt to taste, and serve.

GRILLED QUAIL

I love to hunt and fish. To be in a duck blind with my sons, Wyatt and Walker, or to be sitting in a deer stand with my daughter, Daisy, is one of my very favorite pastimes, and we always leave with memories and a story or two, and hopefully something good to cook. My favorite thing to hunt is upland birds, specifically the bobwhite quail. Hunting quail is about so much more than just shooting some birds. It's about taking that walk with your granddad, and the smell of the air on a sunny fall day. When my Pa-King passed away, he gave me his shotguns, one of which was a 1952 16-gauge Browning Belgium, also known as the "Sweet 16." It's probably the most legendary bird gun ever. I hunt quail with it every year and it still knocks 'em down. You couldn't pay me a million dollars for that gun because it was Pa-King's gun. When I'm using it, it's like he's right there with me.

Oh gosh, and the dogs! Watching a pair of bird dogs work a bean field is like watching real-life art right in front of you. Seeing a wise old Ryman setter or a German shorthair lock up on point while the other dogs respect the primary dog's point just never gets old for me.

Up until the 1980s, where we live, you could walk out your front door and kick up a covey of quail within a hundred yards of your house. Sadly, because of parasites, predators, farming practices, and other reasons, the legendary bobwhite has all but disappeared in the South. When I was young, folks would get permission from families to bird hunt. My Pa-King and my Uncle Doc would come over to my Paw-Paw Martin's, let the dogs out, and just start walking for miles. They'd always get up two or three coveys of birds with probably fifteen birds per covey. They'd come home with a bunch and my Mi-Mi would fry them up for all of us for supper. Today, you can hunt all day and there's a good chance your dog won't find a single covey. But I still love to take that walk.

Assuming I'm lucky and get a few, my favorite way to cook quail is simply grilled and basted with my vinegary Jack's Creek Sauce. Of course, you can buy quail, too.

Put your forks and knives down and eat these birds with your hands. It's messy and fun.

Prepare a hot grill (2 to 3 seconds using the Hand Test, page 46). Clean and oil the grill grates well.

Pat the birds dry with paper towels. Rub each bird with a light coating of olive oil. Sprinkle with salt inside and out.

(recipe continues)

4 to 6 servings

12 whole quail, feathered and cleaned

¼ cup olive oil

2 tablespoons Diamond Crystal kosher salt

2 cups Jack's Creek Sauce (page 95)

Set the birds on the grates, breast-side down, and cook until beginning to brown on the bottom, about 2 minutes. Flip and grill for 1 minute longer. Using a shovel, pull the coals that are directly below the birds to the perimeter of the grill. Cook the birds until golden brown and cooked through but still juicy, about 10 minutes, turning them over and basting them with the Jack's Creek Sauce every couple of minutes.

Transfer the birds to a platter and let rest for 5 minutes. Serve family-style, 2 or 3 quail per person.

CRILLED
SUGAR SNAP PEAS

Remember when you were a kid and y'all would go pick blackberries? I don't know about you, but I'd eat a berry for each one I threw in the basket. For me, sugar snap peas are the same; you start out with a bunch, then find yourself eating half of them as you're preparing them to cook. I freaking love 'em.

Sugar snap peas might seem too sweet, crunchy, and delicate for grilling, but they taste amazing—almost like a completely different vegetable—when they're well charred, plus they get very crispy, almost like chips. Because they contain so much moisture, sugar snaps will take longer than you think to pick up some color—you'll have to cook most of that water out before they really start to char. Make sure you spread them out in a single layer on the grill, or they'll steam instead of charring. I like to toss them with Jack's Creek Sauce, which will make them taste even more like barbecue.

Prepare a hot grill (2 to 3 seconds using the Hand Test, page 46). Clean and oil the grill grates well.

In a large bowl, toss the sugar snaps with the olive oil until coated and season with the salt. Transfer to a grill basket (or a wire rack set on top of the grill) and cook until the sugar snaps are deeply charred on one side, about 5 minutes. Turn and continue to cook until charred and tender and crispy around the edges, another 3 minutes.

Return the sugar snaps to the bowl. Add the pepper flakes and lemon zest. If desired, drizzle with Jack's Creek Sauce. Toss to combine and serve immediately.

2 to 4 servings

1 pound sugar snap peas, trimmed and strings removed

2 tablespoons olive oil

1 teaspoon fleur de sel or other flaky salt

1 teaspoon red pepper flakes

Finely grated zest of 1 lemon

Jack's Creek Sauce (optional; page 95)

USING GRILL BASKETS

Because the grates on my custom grill are about 1½ inches apart, I often use a grill basket or wire rack when I'm grilling smaller vegetables and beans. I like wire-mesh grill baskets with a wide, flat bottom; and a handle is nice for moving it around over the fire (and in the case of purple hull peas or butterbeans, directly on top of the coals). In a pinch, you can also use a large fine-mesh sieve or colander, but this will give the food less contact with the heat of the grill, so you'll need to cook in smaller batches. I also use a sturdy wire cooling rack (one with crosshatch bars) that I set on top of the grill grates. You can also buy a yakitori grill rack, which will be more durable than a wire rack.

GRILLED GREEN BEANS
WITH MEMPHIS DRY RUB

4 servings

2 pounds green beans, trimmed

2 teaspoons vegetable oil

1 teaspoon fleur de sel or other flaky salt

2 teaspoons Memphis-Style Seasoning (recipe follows)

You know how you go to the Chinese buffet and they have those smoky, wok-fried green beans? My memories of munching on those things as a kid are what inspired this recipe.

A hot grill turns some boring-ass green beans into something extremely savory and slightly smoky, with a lightly crispy skin. These beans make for a great side dish with any meat cooked with fire, but they're delicious enough on their own for snacking, especially when sprinkled with some of my Memphis-Style Seasoning for an extra hint of sweetness and heat.

A lot of grilled green bean recipes will have you blanch the beans first. You can do this, sure, but who wants to go inside to blanch something when you're cooking over a fire? Throwing them directly on a hot grill will cook and char them before they can dry out too much. You can make these beans ahead of time and refrigerate them until you're ready to use them. (I like to cut them up, toss them with olive oil and lemon juice, and add them to salads.)

Prepare a hot grill (2 to 3 seconds using the Hand Test, page 46). Clean and oil the grill grates well.

In a large bowl, toss the green beans with the oil and salt until coated. Transfer to a grill basket (or a wire rack set on top of the grill), piling them a few beans high so the ones on top will steam as the ones below char over the fire. Toss the beans every couple of minutes, just until they're tender and slightly charred, about 10 minutes total.

Return the beans to the bowl, add the Memphis-Style Seasoning and toss to coat. Serve immediately or refrigerate for later.

MEMPHIS-STYLE SEASONING

Makes about 4 cups

⅓ cup fine sea salt

1⅓ cups paprika

1⅓ cups chile powder

¼ cup ground cumin

2 tablespoons onion powder

1 tablespoon plus 1 teaspoon garlic powder

1 tablespoon plus 1 teaspoon freshly ground black pepper

1 tablespoon plus ½ teaspoon ground coriander

1 teaspoon ground celery seeds

1½ teaspoons ground thyme

¾ teaspoon ground cloves

½ teaspoon ground allspice

½ teaspoon ground cinnamon

½ teaspoon ground oregano

½ teaspoon ground rosemary

1 tablespoon dried thyme leaves

2 tablespoons yellow mustard seeds

¾ teaspoon monosodium glutamate (MSG)

In a medium bowl, whisk together all the ingredients. Store in an airtight container in a cool, dry place for up to 1 month.

GRILLED
OKRA

For the most part, I hated okra when I was a kid. We only ate it when we were in Mississippi during the summer, and a lot of folks down there boiled their okra, which resulted in what the comedian Jerry Clower referred to as "slick, slimy boiled okry." But when it's fried (like anything else) it tasted great.

Okra is now one of my favorite vegetables, and I can trace my appreciation back to when I started charring them on a Smoky Joe grill outside my dorm room. Most vegetables look sexier after they come off the grill, but okra is an exception visually. Still, okra can take an absolute beating on the grill and come out better for it, even if it goes from a beautiful green or red to a dull, camel brown as it cooks. Most folks go wrong by undercooking it, taking it off the grill before all the slimy stuff inside has a chance to cook out—okra is so full of moisture that it takes a while for it to give up the ghost and start to turn. Make this dish as soon as your coals are ready; if you wait for the fire to die down, it'll take the okra longer to cook, which will turn them mushy. You can also split the okra in half lengthwise before grilling for a crispier result (which kids freakin' love!); cooking time will be reduced by about half. Don't be surprised if this becomes your kids' favorite vegetable once you cook them this way.

I'm going to repeat myself to the right, but do yourself a favor and do not buy okra that is longer than your middle finger. Any longer than that and they become fibrous and tough as they cook.

Prepare a medium-high grill (4 to 5 seconds using the Hand Test, page 46).

In a large bowl, toss the okra with the olive oil and salt to combine. Transfer to a grill basket (or a wire rack set on top of the grill) in a single layer and cook, turning occasionally, until the okra is deeply charred and cooked through, 20 to 25 minutes.

Transfer the okra to the bowl, add the pepper flakes and lemon zest, and toss to combine. Serve immediately (the okra will soften as it sits).

2 to 4 servings

1 pound okra (see Note)

2 tablespoons olive oil

2 teaspoons fleur de sel or other flaky salt

1 teaspoon red pepper flakes

Finely grated zest of 1 lemon

NOTE Choose a shorter, plumper okra such as Star of David variety; the longer ones tend to be hard and stringy.

GRILL-BASKET
BUTTERBEANS

2 to 4 servings

Kosher salt

1 pound shelled fresh
butterbeans (about 2 cups)

2 tablespoons olive oil

1 teaspoon Big Hoss Rub
(page 96)

Lemon wedge

1 teaspoon fleur de sel or other
flaky salt

Butterbeans (also known as lima beans to people up North) are a Southern staple, and we get them fresh, in their pods—not in cans. Because beans need some time to cook through, this is one case where I do blanch the vegetable before cooking it on the grill, but the contrast of texture—crunchy and silky— is addictive.

When grilling butterbeans (and Grill-Basket Purple Hull Peas, page 72), I like to set the grill basket directly on top of the hot coals, rather than on the grill grates (don't worry, they can take the heat). I toss them frequently as they cook, which steams the beans while they absorb some smoke from the fire. When the beans are almost tender throughout (whatever the bean equivalent of "al dente" is), I'll let the basket sit on the heat for a few more minutes without disturbing it. This will char the bottom layer of beans that's in direct contact with the coals, so when you mix them all together in a bowl, you'll have bits of crispy charred beans mixed in with the soft, buttery ones.

Set up a bowl of ice and water. Bring a large saucepan of well-salted water to a boil, add the butterbeans, and cook until firm-tender (NOT mushy!), 10 to 12 minutes. Transfer to the ice bath to cool, then spread the beans out on a towel to dry.

Prepare a hot grill (2 to 3 seconds using the Hand Test, page 46).

In a large bowl, toss the butterbeans with the olive oil to coat well. Transfer to a grill basket.

Get a cold glass of wine or a beer and pull up a 5-gallon bucket to sit on, because this is gonna take some attention. Place the basket directly on the hot coals and cook, tossing every 30 seconds or so, until tender throughout, 20 to 25 minutes. Continue cooking without moving the basket until the bottom layer of beans is nicely charred, about 5 minutes longer.

Return the butterbeans to the bowl, add the dry rub and toss to coat. Squeeze the lemon wedge over, finish with the fleur de sel, and serve warm.

CRILL-BASKET
PURPLE HULL PEAS

4 servings

Kosher salt

3 cups fresh purple hull peas

1 tablespoon olive oil

Finely grated zest of ½ lemon

1 teaspoon red pepper flakes

1 teaspoon fleur de sel or other
flaky salt

Chow-chow, optional

Hot sauce, optional

Black-eyed peas are a popular field pea all over the South, but in the mid-South, their cousin, the purple hull pea, is the OG field pea. In my opinion, they are creamier and earthier in flavor, and I flat out think they're a better pea! I remember sitting below the big pin oak tree in front of my grandparents' carport, where Maw-Maw would have me shell bucket after bucket of purple hull peas. It would make me so mad because I'd be in a rush to get done so I could go shoot hoops or whatever. And just when I could see the bottom of the bucket, she'd dump in another load and say, "Keep shellin', sonny boy." By the time I was done, my fingers would be stained purple, and let me tell you something, it'll take a day or two for that stain to go away. At the time, I wanted to be doing anything else, but now I'd give anything to be back under that tree shelling peas with her.

You'll find purple hull peas fresh in the late spring through fall, or you can buy them frozen. My version finishes the boiled peas over a hot fire, which gives them a smoky flavor and a bit of char.

My family (and many others) always eat purple hull peas with chow-chow, a sweet-and-sour relish, and I suggest you do the same. To do it right, spoon some chow-chow over the warm peas, then take your fork and get a little bit of chow-chow, then fill it up with peas. A good hot sauce to drop on along the way is a must for us, too. Add some cornbread or Hoecakes (page 78), and you've got a meal that any meat lover will tear through.

Bring a pot of well-salted water to a boil over high heat, add the peas, and cook until slightly tender, about 10 minutes. Drain the peas and transfer to a large bowl. Add the olive oil and toss to coat well.

Prepare a hot grill (2 to 3 seconds using the Hand Test, page 46).

Transfer the peas to a grill basket (or a fine-mesh metal sieve). Place the basket directly on the hot coals and cook, tossing every minute or so, until almost tender throughout, about 20 minutes. Continue cooking without moving the basket until the bottom layer of beans is nicely charred, about 5 minutes longer.

Return the peas to the bowl, add the lemon zest and pepper flakes and toss to combine. Finish with the fleur de sel and serve warm with chow-chow and hot sauce, if desired.

CAST-IRON COOKING ON THE GRILL

Once I've got my fire ready for grilling, I don't want to go back inside to prep or cook anything. Pretty much anything you can cook on the stovetop you can cook on top of a grill. (That either sounds obvious to you, or you might be smacking yourself on the forehead right now.) You can use any kind of pots and pans on top of the grill (so long as they don't have plastic handles!), but I do most of my grill-top cooking in a large cast-iron skillet. Mine is a big one, about 14 inches in diameter, because I want the flexibility of the larger surface area. That being said, you can always use one or more smaller skillets.

There are a couple of things I especially enjoy making in a skillet on the grill—hoecakes (savory corn bread pancakes) and fish. While you can grill fish directly on the grates, you'll run into a couple of issues: First, fish loves to stick to the grill, even a clean, well-oiled one. Second, I like my fish to be evenly browned, which is much easier to do in a skillet. When you're cooking fish directly on grill grates you need to move it around a lot to achieve the same results, and you risk tearing that fish apart every time you touch it.

One thing people frequently mess up when using cast-iron on the grill is they get the pan too dang hot. The grill is going to be much hotter than most stovetops, so it won't take long for that skillet to heat up. Just before I'm ready to cook, I'll put the skillet on top of the grill for a few minutes, then add some oil. When that oil starts to shimmer, the pan is ready to go.

WHOLE CRAPPIE

2 servings

2 whole head-on crappie or similar fish (about 12 ounces each), scales, gills, guts, and fins removed

3 tablespoons peanut oil

2 teaspoons fleur de sel or other flaky salt

1 lemon, thinly sliced

2 small bunches fresh herbs (any combination of rosemary, parsley, thyme, and oregano)

With its soft, white flesh and sweet flavor, crappie is my favorite fish on the planet to eat. They are also so much fun to catch. Crappie love hanging out around any kind of structure: rocks, logs, whatever. A dead Christmas tree is the favorite way to build a crappie hole, so every January folks would take their Christmas tree and throw it into a pond, in eight to ten feet of water. Come spring, they'd have a secret crappie bed and could catch as many fish as they could eat.

One whole crappie is the perfect size for a single serving (though I'll often eat two), so that's how I like to cook them. They're easy to overcook, so you want to take them out of the pan as soon as the flesh turns opaque; the fish will continue to cook for a couple of minutes as it rests.

Crappie are rarely found at fish markets, so if you don't catch your own, you can substitute with similar-sized blue gill, bream, or perch.

Serve the fish with Grilled Collard Greens (page 54), Hoecakes (page 78), or "Arsh" Potatoes (page 227). And you definitely want a bottle of bubbles to drink with this fish.

Prepare a hot grill (2 to 3 seconds using the Hand Test, page 46).

Pat the fish dry with paper towels. Make two 2-inch slashes on each side of the fish through the thickest part of the flesh. Rub each fish with 1 tablespoon of the oil. Sprinkle with the fleur de sel inside and out. Stuff each fish with lemon slices and herbs.

Set a 12- or 14-inch cast-iron skillet on the grill and let it warm up for a couple of minutes. Add the remaining 1 tablespoon oil. When the oil shimmers, add the fish to the pan and cook, undisturbed, until it releases easily from the pan and is crispy, 6 to 8 minutes. Flip and continue to cook until crispy on the other side and just cooked through, another 4 to 5 minutes. Serve.

CAST-IRON
CATFISH FILLETS

In the South, farm-raised catfish is the king of freshwater fish. It's also a romantic soft spot for me. Anybody in the South who's got a pond usually had it stocked with catfish, as did both of my grandfathers. My Pa-King would head down to the pond to feed his fish, and I'm telling you the fish literally could sense the vibration of that red-belly Ford tractor when he drove up to feed them. By the time we got up to the bank, they'd be churning the water around while they waited for him to sling a scoop of feed into the pond, like a bunch of bird dogs waiting for you to throw some scraps their way. We always had our hooks baited and ready to go before he slung the feed out so we could start catching them.

But my Aunt Jewell and Uncle Marvin had the best fishpond in the history of mankind. You could tie a crescent wrench on a hook, throw it in, and catch a fish. Some of my fondest memories as a kid were when Paw-Paw would fry fish in the carport while my Maw-Maw, mom, and Aunt Cathy would make hushpuppies, fries, and slaw. My Pa-King and Mi-Mi would come over and we'd all eat as a family. It was special.

If you're reading this and don't like catfish, then that tells me you've probably had the wrong kind of catfish. A lot of catfish you'll encounter at the supermarket or a cheap restaurant has either been caught in a domestic river (and are known as mudcats) or raised in an Asian fish farm, where the environment is muddy, so the fish tastes like garbage. If I'm not catching my own (blue catfish is the best wild species for eating), I use a domestic farm-raised, grain-fed catfish, which has white, delicate flesh—a bit denser than crappie—and a clean flavor. Of course I'm partial, but Mississippi is legendary for its catfish farms and that's all I serve at Martin's. Most of the Southern states claim this type of farming as an integral part of their state's agriculture industry. If you can't find catfish, you can substitute another medium-dense fish, such as cod, haddock, or flounder.

Prepare a hot grill (2 to 3 seconds using the Hand Test, page 46).

Pat the fish dry with paper towels. Use 2 tablespoons of the peanut oil to rub the catfish fillets on both sides. Season with the fleur de sel and the rub.

Set a 12- or 14-inch cast-iron skillet on the grill and add the remaining 1 tablespoon oil. When the oil shimmers, add the catfish and cook until golden brown on the bottom, 2 to 3 minutes. Flip and cook until just opaque throughout, 2 to 3 minutes longer.

Serve warm with lemon wedges or Jack's Creek Sauce.

4 servings

4 skinless catfish fillets (6 to 8 ounces each)

3 tablespoons peanut oil

2 teaspoons fleur de sel or other flaky salt

2 teaspoons Big Hoss Rub (page 96)

Lemon wedges or Jack's Creek Sauce (page 95), for serving

NONIE SUE'S
SCRUB

When my Maw-Maw's garden was teeming with summer squash, she'd chop some up along with slices of okra, potatoes, and onions, toss the vegetables with cornmeal and flour, and fry it in cast-iron skillet. She called this crispy, hash-like side "scrub," but I have no idea why. Other families in the area made similar dishes, but I've never seen it outside of my hometown of Corinth, Mississippi.

In a large bowl, combine the squash, okra, potatoes, onion, cornmeal, flour, and salt and toss to combine.

In a large cast-iron skillet, heat the vegetable oil over a medium-hot fire (or a medium flame on the stovetop). When it shimmers, add the vegetable mixture and spread it into an even layer. Cook without disturbing for 2 minutes, then stir and continue cooking, stirring occasionally, until the vegetables are browned all over, 8 to 10 minutes total. Serve warm.

4 to 6 servings

2 medium yellow squash, cut into ¼-inch dice (about 2 cups)

2 cups sliced okra, stem ends removed (from about 1¼ pounds)

2 medium red potatoes, cut into ¼-inch dice (about 1½ cups)

1½ cups diced onion (about 1 large onion)

½ cup fine white cornmeal

⅓ cup all-purpose flour

2 teaspoons Diamond Crystal kosher salt

½ cup vegetable oil

HOECAKES

10 to 12 hoecakes (1 or 2 per person)

2½ cups medium-ground white cornmeal

¾ teaspoon freshly ground black pepper

½ teaspoon Diamond Crystal kosher salt

1 egg, beaten

3 cups whole buttermilk

¼ cup lard or bacon grease, melted, plus more for cooking

4 tablespoons butter, melted, for brushing

In Nashville, pulled pork is traditionally served on top of a hoecake, which is an unleavened round of cornbread batter cooked in a cast-iron skillet or on a griddle. This is probably the city's main contribution to the history of barbecue in the American South. So when we were writing the menu for the original Martin's Bar-B-Que, Bo said, "Pat, you can't open a barbecue joint in Nashville and not have pulled pork on hoecakes—that's just offensive."

Hoecakes look like pancakes—made correctly, they're soft and airy—but they're savory, not sweet. (We don't put sugar in any version of corn bread; where I come from, that makes it a corncake.)

As the story goes, sharecroppers would bring cornmeal to the field, and when it was time for a break, they'd mix it with spring water, build a fire in the field, and cook their corn bread on the back of a hoe for lunch. However the name came about, like their namesake, hoecakes should be sturdy enough to shovel up whatever else is on your plate. Because we have lots of leftover hog grease from our barbecue, we use it for cooking our hoecakes, but you can use lard or bacon grease instead.

One more thing: Make 100 percent sure that the buttermilk you buy is whole (3.25% butterfat). For whatever reason, many groceries do not stock whole buttermilk, but a lower-fat buttermilk will ruin the texture of your hoecakes. If you can find a local dairy, do yourself a favor and go buy your buttermilk directly from them—it will be otherworldly better! If you can only find nonfat, 1%, or 1.5% buttermilk, add a splash of heavy cream to it, or use whole milk yogurt as a substitute.

Prepare a medium-high grill (4 to 5 seconds using the Hand Test, page 46).

In a medium bowl, whisk together the cornmeal, pepper, and salt.

In a separate bowl, whisk together the egg and buttermilk to combine. While whisking, add the warm pork fat to the egg/buttermilk mixture, slowly to prevent the egg mixture from cooking. Add the buttermilk mixture to the cornmeal mixture and use a whisk to stir until smooth but do not overmix. It should have the same consistency as pancake batter.

Set a cast-iron skillet on the grill and let it heat up for a few minutes. Brush the skillet with 1 teaspoon of the lard and heat until it looks shiny. Working in batches, scoop ⅓ cup batter into the pan for each hoecake and cook, without moving, until the batter starts to slightly lift around the edges, 3 to 4 minutes. Flip the hoecakes, brush the tops with the melted butter and cook until the bottom is golden brown and crispy, 3 to 4 minutes longer. Place the cooked hoecakes on a platter and cover with a kitchen towel to keep warm.

Repeat until all the batter is cooked. Serve immediately; hoecakes will dry out if you try to rewarm them.

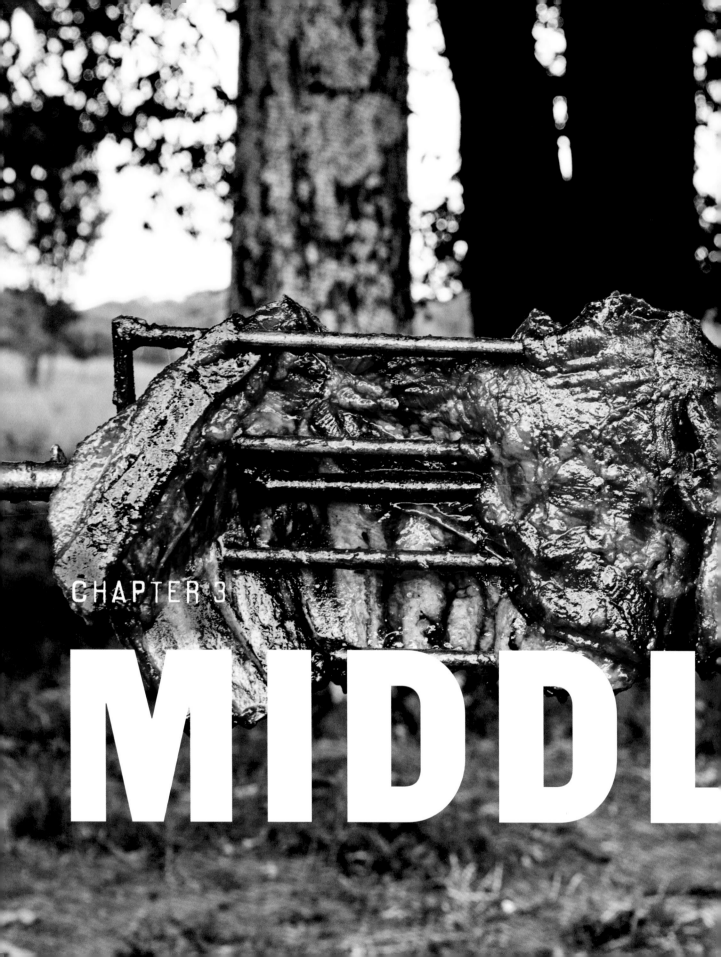

CHAPTER 3

MIDDL

.E AGE

OPEN-PIT AND SPIT BARBECUE

ONCE YOUR BED OF RED-HOT COALS HAS cooled down a bit, you're ready to cross the line from grilling to barbecue. Open-pit barbecue is the nexus of these two live-fire cooking styles: The meat is cooking over—or rather, *near*—hot coals, and there's a lot of air flow around the food and the fire. But unlike grilling, the fire is now configured to produce much less heat—by feeding it fresh coals less often, and spreading them around a bit more—so minutes of cooking time turn into hours, letting the meat slow-cook to break down the collagen, and exposing it to a good amount of smoke during the process. And with the change in technique, time, and heat comes a change in the types of meat we cook. A pork loin chop or a nice tender steak, you grill over relatively high heat to get a good charred crust and a just-cooked interior. When I barbecue, typically I'm cooking tougher cuts with more connective tissue to dissolve, like ribs, shoulders, and of course, whole hogs.

Open pit is as old-school as barbecue gets, especially if you are taking into account the historical significance of it: Indigenous cultures around the world have been slow-cooking meat over an open fire for ages. Open pit is also the most finicky method, because your fire and meat are fully exposed to the elements. You need to take into account the potential for wind and rain; and I'd avoid open-pit barbecue in the dead of winter, because the top half of the meat will cool down quickly every time you flip it.

One of the great things about open-pit barbecue, though, is you can see what you're cooking throughout the process, and it's easier to respond to what's happening in and around the fire and meat in real time. For example, if you have a flare-up, you can pat it out right away with a shovel, whereas a flare-up in a closed pit, if not managed correctly, can turn into a pit fire. You can also monitor the temperature of your meat as it's cooking, and adjust your fire as needed. For instance, you can watch/listen for the right sizzle: If the surface of the meat is sizzling, you know it's too hot. (In any style of barbecue, the only sizzling you should hear is the sound of juice or fat slowly dripping onto a bed of coals.) Conversely, if the top of your meat is cool to the touch, then you know it's time to flip it.

On an open pit, I'll cook everything from ribs and whole chicken (and other small animals, such as rabbit) up to a whole suckling pig, as well as cabbage and other large, sturdy vegetables. This method also opens the door to spit barbecue (see Spit Barbecue, page 131). A spit allows you to cook a bunch of meat at the same time: You can load it up with multiple racks of ribs, a few bone-in pork loins, or even a whole pig. We'll cover both of these techniques in this chapter.

OPEN-PIT BARBECUE

THE GRILL

The custom-fabricated setup I use for grilling (see My Custom-Fabricated Grill, page 42) is the same thing I use for open-pit barbecue. My grill sits about 12 inches off the ground, so if you don't have a similar setup, you can prop a grill grate up on two rows of cinder blocks, or use rebar and cinder blocks.

THE TOOLS

In addition to your grill or open-pit setup, you'll need a **FLAT-HEAD SHOVEL** for moving coals, a pair of **HEATPROOF GLOVES** for handling the meat, and **SOMETHING TO MOP WITH**. This can be an unused kitchen mop (especially handy when cooking whole pigs) or a long-handled grilling mop. But more often than not, I just dip a kitchen towel into my mopping liquid and use that to baste the meat (see Mops, page 107). If you're cooking a whole pig, you'll need a **MEAT CLEAVER, HATCHET, OR LARGE, STURDY KNIFE** for separating the pork ribs from the backbone, and the larger bones from the larger joints.

OPEN-PIT BARBECUE
IS THE NEXUS OF BOTH
GRILLING AND PIT
BARBECUE: THE MEAT
IS COOKING OVER—OR
RATHER, *NEAR*—HOT
COALS, AND THERE'S
A LOT OF AIR FLOW
AROUND THE FOOD AND
THE FIRE.

GETTING READY TO COOK

My technique for cooking open-pit barbecue begins with cooking meat over a medium-hot bed of coals during the front end of the cook, then pulling those coals away to form a ring around the perimeter of the grill for the duration of the process. Following the instructions in Feeder Fires for Grilling and Open-Pit Barbecue (page 37), prepare a space for your grill and build a feeder fire behind the grill. Make this feeder fire about 1 hour before you're ready to start cooking.

You want to clear a space around your grill to leave room for a foot-wide coal bed that surrounds the footprint of the grill on all four sides. (You'll pull the coals under the grill from there to adjust the cook temperature.) If you're using a fresh patch of land, burn it off with a layer of hot, burning coals for 15 to 20 minutes, then repeat once more to ensure the ground below is free of moisture.

MAINTAINING THE HEAT

No matter what I'm cooking on an open pit, I always start open-pit barbecue by laying down a bed of fresh coals. I'll let these coals burn down until they're about medium to medium-low heat, which, depending on wind, takes 8 to 10 minutes. Once the coals get to this point, they start to cool off at a faster rate, meaning they'll quickly go from medium-hot to low in the open air. For open-pit barbecue, you're looking to maintain a heat level throughout the cook that allows you to hold your hand just above the grill grates for 7 to 10 seconds—or sometimes even slightly longer than that.

STOKE YOUR COALS EVERY 10 MINUTES OR SO

You do that just by taking your shovel and gently pushing them around a little, maybe even flipping a few here and there. If you stoke them and the air exposure doesn't increase the bed's heat, then you know it's time to add a few more coals from the feeder fire. I want you to use your hand, and not your eyes, to gauge the heat of the coal bed, because during the day it's tougher to read how bright your coals are glowing by sight.

ADD NEW COALS EVERY 15 TO 20 MINUTES

Do this more frequently if it's breezy outside—to keep the heat where you need it. If you miss this window, just scatter a few fresh, hot coals strategically around the bed to get you back to where you need to be.

BE PATIENT

One last thing before you start cooking. During the first hour or so of your cook, you'll swear to yourself that there's no way your meat is gonna get done in time. You won't see much color change, and your head will start playing games with you. This is the point where you're at risk of fouling everything up, as your first instinct is to add more coals to your bed. Don't do it. Just trust me and be patient. Around the second hour of your cook, you'll (finally) start to notice some changes. So just stay the course and trust the feel of your hand when gauging the temperature of your bed. If your meat is sizzling on the surface or quickly browning, your pit is too hot, so pull some coals out from under the meat toward the perimeter of the bed until you get the temperature where it needs to be.

BREEZY BARBECUE

The goal of open-pit barbecue is to deliver a consistent temperature to your meat. Wind is the enemy of that endeavor, as it can blow heat and smoke away from your food. The best way to combat this is to set up your pit in a spot that's guarded from the wind. But if you can't, or if the breeze is blowing across your fire, you should flip your meat more frequently—every 10 to 12 minutes instead of every 15 minutes. Wind also dries up mop more quickly, so be sure to mop before and after every flip, and maybe in between to keep the meat looking tacky.

THREE KINDS
OF PORK RIBS

Ribs are the steak of the barbecue world, a high-ticket item that you use to reward yourself after a hard week (which is why I see spikes in rib sales on the weekend).

I'll say this up front: I'm not a huge fan of **BABY BACK—AKA LOIN BACK—RIBS**. For years, advertisements have told us that we're supposed to "want our baby backs," and we've taken that message to heart. I'm not gonna let my personal preferences or pride get in the way of my customers' happiness, though, so I serve them in my restaurants. They are mild in flavor; most of what you'll taste is from a rub or a sauce. For me, I'd choose spareribs or their siblings, St. Louis-style ribs. But we'll get to cooking both spares and baby backs in a few pages.

BABY BACKS ARE ATTACHED TO A PIG'S BACKBONE BENEATH THE LOIN MUSCLE. (If you've eaten a bone-in loin chop before, that was a baby back rib attached to the meat.) They're named for their size, not the age of the pig from which they came. The rack tapers from about 6 inches across, down to about 3 inches on the shorter end, and the ribs themselves are curved where they meet the backbone. Most of the meat is located on top of the ribs—rather than between the ribs. This meat tends to be lean and tender, and doesn't taste like much compared to spares, which have more collagen and intramuscular fat. A full rack technically contains 13 ribs (but we only count 12 because the thirteenth bone is nothing but a nub) and weighs 1 to 2 pounds, about half of which is bone mass—most adults can eat a whole rack of baby backs without getting too full.

SPARERIBS ARE FROM A PIG'S LOWER RIB CAGE, TOWARD THE BELLY. If you think of the baby backs as the top of the ribs, the spares are the bottom, and they are what's leftover (or spare) once the belly meat has been removed. Spareribs are longer and flatter than baby backs. One side of the rack has exposed bone where it was cut from the baby backs, and on the other side, you'll find a flap of fatty meat, cartilage, and small bones known as the rib tips. Unlike baby backs, most of the meat on spareribs is located between the bones. Like baby backs, a full rack of spares also includes 13 ribs, but again the thirteenth rib doesn't really count for our purposes because it's about the size of your pinky. An untrimmed slab will weigh 4 to 5 pounds, enough for 2 to 3 people. This cut also gives you the most meat for your dollar.

ST. LOUIS-STYLE RIBS are what you'll most likely encounter if you're shopping for ribs at a grocery store. These are spares that have been trimmed by removing the rib tips and skirt flap. You can spot a St. Louis-style rack right away: It's a neat rectangle, compared to the irregular shape of an untrimmed slab of spares. A full St. Louis-style slab contains 13 ribs and weighs about 3 pounds, enough for 1 to 2 people.

HAVING SPENT YEARS TAKING ORDERS FROM CUSTOMERS AT MY RESTAURANTS, I'VE REALIZED THAT MANY PEOPLE THINK SPARERIBS ARE TOUGH AND CHEWY. But when cooked correctly, they are just as tender as baby backs, have a lot more flavor, and they're twice the size, so you get more pork for your buck. The muscles holding spareribs together are tougher than that of baby backs, which is why we cook them slowly to break down all of the connective tissue. Cooked properly, spares can be as tender as you desire.

NO MATTER WHAT KIND OF RIBS I'M COOKING—AND NO MATTER WHAT TECHNIQUE I'M USING—I NEVER REMOVE THE PAPERY MEMBRANE FROM THE CONCAVE SIDE OF THE RACK. You'll hear a lot of people saying that you should. It's a practice that's spilled over from competition barbecue, where the conventional wisdom says that the membrane prevents the flavors of rub, sauce, and smoke from reaching the meat. This ain't nothing but a bunch of bull. Membranes are porous, so flavors can pass right through. It's true that the membrane is tough when it's raw, but after cooking it becomes papery and easy to chew. We've served hundreds of thousands of ribs at my restaurants, all of them with the membrane on, and I can't think of one time anyone complained about it. Also, the membrane is an insurance policy in case you overcook your ribs to the point of being *too* tender; the membrane will hold the ribs together and your rack won't fall apart on you. If you are determined not to serve ribs with a membrane on them, then right before serving, simply take the tip of a knife and slide it under the membrane, lifting it off the bone enough that you can pinch the membrane with your fingers. Then take a paper towel, grab the membrane, and pull it right off.

THE RIB RECIPES IN THIS CHAPTER CAN BE MADE WITH ANY OF THESE THREE STYLES OF PORK RIBS—YOUR ONLY VARIABLE WILL BE COOKING TIME. Baby backs and St. Louis-style ribs will cook in about the same amount of time, while untrimmed spares will take a while longer.

WE'VE SERVED HUNDREDS OF THOUSANDS OF RIBS AT MY RESTAURANTS, ALL OF THEM WITH THE MEMBRANE ON, AND I CAN'T THINK OF ONE TIME ANYONE COMPLAINED ABOUT IT.

SPARERIBS

T hese spareribs are my favorite thing to make on an open pit. I rub them down with my all-purpose Big Hoss Rub, then mop them with Jack's Creek Sauce as they cook. This combination makes the ribs slightly spicy and tangy, without overpowering the flavor of the pork. (If you want to skip the dry rub, you can season the ribs with salt before throwing them on the grill.) The moisture of the mop helps grab some of the smoky flavor, though open-pit ribs will be noticeably less smoky than those cooked in a closed pit, because so much of the smoke blows away.

Texturewise, I like my ribs tender, but with some bite. In other words, you should be able to take a bite of meat off the finished ribs without ripping all of the meat from the bone. My ribs also don't have that all-over "bark" that competition barbecue guys lust after, but they will get caramelized and crispy in parts.

As the ribs cook, I alternate between flipping and rotating them about every 12 to 15 minutes, for a total of 2½ to 3½ hours or so. Because you're working with an open pit, your bed of coals isn't going to produce a perfectly even temperature. So moving the meat around frequently ensures that every part of the rib is exposed to the same amount of heat. It's extra important to remember to rotate the ribs throughout the cook on an open pit, or you could end up with unevenly cooked meat.

My grill grate holds four racks of spares, but you can scale this recipe down, or up, depending on the size of your setup and the amount of ribs you want to make.

Evenly coat the ribs with the dry rub (see How to Apply Rub, page 97) and let sit for an hour or so before cooking so the rub can slightly cure the meat. If time allows, season the ribs the night before, then place them on a wire rack set inside a sheet pan and refrigerate.

Prepare a bed of coals (see Getting Ready to Cook, page 85) below the grill grate and let them burn down until they're medium to medium-low (you should be able to hold your hand just above the grill grate for 7 to 10 seconds).

Place the ribs membrane-side up (meat-side down) on the grate and let them cook, undisturbed, for 5 to 10 minutes. Flip the ribs over and cook for 5 minutes longer.

Using a shovel, pull the coals below the grill grate toward the perimeter of the grill to make a four-sided bed of coals, about 4 inches high, around the grate. Lay a few logs or wood slats around the perimeter of the grill on top of the coals. At this point, there should be nothing but smoldering ash below the ribs; the heat radiating from the ring of coals will do the cooking from here on out.

(recipe continues)

8 to 12 servings

4 slabs untrimmed spareribs (4 to 5 pounds each), or St. Louis-style ribs (2½ to 3½ pounds each)

½ cup Big Hoss Rub (page 96), or Diamond Crystal kosher salt

1 gallon (4 recipes) Jack's Creek Sauce (page 95)

Sweet Dixie BBQ Sauce (optional; page 100)

IT'S EXTRA IMPORTANT TO REMEMBER TO ROTATE THE RIBS THROUGHOUT THE COOK ON AN OPEN PIT, OR YOU COULD END UP WITH UNEVENLY COOKED MEAT.

Flip the ribs back over, meat-side down again, and cook for 15 minutes. Rotate the ribs 180 degrees (without flipping). Wait 15 minutes, then flip the ribs over. After 15 minutes, rotate the ribs again. You'll be repeating this pattern for a while.

As your wood burns down, push or shovel some coals from the perimeter of the grill inward (about a half shovelful per side) and add new wood to the top of the coal bed. Adding the new wood produces additional hot coals for you to push in later. You'll probably need to do this about every 30 minutes or so throughout the cook, more often on windy days. Check the ambient temperature around the ribs with your hand every so often; you're aiming for 225° to 250°F, or 7 to 10 seconds with the hand test. If you can hear the surface of the ribs sizzling, that means your fire is too hot. In any barbecue, the only sizzling you should hear is the sound of juice or fat dripping onto a bed of coals; you never want the surface of the meat itself sizzling. If this happens, just flip the ribs over and let the coals die down a little longer before pushing new ones toward the grill, and push fewer coals when you do, until the sizzling stops.

One hour into your cook, begin lightly mopping the ribs with the Jack's Creek Sauce after every time you touch them. Flip the ribs, mop with sauce, wait 15 minutes. Rotate the ribs, mop with sauce, wait 15 minutes. And so on.

Continue this process until the ribs are ready to eat. A rack of untrimmed spareribs will take between 3 and 3½ hours to cook, and St. Louis-style ribs will take around 2½ hours. I use my eyes and hands to know when the ribs are done. The meat will have a beautiful mahogany color (from all the mopping) and will begin to pull back from the ends of the bones. I can put on a pair of gloves, pick the rack up in the middle, membrane-side down, and the ends will bow down so the ribs resemble a frown. The rack should be flexible enough that I can break it into two pieces by giving it a hard wiggle. You can also test for doneness by pressing your finger between two ribs; if you can push your finger into the meat, it's done. If you don't trust your other senses and want to use an instant-read thermometer, insert it into the meat between two ribs (making sure not to hit any bones); they're finished when the thermometer reads between 185° and 190°F.

If the ribs aren't finished, or if you lost your dentures and want super-tender ribs, continue cooking the ribs as before, checking them for doneness every time you flip or rotate.

When the ribs are finished, transfer them to a cutting board. Using a sturdy knife, cut the flaps of brisket meat away from the ribs. You can snack on this bonus meat yourself, give it to your messy uncle, or use it to make a Rib Meat Sandwich (page 99).

Cut the racks into individual ribs and serve—with barbecue sauce, if you like.

IN ANY BARBECUE, THE ONLY SIZZLING YOU SHOULD HEAR IS THE SOUND OF JUICE OR FAT DRIPPING ONTO A BED OF COALS; YOU NEVER WANT THE SURFACE OF THE MEAT ITSELF SIZZLING.

YOU DIDN'T TAKE AN ENTIRE AFTERNOON WORKING HARD TO COOK GREAT RIBS, ONLY TO USE THEM AS A VEHICLE FOR SOME THICK SAUCE. IF THAT'S WHAT YOU REALLY WANT, BUST OPEN A BAG OF POTATO CHIPS AND DIP AWAY.

Jack's Creek
9/6

JACK'S
CREEK SAUCE

If you think of a vinaigrette as a balance between fat and acid, barbecue is the same thing: fatty meat with an acidic sauce. The fattier the meat, the more acidic you need a sauce to be. This is why I have an issue with using rich, thick, super-sweet barbecue sauces on fattier meats: I only taste the sauce, which is an imbalance. Some folks think this is what they really want in their barbecue, but I'll tell them they don't. You didn't take an entire afternoon working hard to cook great ribs, only to use them as a vehicle for some thick sauce. If that's what you really want, bust open a bag of potato chips and dip away.

The classic West Tennessee barbecue sauce is vinegar-based, but unlike the vinegar sauces from the Carolinas, ours contains sugar, which varies in amount from one joint to the next. When I was learning whole-hog barbecue from Harold Thomas, I never had the balls to ask him for his sauce recipe (which he would've kindly shared), so I backed into this in my college dorm room as I was preparing to cook my first hog. I continue to use it as both mop and sauce today.

I named this sauce after the small town of Jacks Creek, which is roughly the midpoint between West Tennessee's main barbecue hubs: Henderson and Lexington. Although Jacks Creek doesn't have much barbecue itself, we consider it the unofficial ground zero of the regional style, so naming my sauce "Jack's Creek" was my way of paying homage to our style of whole-hog barbecue.

In a blender, combine all the ingredients and blend until smooth, 1 to 2 minutes. Transfer to an airtight container and refrigerate for up to 1 month.

Makes about 4 cups

1¾ cups apple cider vinegar
1¾ cups distilled white vinegar
1¼ cups granulated sugar
½ cup Big Hoss Rub (page 96)
3 tablespoons red pepper flakes

BIG HOSS RUB

Makes about 5 cups

1½ cups packed light brown sugar

1 cup Diamond Crystal kosher salt

1 cup garlic salt

½ cup granulated sugar

½ cup sweet paprika

3 tablespoons lemon pepper

2 tablespoons chile powder (see Note)

1 tablespoon plus 1 teaspoon mustard powder

1 tablespoon freshly ground black pepper

1 tablespoon cayenne pepper

1 teaspoon ground ginger

½ teaspoon ground cinnamon

NOTE Not to be confused with chili seasoning, this is pure ground dried chiles. I like Santa Cruz brand, made from Hatch chiles.

I came up with this dry rub recipe in my college dorm room in 1991 and loved it so much, I haven't changed it since. That said, I don't think my rub recipe has anything to do with the quality of my barbecue. Sauces and rubs have been overromanticized by both professional and amateur barbecue enthusiasts alike—including myself, in my early days. Everyone thinks they have to come up with a "secret" recipe to make their meat stand out, which we can blame on the idiosyncrasies of competition barbecue. But about ten years ago I realized that what makes a good rub isn't proprietary ingredients—it's balance. If you can find the right ratio of salt, sugar, acidity, and heat using just a few ingredients, your rub is as good as any.

Don't believe me? As proud of this recipe as I am, as an experiment you could just take its main components—salt, sugar, lemon pepper, and cayenne—and use that on one rack of ribs and some complicated rub on another. Once the ribs are cooked, you won't be able to taste much difference between the two. That's because a rub's primary function is to help the meat develop a crust, or bark, on its surface as it cooks. For this you need salt (to help draw out the moisture) and some sugar for the caramelization. I like a good amount of zesty acidity in my rub, so I add mustard powder, ground ginger, and lemon pepper (which you can find at most grocery stores, or make your own by combining 1 part citric acid to 3 parts ground pepper). Cayenne adds a hint of spiciness, and paprika and chile powder mostly add color. The rest of the ingredients will add some flavor, but not much.

My point is: If you want to use your own rub recipe—which I highly encourage—in your barbecue, just make sure it's balanced.

In a medium bowl, whisk together all the ingredients. Store in an airtight container in a cool, dry place for up to 1 month.

I REALIZED THAT WHAT MAKES A GOOD RUB ISN'T PROPRIETARY INGREDIENTS— IT'S BALANCE. IF YOU CAN FIND THE RIGHT RATIO OF SALT, SUGAR, ACIDITY, AND HEAT USING JUST A FEW INGREDIENTS, YOUR RUB IS AS GOOD AS ANY.

HOW TO APPLY RUB

Dry rubs have two functions: They add flavor and, because they contain sugar, add caramelization to the surface of the meat. Some barbecue folks like to dump loads of rub on their meat and work it into the cavities and crevices. This excessive seasoning can overpower the flavor of the meat, and you'll often find little pockets of uncooked rub in the crannies. I err on the side of underseasoning meat with rub, and apply it only to exposed meat—it's a waste to put rub on the animal's skin, as it won't penetrate and season the meat below. It takes a lot less than you think to end up with the flavor and texture you're looking for.

The best way to apply rub is to get a "dredge shaker," which is a large spice shaker with a handle (you'll often see these at pizza parlors filled with cheese or pepper flakes). Fill it with rub and move it back and forth (rather than using an up and down motion) over the meat until you have a light, even coating. Think of it like seasoning a burger or steak: You wouldn't coat the thing in salt, right? If you don't have a shaker, then use your fingers, grabbing a large pinch and evenly broadcasting the rub 6 to 8 inches over the meat.

RIB MEAT
SANDWICH

There's a big bone at the front of a rack of untrimmed spareribs that's surrounded by meat and ligaments running every which way. I consider this "brisket" a piece of bonus meat, a treat for the pitmaster and his buddies, and it makes a dang-tasty sandwich. One slab of ribs should give you enough of this bonus meat for 1 large or 2 small sandwiches. If you want to make more sandwiches, or if you've cooked St. Louis-style ribs, you can pull some rib meat right off the bones. Normally, I think slaw is a must on barbecue sandwiches, but I love the flavor of ribs so much, I'm okay eating this without slaw.

Pull the meat into large shreds, discarding any small bones. Stack the meat on bread and drizzle with the sauce of your choosing.

1 or 2 servings

1 piece brisket (rib tips) from Open-Pit Spareribs (page 91), or a few ribs' worth of meat

White bread or burger buns

Jack's Creek Sauce (page 95) or Sweet Dixie BBQ Sauce (page 100)

SWEET DIXIE
BBQ SAUCE

Makes about 4 cups

2⅔ cups apple cider vinegar

1 cup ketchup

¼ cup unsulfured molasses

¼ cup honey

1 tablespoon soy sauce

1 tablespoon plus 1 teaspoon
Diamond Crystal kosher salt

½ cup granulated sugar

1 tablespoon plus ¾ teaspoon
mustard powder

1 teaspoon chile powder (see
Note)

½ teaspoon red pepper flakes

¼ teaspoon onion powder

NOTE Not to be confused
with chili seasoning, this is
pure ground dried chiles. I like
Santa Cruz brand, made from
Hatch chiles.

I almost always prefer a vinegar-based sauce on my barbecue (that's the West Tennessee way), but when I opened Martin's, even my ignorant ass knew enough about the restaurant business that society would demand a thick, tomato-based sauce, and I didn't want to give folks a stupid reason not to eat there. So I came up with a compromise: a tomato-based sauce that's on the thinner side and not overly sweet, which I use to finish ribs and chicken (or drizzle on a rib-tip sandwich). You might notice that the sauce isn't cooked: This both saves on prep time and keeps the sauce nice and loose.

In a blender, combine all the ingredients and blend until the sugar is dissolved, about 3 minutes. Transfer to an airtight container and refrigerate for up to 1 month.

PHOTO COURTESY OF ROBERT LERMA

OPEN-PIT
BABY BACK RIBS

4 servings

4 slabs baby back ribs (about 1½ pounds each)

½ cup Big Hoss Rub (page 96), plus more for serving, or ¼ cup Diamond Crystal kosher salt

1 gallon (4 recipes) Jack's Creek Sauce (page 95)

1 cup Sweet Dixie BBQ Sauce (page 100), plus more for serving

If you're going to cook baby back ribs, this is the way to do it. You'll notice that the method is nearly identical to the Open-Pit Spareribs (page 91)—with the cooking time close to the St. Louis-style ribs—with some slight but meaningful tweaks. Because baby backs don't have as much fat as spares, I start mopping them earlier in the cook to moisten them. And because they don't offer much flavor, I finish the baby backs with a thicker, tomato-based barbecue sauce, or I'll sprinkle them with dry rub after they come off the pit.

Season the ribs with the dry rub (see How to Apply Rub, page 97) and let sit for 1 hour or so before cooking so the rub can slightly cure the meat. If time allows, season the ribs the night before, then place them on a wire rack set inside a sheet pan and refrigerate.

Meanwhile, prepare a bed of coals (see Getting Ready to Cook, page 85) below the grill grate and let them burn down until they're medium to medium-low (you should be able to hold your hand just above the grill grate for 7 to 10 seconds).

Place the ribs membrane-side up (meat-side down) on the grates and let them cook, undisturbed, for 5 to 10 minutes. Flip the ribs over and let cook for 5 minutes longer.

Using a shovel, pull the coals below the grill grate toward the perimeter of the grill to make a four-sided bed of coals around the grate. Lay a few logs or wood slats around the perimeter of the grill on top of your coals. At this point, there should be nothing but smoldering ash below the ribs; the ring of coals will do the cooking from here on out.

Mop the ribs with the Jack's Creek Sauce and flip them over. Wait 15 minutes, then rotate the ribs 180 degrees (without flipping). Mop the ribs again and wait 15 minutes, then mop and flip the ribs over. After 15 minutes, rotate the ribs again.

As your wood burns down, push or shovel some coals from the perimeter of the grill inward (about a half shovelful per side) and add new wood to the top of the coal bed. You'll probably need to do this about every 30 minutes, more often on windy days. Check the ambient temperature around the ribs with your hand every so often; you're aiming for 250° to 275°F, or 7 to 10 seconds with the hand test. If you can hear the surface of the ribs sizzling, that means your fire is too hot. If this happens, just flip the ribs over and let the coals die down a little longer before pushing new ones toward the grill, and push fewer coals when you do, until the sizzling stops.

About 1½ hours into your cook, put the mop away and begin brushing the ribs with the Sweet Dixie BBQ Sauce after every time you touch them. Flip the ribs, brush with sauce, wait 15 minutes. Rotate the ribs, brush with sauce, wait 15 minutes. And so on.

Continue this process until the ribs are ready to eat. A rack of baby backs should take 2 to 2½ hours to be finished. I use my eyes and hands to know when the ribs are done. The meat will begin to separate from the bones, and I can put on a pair of gloves, pick the rack up in the middle, membrane-side down, and the ends will bow down so the ribs resemble a frown. The rack should be flexible enough that I can break it into two pieces by giving it a hard wiggle. You can also test for doneness by pressing your finger between two ribs; if you can push your finger into the meat, it's done.

If the ribs aren't finished, continue cooking the ribs as before, checking them for doneness every time you flip or rotate.

When the ribs are done, transfer them to a cutting board. Cut the racks into individual ribs and serve with Sweet Dixie BBQ Sauce or sprinkle with Big Hoss Rub.

MOPS

I almost always use a mop when doing open-pit or spit barbecue. (By contrast, I don't use a mop when cooking with a closed pit, because there's enough humidity trapped inside the pit to keep the meat moist, and mopping it will slow the cooking down.)

Not to be confusing, but a mop is simply some kind of liquid that you dab onto the surface of the meat periodically as it cooks—sometimes applied with an actual mop, which is why the liquid has its name. A mop serves a few purposes: First, it keeps the surface of the meat moist. As meat cooks, its surface releases moisture, much like you sweat on a hot day (or like I sweat on any day). By mopping the surface of the meat, it prevents more moisture from within from evaporating. Surface moisture, it turns out, also attracts smoke, so keeping the surface of the meat wet will help your meat absorb more delicious smoke flavor.

Depending on what's in your mop, it will also add some flavor. If I want a classic barbecue flavor, I'll use a vinegar-based mop that's been sweetened with sugar or sorghum and seasoned with some pepper flakes or dry rub. Most of the recipes in this chapter call for using my Jack's Creek Sauce (pag 95), which is a combination of vinegar, sugar, pepper flakes, and my house dry rub. Most of the time, however, I just grab a large jug of cider vinegar, dump some sugar and pepper flakes into it, and shake it up. If you don't want your mop to add much flavor to the meat, you can simply use vinegar, apple juice, cheap beer or wine, or even water—because all of these ingredients are mostly water, the difference in flavor will be subtle, if at all noticeable. If your mop contains sugar, that will also aid in browning the meat, as the sugars will caramelize on the surface, giving you a gorgeous deep mahogany color. Just don't use a mop that tastes super sweet; a high-sugar mop can eventually burn and taste bitter.

If applied incorrectly, a mop can also *remove* flavor from your barbecue. Brushing a mop onto the meat, or applying too much mop, can wash away any dry rub or salt sticking to its surface. To mop correctly, you should dab your mop-soaked brush (or a kitchen towel, if you don't have a brush) gently on the meat.

Be sure you have *plenty* of mop ready before your cook. It evaporates quickly, so you'll be burning through the stuff much faster than you think.

WHOLE CHICKEN
WITH ALABAMA WHITE SAUCE

This chicken is my ode to Alabama white sauce, a tangy blend of mayonnaise, vinegar, and spices that was created almost a hundred years ago at Big Bob Gibson Bar-B-Q in Decatur, Alabama, about thirty miles south of the Tennessee border. It has since become a cult item in the world of barbecue, and my buddy Chris Lilly (Gibson's pitmaster and competition barbecue legend) has made enough of the original recipe to float the USS *Nimitz*. I started working on my own version of white sauce a couple months before I opened my first barbecue joint. While you'll often see the sauce used on chicken wings, legs, or half chickens, I like to dunk a whole barbecue bird in the stuff when it's close to being cooked through, then finish the chicken over the fire, which turns the sauce into a rich, shiny glaze.

To help the chicken cook evenly and expose more of it to the smoky fire, I butterfly (aka spatchcock) it first. But my method is unconventional. Frankly, it's backward: Instead of removing the chicken's backbone (as is the established method), I split the bird through the breastbone. This technique was born years ago out of a screwup: I accidentally cut down the wrong side of a chicken, but I cooked it anyway, and I actually preferred the results. The breast and leg meat cooked more evenly, and to me it just looks right: When you lay the bird out flat, the legs fold neatly around the breast to create a tight square of meat. If you think I'm full of it, try my "reverse spatchcock" method once, and see for yourself.

To keep your bird from drying out over the dry heat of the fire, I highly recommend using a brined chicken. Many of the chickens you buy at the grocery store have already been injected with brine, or "plumped." The label will tell you if it's been brined, and how much of its total weight is brine (look for something that has been plumped by at least 9 percent brine or broth). Organic chickens have probably not been plumped, and the same goes for anything you buy from a local farmer. In those cases, you can dry-brine the chicken: Season it all over, inside and out, with kosher salt (about 1 teaspoon of Diamond Crystal per pound), then place it on a wire rack set over a sheet pan and refrigerate it, uncovered, for at least 6 and up to 24 hours.

4 servings

1 whole chicken (3½ to 4 pounds), brined or dry-brined

1 tablespoon Big Hoss Rub (page 96)

1 cup apple cider vinegar

1 cup apple juice

Pat's Alabama White Sauce (page 113)

Using kitchen shears, split the chicken by cutting up from the cavity, through the breast side. Cut close to the breastbone and through the wishbone. Season the chicken with the dry rub (see How to Apply Rub, page 97).

In a bowl, whisk together the vinegar and apple juice; this will be your mop.

Prepare a bed of coals (see Getting Ready to Cook, page 85) below the grill grate and let them burn down until they're medium to medium-low (you should be able to hold your hand just above the grill grate for 7 to 10 seconds).

(recipe continues)

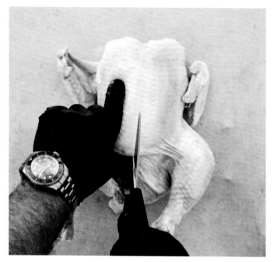

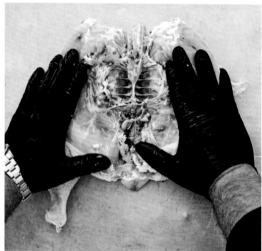

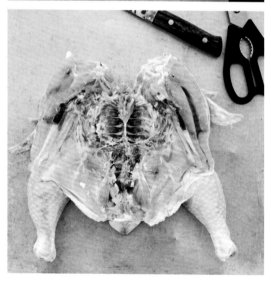

Open up the chicken so that it lies flat and place it skin-side down on the grill grates. Cook, undisturbed, for 5 to 10 minutes. Flip the chicken over and let it cook for 5 minutes longer.

Using a shovel, pull the coals below the grill grate toward the perimeter of the grill to make a four-sided bed of coals around the grate. Lay a few logs or wood slats around the perimeter of the grill on top of your coals. At this point, there should be nothing but smoldering ash below the chicken; the ring of coals will do the cooking from here on out.

Flip the chicken over and wait 15 minutes, then rotate it 180 degrees (without flipping). Wait 15 minutes, baste the chicken with some mop, and flip over. Continue alternating between flipping and rotating the bird every 15 minutes, basting it with the mop every time you move it.

As your wood burns down, push or shovel some coals from the perimeter of the grill inward (about a half shovelful per side) and add new wood to the top of the coal bed. You'll probably need to do this about every 30 minutes, more often on windy days. Check the ambient temperature around the chicken with your hand every so often; you're aiming for 250° to 275°F, or 7 to 10 seconds with the hand test.

Continue this process until the chicken is almost cooked through (the thickest part of the leg should be around 160°F), about 2 hours.

Pour the Alabama white sauce into a large bowl or baking pan and add the chicken, turning it until it's well coated in the sauce. Return the chicken to the grill grates, skin-side down, and cook until the sauce is clearly reducing on the skin, about 10 more minutes. Coat the chicken in the sauce once again, then transfer to a cutting board and let rest for about 10 minutes; the heat of the cooked chicken will turn the sauce into a shiny glaze. Carve the bird into pieces and serve.

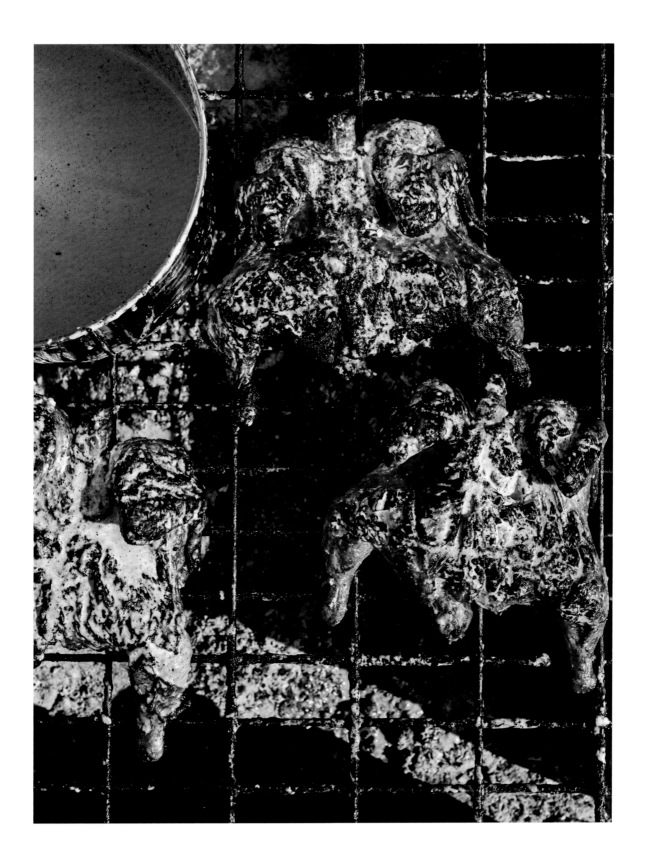

ALABAMA
WHITE SAUCE

A lthough this is based on Big Bob Gibson's original recipe—he generously gave it away to anyone who asked—I wanted my version to be less sharp-tasting, so I swapped distilled vinegar out for cider vinegar, and added a little cinnamon and a bit of honey, not for sweetness but to balance out the acidity of the vinegar. When it's at refrigerator temperature, my sauce is thick and pungent, so it's best to let it warm up to room temperature before you use it (don't worry; it's plenty acidic to stay fresh). In addition to being a glaze for grilled chicken, it makes a fine sauce for smoked wings, and Martin's guests love it as a dip for French fries.

In a medium bowl, whisk together all the ingredients. Transfer to an airtight container and refrigerate for up to 2 weeks.

Makes about 4 cups

2½ cups mayonnaise

1¼ cups apple cider vinegar

1½ teaspoons Worcestershire sauce

2 tablespoons honey

1 garlic clove, finely grated

1 tablespoon Diamond Crystal kosher salt

1 tablespoon freshly ground black pepper

1½ teaspoons chile powder (see Note)

1½ teaspoons red pepper flakes

1½ teaspoons cayenne pepper

¾ teaspoon ground cinnamon

NOTE Not to be confused with chili seasoning, this is pure ground dried chiles. I like Santa Cruz brand, made from Hatch chiles.

SLOW-GRILLED
CHICKEN THIGHS

4 servings

8 bone-in, skin-on chicken thighs (about 3 pounds total)

2 tablespoons vegetable oil

2 teaspoons Diamond Crystal kosher salt

1 cup Jack's Creek Sauce (page 95)

To me, chicken breasts are the poultry equivalent of baby back ribs: They're high in hype and low in flavor. I'm a dark meat man; those muscles have more intramuscular fat and were constantly used, developing character. So unless I'm grilling a whole chicken, I'll stick to thighs, which have more flavor and are far more forgiving on the grill—this leaves lots of time for building up a nice layer of sticky, tangy glaze. My kids love this recipe alongside some Smashed Potatoes with Crisped Cheddar (page 228).

Prepare a medium-hot fire (4 to 5 seconds using the Hand Test, page 46). Clean and oil the grill grates well.

Rub the chicken all over with the oil and season with the salt. Place the chicken, skin-side down, on the grill and cook for 15 minutes, then flip and cook for another 15 minutes.

As your wood burns down, push or shovel some coals from the perimeter of the grill inward (about a half shovelful per side) and add new wood to the top of the coal bed. You'll probably need to do this about every 30 minutes, more often on windy days, as you try to maintain a medium to medium-low fire below the chicken throughout the cook. Check the ambient temperature around the chicken with your hand every so often; you're aiming for 225° to 250°F, or 7 to 10 seconds with the hand test.

After 30 minutes, brush the thighs with the Jack's Creek Sauce. Continue cooking, turning and brushing with sauce every 5 to 7 minutes until well glazed and cooked through, about 30 minutes longer. Transfer the chicken thighs to plates and serve. I strongly suggest you eat these with your bare hands.

OPEN-PIT RABBIT
WITH ALABAMA WHITE SAUCE

2 servings

1 whole rabbit (about 2½ pounds), cleaned

2 tablespoons Diamond Crystal kosher salt

2 cups white wine or light (non-hoppy) beer

1 cup Pat's Alabama White Sauce (page 113)

Fleur de sel or other flaky salt

Lemon wedges, for serving

In the South, much like other parts of the country where agriculture is an economic driver, hunting and fishing is really big. My family fishes for crappie and catfish, and we hunt quail (see Grilled Quail, page 61) and rabbits. My Uncle Grady was paralyzed and bound to a wheelchair from an accident as a young adult, which kept him from hunting anymore. But even then, in the evenings my Aunt B would roll him outside on their carport, and she'd turn their pack of beagles out to run. He'd sit there and smile, listening to them work, tilting his head saying to me, "Listen, Patrick, you hear 'em? They're running a rabbit now."

Besides quail, rabbit is my favorite wild game to eat. It cooks easily, has a clean, chicken-like flavor, and is not at all gamey. As with whole chicken, I like to coat the rabbit in Alabama white sauce right after it comes off the pit, but you can skip this step and serve it with a vinegar-based barbecue sauce, or it's sublime with just a squeeze of lemon juice. Serve this with Charred Carrots with Sorghum and Buttermilk (page 53) or "Arsh" Potatoes (page 227) and a bottle of light, fruity red wine, and you've got about as elegant of a barbecue meal as you can get.

Lay the rabbit, belly-side down, on a cutting board and push firmly on its back until it lies flat (you might crack a few bones; that's fine). Season the rabbit all over with the kosher salt and place it on a wire rack set inside a sheet pan. Refrigerate, uncovered, for at least 6 hours or up to 1 day ahead.

Prepare a bed of coals (see Getting Ready to Cook, page 85) below the grill grate and let them burn down until they're medium to medium-low (you should be able to hold your hand just above the grill grate for 7 to 10 seconds).

Place the rabbit on the grill grates, belly-side up, and cook, undisturbed, for 5 to 10 minutes. Flip the rabbit over and let cook for 5 minutes longer.

Using a shovel, pull the coals below the grill grate toward the perimeter of the grill to make a four-sided bed of coals around the grate. Lay a few logs or wood slats around the perimeter of the grill on top of your coals. At this point, there should be nothing but smoldering ash below the rabbit; the ring of coals will do the cooking from here on out.

Flip the rabbit over and wait 15 minutes, then rotate it 180 degrees (without flipping). Wait 15 minutes, mop the rabbit with wine or beer, and flip over. Continue alternating between flipping and rotating the rabbit every 15 minutes, basting it with the mop every time you move it.

As your wood burns down, push or shovel some coals from the perimeter of the grill inward (about a half shovelful per side) and add new wood to the top of the coal bed. You'll probably need to do this about every 30 minutes, more often on windy days. Check the ambient temperature around the rabbit with your hand every so often; you're aiming for 250° to 275°F, or 7 to 10 seconds with the hand test.

Continue this process until the rabbit is cooked through (the USDA tells you to cook it to 160°F, but I like mine around 140°F), 1 to 1½ hours. Transfer the rabbit to a cutting board and brush all over with Alabama white sauce. Let rest for about 10 minutes; the heat of the cooked rabbit will turn the sauce into a shiny glaze. Carve the rabbit into pieces, sprinkle with fleur de sel, and serve with lemon wedges.

WHOLE CABBAGE

Cabbage gets a bad rap as being this boring vegetable, thanks in part to the mushy, boiled cabbage many of us ate in school cafeterias when we were young. (If this wasn't the case where you grew up, consider yourself lucky.) But cabbage can really take a beating before it gets to that point, and that's what I intend for you to do here. This is a stupid-simple dish you can cook alongside anything else you're doing on the open pit or spit. The finished product is smoky and tender, but it still holds its texture with a little crunch. I don't do much to the cabbage at all besides giving it a generous sprinkle of salt before it goes on the pit. When it's done, you can drizzle the cabbage with an acidic barbecue sauce, or I like to quickly dunk it in Alabama white sauce, pile the wedges up on a platter, and serve it family-style.

4 servings

1 head red or green cabbage
   (2 to 2½ pounds)

¼ cup vegetable oil

Kosher salt

About ½ cup Jack's Creek
   Sauce (page 95) or 1 cup
   Pat's Alabama White Sauce
   (page 113), for serving

Prepare a bed of coals (see Getting Ready to Cook, page 85) below the grill grate and let them burn down until they're medium to medium-low (you should be able to hold your hand just above the grill grate for 7 to 10 seconds).

Meanwhile, remove the tough outer layer of leaves from the cabbage. Turn the cabbage stem-side-up, and cut the head into quarters through the core. You want the core to hold the four wedges together, so watch that you don't cut the core out of one side. Brush the cabbage all over with the oil. Generously salt the cut sides of the cabbage wedges. Place the cabbage wedges, cut-side down, on the grill grates and cook, undisturbed, for 5 minutes. Turn the wedges so the other cut side is down and cook for 5 minutes longer.

Using a shovel, pull the coals below the grill grate toward the perimeter of the grill to make a four-sided bed of coals around the grate. Lay a few logs or wood slats around the perimeter of the grill on top of your coals. At this point, there should be nothing but smoldering ash below the cabbage; the ring of coals will do the cooking from here on out.

Continue cooking the cabbage wedges, turning them from one cut side to the other every 15 minutes, until well charred and just soft throughout when pierced with a knife, 45 minutes to 1 hour total.

As your wood burns down, push or shovel some coals from the perimeter of the grill inward (about a half shovelful per side) and add new wood to the top of the coal bed. You'll probably need to do this about every 30 minutes, more often on windy days. Check the ambient temperature around the cabbage with your hand every so often; you're aiming for 250° to 275°F, or 7 to 10 seconds with the hand test.

When the cabbage is finished, transfer to a platter and drizzle with the Jack's Creek Sauce, or toss in a bowl with the Alabama white sauce, and serve.

SOURCING PIGS AND HOGS FOR BARBECUE

Before we get into this book's first whole-swine barbecue recipe, it's time for a primer on how to source and prepare pigs and hogs (hogs are swine larger than 120 pounds). The three main things you'll have to consider are size, breed, and in what state of processing the pig will come to you.

— SIZE —

When deciding what size of pig you want to cook, ask yourself: 1) How many people do I want to feed? and 2) How much time do I have? This book will give you instructions for four different whole-pig/hog methods, listed in the chart below, along with the weight of the swine you'll need, and the approximate start-to-finish cooking time. If you're wondering why it isn't a perfect 1:1 ratio of weight to meat as you look across this chart, it's because younger pigs will tend to give you a larger percentage yield of meat, as they have less collagen and fat.

METHOD	WEIGHT OF PIG/HOG (DRESSED)	APPROXIMATE COOKING TIME	COOKED MEAT YIELD	APPROXIMATE SERVINGS*
OPEN PIT (page 126)	**30 TO 50 POUNDS**	**4 TO 5 HOURS**	**ABOUT 45 PERCENT**	**14 TO 23 POUNDS OF MEAT**; enough for **50 TO 90 SERVINGS**
SPIT (page 139)	**70 TO 100 POUNDS**	**8 TO 12 HOURS**	**ABOUT 40 PERCENT**	**30 TO 40 POUNDS OF MEAT**; enough for **140 TO 150 SERVINGS**
IN THE GROUND (page 197)	**125 TO 155 POUNDS**	**16 TO 18 HOURS**	**ABOUT 33 PERCENT**	**ABOUT 40 TO 50 POUNDS OF MEAT**, enough for **150 TO 190 SERVINGS**
CLOSED PIT (page 148)	**175 TO 190 POUNDS**	**20 TO 24 HOURS**	**ABOUT 33 PERCENT**	**53 TO 63 POUNDS OF MEAT**; enough for **200 TO 240 SERVINGS**

*When I say a "serving," I'm referring to 4 to 5 ounces of cooked pork, which is the amount I put on a typical Pulled Pork Sandwich (page 189). If you're going to serve plates of pork, plan on a typical serving being 7 to 8 ounces, and reduce the number of servings accordingly.

— BREEDS —

I love cooking heritage-breed pigs and promote them because they often have unique flavor, good intramuscular fat, and are worth every extra dollar that you spend on them. They bring us closer back to the way barbecue tasted in the old days. Commodity pigs have been bred for decades to produce leaner meat, and are not helped by their typical environment and handling, which leaves them in crowded conditions and pretty beat up. But not all heritage breeds make good whole-hog barbecue. Larder hogs (we call them "swallow belly" hogs), such as Mangalitsa, for example, have too much fat on them and make them too

risky (fire) and too expensive (yield). They taste incredible, but you've just got to watch that pit like a hawk so you don't burn it up. Those breeds are better suited for charcuterie.

My favorite breeds of hog for barbecuing whole are Chester White (commonly found all over the United States), Berkshire, and Red Yorkshire. Berkshires make great barbecue and are my actual favorite breed, but depending on their diet they can be too fatty, and you'll have to remove some of their lard before you cook. Durocs work fine as well and offer lots of belly meat, but their hams are on the smaller side and tend to overcook.

— SOURCING —

If you live in pork country, it's pretty easy to find and call a local farmer who'll sell you a pig or hog of your desired size, or they can tell you where you can buy their pigs—usually a local USDA-inspected pork processing plant. While you're at it, ask them what they feed their hogs. If they've exclusively been "pasture-raised," these are not the hogs you're looking for; they are generally too lean for barbecue. You want a hog that has at least been finished with a grain-based diet, so they'll have plenty of fat.

Depending on the season, you'll want to do this at least a couple of weeks in advance—even more if you have very specific requests.

If you can't find a local farmer, search your area for a USDA-inspected meat-processing plant that sells to the public (these are common in smaller rural towns, and a lot of them have a retail storefront), which should be able to get you the type of pork you need. If this isn't an option, most local butcher shops, wholesale meat packers— and even some independent grocery stores—will special order one for you. Just make sure to do a little recon in advance to find out the kind of lead time they'll need. I'd rather you don't order a commodity packer from a larger plant or supermarket—because of the way they're raised, their meat is lean and they tend to be beat up and bruised from overcrowding.

Whoever you're ordering from, you're gonna need to have a conversation with your supplier to make sure you get what you want. I don't need some supplier telling me his opinion on hog sizes, how I should cook it, what he and his buddies cooked in college, blah blah blah, but you can bet someone will want to have that discussion with you. Some butchers will tell you they'll get you the size you requested and then they get one much smaller or larger—and then expect you to take it. Tell them nicely but firmly that what you're ordering is what you are expecting to pick up. If they aren't able to lock in a specific breed, be sure to specify you want a "meat hog," not a "larder hog."

— SIZE —

For smaller pigs for open-pit and spit barbecue, you'll likely need to go direct to the farmer or to a butcher shop. Any size of pork processer sells mostly 120-pound hogs for primal cuts like chops, and 300-plus pound hogs for ground pork and other commercial products. This means you want to find your source well in advance of your cook, and make sure they can deliver you the size you want. These guys are not used to selling 185-pound one-off hogs, so you might need to bribe them with a case or two of beer or slide them a Ulysses S. Grant to make sure they'll get you what you want. This is important because it's pretty common for you to agree on the weight you need, only to show up and be given a hog that's 40 to 50 pounds lighter. Be diligent, and follow up with your source before picking up the hog to ensure you get what you need.

So assuming you've already talked to your supplier about breed and size, use this list of questions to make sure you cover all the bases during your conversation, and for getting ready to pick up and take the pig home:

WILL THE PIG COME DRESSED? You definitely don't want to do this yourself, unless your daddy was a hog farmer and has the equipment to do it. A "dressed" or "off the hoof" pig has had its hair scalded off and removed, belly slit open, and organs removed. Sometimes the eyelids will also be removed. Be sure to ask them to check for and remove the lymph nodes, which can ruin a whole hog. (As a backup, I've included instructions for spotting and removing these on page 175.) A dressed pig will weigh about 30 percent less than the live animal. Also, if they ask you if you want the hog to be split or butterflied, say no. You want to handle that part yourself (to ensure the skin stays intact); see West Tennessee Whole Hog, pages 173–76 for detailed instructions.

WILL THE HEAD, FEET, AND TAIL BE INTACT? If you're buying a large hog, ask that they remove the head, which will help prevent the shoulders from "dragging"—that is, cooking too slowly. (If you're buying a whole pig for a spit cook, keep the head on the animal.) Preferably, they'll leave the feet on, which makes moving and flipping larger pigs and hogs easier. You also don't need the tail, unless you have a hungry dog.

ARE THE HIND LEGS TUCKED? Pigs that weigh less than 120 pounds will often come with its hind legs tucked up under the belly, but you'll want the legs sticking out for all of the barbecue methods in this book. If your supplier can't get you a pig with its back legs extended, you'll need to pull on them real hard to pop them back out—you'll likely break their legs or pop their hip bones out in the process, but this isn't a big deal. If you're dealing directly with a farmer or USDA plant, you won't have this issue.

WILL THE PIG ARRIVE FROZEN? This is SO important, because it can take a week to thaw a frozen pig, and where the heck are you going to do that? Make sure you're getting a fresh pig (killed and processed within a week of delivery) or one that will be fully thawed when you get it. If it does come frozen, ask your supplier to "slack" (thaw) it for you. If you do find yourself in a pinch with a frozen pig, and you don't have a week and a cooler big enough for a pig to camp out in, lay the pig in the largest cooler you can find (I use a 250-quart YETI cooler) and fill it with cold water. Leave the hose in the cooler, running at a slow, steady stream overnight. Monitor the temperature closely; you'll need to keep the hog at or below 40°F, to avoid any food safety concerns.

WHAT ABOUT THE BACKBONE? Your supplier might offer to split the backbone for you, but I'd rather you do that yourself (butchers tend to cut too deep, which can lead to the pig's skin tearing during the cook). Instructions for splitting the spine are in West Tennessee Whole Hog on pages 173–76.

COLD MEAT ABSORBS SMOKE MORE EASILY, AND THE LONGER IT'S COLD, THE DEEPER THE SMOKE WILL PENETRATE, SO TRY TO KEEP THE HOG AS CLOSE TO REFRIGERATOR TEMPERATURE AS POSSIBLE BEFORE YOU PUT IT IN THE PIT.

WHEN SHOULD YOU PICK UP THE PIG?

Cold meat absorbs smoke more easily, and the longer it's cold, the deeper the smoke will penetrate, so try to keep the hog as close to refrigerator temperature as possible before you put it in the pit. (Also, keeping it at any temperature above 40°F for more than three hours or so could be a serious food safety risk.) The easiest way to do this is to schedule your hog pickup for a couple hours before you want to cook it. (Just make sure it's not gonna come frozen; see above.)

HOW SHOULD YOU PREP YOUR COOLER?

When you're ready to pick up your pig, bring the largest cooler you can find, line it with a tarp or a plastic tablecloth, and fill the bottom with ice. This is going to keep your pig cold until you're ready to cook, so have enough extra ice ready for replenishing the cooler. If you don't have a massive cooler, lay a few bags of ice around the hog and wrap it with a tarp. The biggest factor in warming a hog up is the air passing over it, more so than ambient temperature. So if you're transporting the hog in the bed of a pickup truck, make sure you keep it covered and out of the wind. Before you load the pig up, give the outside of its body a quick scan. It's normal to spot a couple of small bruises or blemishes, but if your pig looks like it lost a street brawl, ask for another. A lot of unhealed bruising in the pig can sour a whole cook.

— PREPARING FOR THE COOK —

Once you've got your hog home, give it another inspection to make sure everything is ready. First, inspect the outside of the pig, shaving off any stray hairs with a disposable razor or sharp knife, or burn them off with a lighter. Rinse the outside of the pig all over with cold water and wipe it down with a wet rag, making sure you wash away any blood or debris that might still be stuck on.

Next, flip the pig on its back and inspect the cavity. Make sure the organs and lymph nodes (see photo, page 175) have been removed. If there's a ton of loose fat inside, remove it. (Most meat packers will have already done this, because they can sell leaf lard. If you find yourself with some, you can render it down for cooking.) Rinse the inside with more cold water (or cheap beer, if fresh water is in short supply) and wipe away any dried blood, bits of leftover guts. If it *looks* disgusting, it *is* disgusting, so get rid of it.

For all sizes of pigs and pit barbecue methods (open, closed, and in the ground), you'll need to split the pig's backbone to help it lie flat as it cooks. The method for this varies slightly depending on the size of the pig, so I've included specific instructions with each recipe.

OPEN-PIT
WHOLE PIG

50 to 90 servings

1 whole pig (30 to 50 pounds dressed)

¾ cup Diamond Crystal kosher salt or Big Hoss Rub (page 96)

1 cup vegetable oil

2 quarts cheap white wine or double recipe Jack's Creek Sauce (page 95), for mopping

Lots of lemon wedges, fleur de sel, and pepper flakes, for serving (optional)

This is the easiest way to cook a whole pig, especially if you're just cooking for a backyard party. I find that pigs in the 30- to 40-pound range are the easiest to source. You can knock one of these pigs out in an afternoon, and the whole process doesn't beat you up like a 24-hour whole-hog cook does.

I use a slightly hotter temperature when cooking a whole pig on an open pit, which will ensure the pig cooks through before it dries out. When smoking smaller pigs, I usually skip the rub and simply salt the pork before throwing it on the pit, baste it with a cheap white wine while it cooks, then finish it with lemon juice, pepper flakes, and more salt. Because the pig is young, it hasn't developed a lot of fat yet, and therefore doesn't have the richer flavor of a mature hog, so I don't want to cover up the flavor of the animal with big-flavored rubs and sauces. I prefer to complement it and not run the risk of burying it. However, I've also included instructions for using a rub and mop for a more traditional barbecue flavor, if that's what you're looking for.

Another difference in cooking a smaller pig this way is there will be more variation in texture compared to a big pig and a long cook. The belly will be soft and pliable, as will most of the shoulder, especially near the shoulder blade bone. The hams, though, won't have had the time to really break down and will be more sliceable than pullable. But that's okay because of how you'll serve it. You'll pull the shoulder and belly meat as you do with a whole hog, but the ham will be carved instead, which makes a really great presentation on the table. For your guests, it can be a choose-your-own-pork-adventure kind of thing. I often serve mine with tortillas to make killer tacos (especially if I've got my friends and former cooks, Marteen or Cho-Cho, with me, because they make the best carnitas, oh gosh).

Clean and prepare the pig for barbecue (see West Tennessee Whole Hog, pages 173–76).

On a work surface, lay the pig on its back. Use a sturdy knife (one you don't mind messing up a bit, as you'll be cutting bones) to cut the rib bones away where the joint meets the spine, working down one side, then the other. Ideally, you're mostly cutting through cartilage, but inevitably you'll nick the hard bones here and there. Just be patient and try to aim the blade at the softer parts of the joints.

If the pig arrived with its hind legs tucked in, pull them out until they're extended—you'll probably end up breaking the legs and/or popping the hip sockets; this is okay. Season the cavity with the salt.

Turn the pig over and use your hands to rub the skin down with oil. Season the skin all over with the salt.

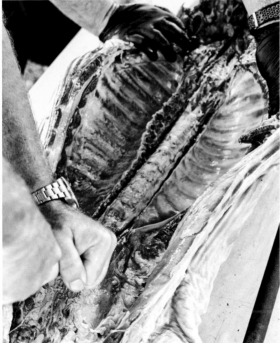

Prepare a bed of coals (see Getting Ready to Cook, page 85) below the grill grate and let them burn down until they're medium to medium-high (you should be able to hold your hand just above the grill grate for 4 to 5 seconds).

Place the pig, cavity-side down, on the pit and cook for 15 minutes. Put on a pair of heatproof gloves and stand alongside the pit. Grab the pig by a front and back leg and flip it over on the grate so the skin side is down. Mop the cavity side of the pig with white wine. Don't mop the skin just yet.

Using a flat-head shovel, pull most of the coals below the grill grate toward the perimeter of the grill to make a four-sided bed of coals around the grate, leaving a light smattering of coals below the pig. Lay a few logs or wood slats around the perimeter of the grill on top of your coals.

Cook the pig for 20 to 30 minutes, then mop the cavity side again and flip the pig over. Mop the skin side and repeat, flipping the pig every 20 to 30 minutes, mopping the top side before and after each flip. Replenish the feeder fire with fresh wood and replenish the coals below the pig as needed. Check the ambient temperature around the perimeter of the pig with your hand every so often; you're aiming for around 250°F to 275°F, or 7 to 10 seconds with the hand test. If you can hear the pig sizzling, or if you see a dramatic color change on the skin after you flip the pig, you're cooking too hot. Move some of the coals below the grate toward the bed ringing the pit.

The pig should take 4 to 5 hours total to cook. If at any point you get a flare-up, meaning flames shooting up from the coals under your pig, pat it out right away with your shovel, or scatter the coals away and let them burn out. Replace the smattering of coals under the pig with some fresh ones.

(recipe continues)

To test for doneness, take the temperature in the middle of the shoulders; it should be 180° to 185°F on an instant-read thermometer. A key point to remember is that, unlike larger hogs (whether a whole hog or a shoulder), you don't want the internal temperature to go above 185°F because the hams will really dry out on you. So once you get close to 180°F, get ready to pull the pig off the pit. You can also test for doneness with your hand. When they're ready, the shoulders will be soft and pliable. Take a knuckle and push down on that shoulder; if it leaves an indention after you remove it, that's a sign you're getting close to being wrapped up.

Transfer the pig to a large platter, cutting board, or clean work surface. Let it rest for 10 minutes or so. If it's breezy outside, cover the pig with a towel or aluminum foil. Using heatproof gloves, grab the top of the pig's spine (near the shoulders) and pull it out, *Predator*-style. Use a large, sturdy knife to remove the shoulders and hams from the carcass. Pull the shoulder meat and slice the ham into ¼-inch-thick slices. You can either slice or chop these up. The belly meat left behind is soft enough to pull with your hands. For each serving, I like to give my guests some sliced or chopped shoulder and ham, along with a pile of juicy pulled belly meat. If you salted the pig instead of using dry rub, finish each serving with a squeeze of lemon juice, a sprinkle of fleur de sel, and a sprinkle of pepper flakes, if you like. If you used a rub and mopped with barbecue sauce, serve some extra Jack's Creek Sauce on the side.

SPIT BARBECUE

This method has a couple of advantages over open-pit barbecue. Because the meat is farther away from the fire, you're less likely to overcook it, and flare-ups won't threaten to burn the meat. I also love how interactive a spit is; you'll need to turn that thing every 15 minutes, and you can see all the way around your meat as it cooks. But choosing between open-pit and spit barbecue really comes down your personal preference and the gear you have; both methods will take about the same amount of time to cook the meat.

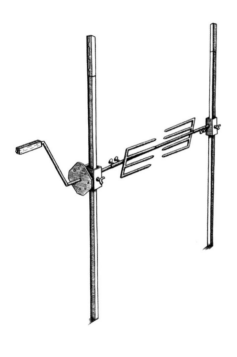

I LOVE HOW INTERACTIVE A SPIT IS; YOU'LL NEED TO TURN THAT THING EVERY 15 MINUTES, AND YOU CAN SEE ALL THE WAY AROUND YOUR MEAT AS IT COOKS.

GEAR

THE SPIT

While the actual method isn't much different from open-pit barbecue, spit barbecue requires some extra equipment. I use a homemade spit that clamps onto metal fence posts (see diagram, left), which my buddy Tyler Brown designed years ago. It has a forked design and you can lock it on every eighth of a turn, which gives you more control over heat exposure. But you can easily buy an off-the-shelf spit to use. Just make sure you get one that can be adjusted up and down (the meat should be placed 30 to 36 inches off the ground) and that you can lock in position in at least eight spots as it rotates. Most manual spits on the market only lock every quarter-turn, which isn't ideal. If you can't find one that locks every eighth-turn, you can drill four extra holes in yours. The forks that will hold the meat in place should be sturdy and at least 6 inches long. If you're going to cook a whole pig on a spit, make sure it can also handle the weight (the largest pig I cook on a spit is around 100 pounds).

TOOLS

In addition to your spit setup, you'll need **A SHOVEL** for moving coals, a pair of **HEATPROOF GLOVES** for handling hot metal and meat, and **SOMETHING TO MOP WITH**. This can be an unused kitchen mop (especially handy when cooking whole pigs) or a long-handled grilling mop. But more often than not, I just dip a kitchen towel into my mopping liquid (which is also called the "mop") and use that to baste the meat. If you're cooking a whole pig, you'll need a **MEAT CLEAVER, HATCHET, OR LARGE, STURDY KNIFE** for separating the pork ribs from the spine, as well as a **ROLL OF 18-GAUGE WIRE** for securing meat to the spit. (You'll only use a few feet at a time.) This last step isn't always necessary; your goal is just to prevent meat from flopping around as it rotates.

GETTING READY TO COOK

Because of the extra distance between the fire and your meat, spit barbecue is done at a higher temperature than open pit, so you'll go through more wood when using a spit.

Prepare a space for your spit, and following the instructions in Feeder Fires for Pit Barbecue on page 32, prepare a feeder fire in a burn barrel. If you don't have one, build a wide bed of coals around the spit and keep it loaded with fresh wood to burn down.

Clear a space around the spit large enough to leave room for two long coal beds that parallel the spit's crossbar. Depending on what it is you are cooking, these beds should be somewhere between 24 to 36 inches long. (How far they should be from the spit is a matter of what you're cooking—see the recipes that follow for recommended distances.) If you're using a fresh patch of land, burn it off with a layer of coals for 15 to 20 minutes, then repeat once more to ensure the ground below is free of moisture.

With spit barbecue, you'll usually leave a light layer of coals burning directly below the meat, which doesn't risk burning the meat because of the extra distance above the ground. Once the ground is burned off, lay a fresh bed of coals and let it burn down to about medium to medium-low heat, which takes about 15 minutes. You'll know your coals are ready when they're no longer glowing red hot, and you can hold your hand for 7 to 10 seconds at the level where the meat will cook.

SPARERIBS
ON A SPIT

4 to 6 servings

2 slabs untrimmed spareribs
(3½ to 4½ pounds each) or
St. Louis-style ribs (2½ to
3 pounds each)

½ cup Big Hoss Rub (page 96)
or Diamond Crystal kosher
salt

Jack's Creek Sauce (page 95)

Sweet Dixie BBQ Sauce
(optional; page 100), for
serving

I love spit ribs because more caramelization—those delicious little crunchy bits—builds up on the meat than you get from closed-pit barbecue, and I find that my spit ribs absorb a bit more smoke than open-pit ribs, probably due to the fact that I'm cooking the meat directly over smoldering coals.

I cook at least two racks of ribs at a time on my spit—any less is a waste of time and fuel—but you can adjust this recipe up or down to accommodate your needs and the size of your rig. Because you'll have a hot metal rod running through the ribs, they'll cook a bit faster than ribs cooked on an open or closed pit.

Evenly coat the ribs with the dry rub (see How to Apply Rub, page 97). If possible, let the ribs sit for up to 1 hour before cooking so the rub can slightly cure the meat.

About 1 hour or so before you begin your cook, start your feeder fire off to the side, ideally in a burn barrel (see page 33). Prepare a bed of coals below the spit and let them burn down until they're medium to medium-high (you should be able to hold your hand at spit level—30 inches above the ground—for 4 to 5 seconds). Make two parallel mounds of coal along the sides of the spit (3 to 4 shovelfuls a side) about a foot away from the center. Lay fresh wood on top of the coals.

Meanwhile, mount the ribs to the spit. If you're using my setup, do this by weaving the tines of the spit's fork through the slab, "sewing" the tines between every other rib. Otherwise, follow the instructions for your spit set-up; basically you just need to attach the meat to the bar or tines and prevent it from flopping around as it rotates.

Depending on your spit setup, you may want to tie the ribs to the prongs with some 18-gauge wire run through the meat and around two or three ribs on each rack. Mount the ribs onto the spit, pushing the two racks together so they resemble one giant rack of ribs.

Check your coal bed and make sure you're getting a good amount of heat (4 to 5 seconds with the hand test) at spit level. If not, add a fresh shovelful of coals. Mop the ribs with Jack's Creek Sauce (see Mops, page 107), and rotate the spit one-eighth turn every 10 minutes, mopping them again each time you rotate the spit.

(recipe continues)

After the ribs have cooked for 30 minutes, use a shovel to pull the coals below the spit toward the sides, leaving a light layer of burning coals below the meat. Continue this process, rotating the ribs an eighth-turn and mopping every 10 minutes, and replenishing your coal beds as needed, until the ribs are ready to eat, 3½ to 4 hours. The ribs are done when you can see the meat starting to pull away from the bone, or if you can push your finger into the meat between two ribs with little resistance. If you want to use an instant-read thermometer, insert it into the meat between two ribs; they're finished when the thermometer reads 190°F.

When the ribs are finished, transfer them to a cutting board. Using a sturdy knife, cut the flaps of brisket meat away from the ribs. You can snack on this bonus meat yourself or use it to make a Rib Meat Sandwich (page 99).

Cut the racks into individual ribs and serve—with barbecue sauce, if you like.

HOLDING AND REWARMING RIBS

I usually eat barbecue right after it comes off the pit, but there are times when you need to keep the food warm for a while before you're ready to serve. If you need to hold barbecue for 3 hours or less, wrap it tightly in a couple layers of plastic wrap, then place it in an insulated cooler. I wrap ribs in individual racks and pulled pork in 2-pound football-shaped bundles.

If it's warm outside, just shut the cooler until you're ready to unwrap and serve the meat. If you're using a super-efficient cooler (like a YETI), it might work *too well* and continue cooking the meat, so leave the top open a crack. If it's cold where you're cooking, the cooler's insulation will be cold as well, so it will chill the meat down instead of holding its temperature. In this case, keep your cooler warm in your car, or heat a brick in a 300°F oven for 1 hour and place it on top of a towel inside the cold cooler.

If you need to hold ribs for longer than 3 hours, wrap them in plastic and refrigerate until they're ready to be reheated. Place the ribs, still wrapped in plastic, in a 250°F oven on the middle rack; they'll take 45 minutes to 1 hour to warm up. Don't worry about the plastic: It doesn't melt and is perfectly safe to use at this temperature, so long as you don't go above 300°F.

You can also rewarm ribs directly over a grill. I'll do this when I want to glaze them with barbecue sauce (Martha has me finish her ribs with honey) or remoisten them with a bit of mop throughout the reheating process. Move enough burning coals below your grill grate to create a medium-hot fire, brush the ribs with the sauce or mop of your choice, and grill them, flipping them every couple of minutes until they're warmed through. I don't like my ribs super sweet, so I usually brush them just once or twice at the beginning, but if you want a sticky, lacquered coating of sauce, continue brushing them before every flip.

PORK LOIN
ON A SPIT

Here's an impressive roast that you can spit-smoke in under 3 hours. (You can double this recipe and cook two loin roasts at the same time.) Pork loin has a mild flavor, but it still cooks up tender and juicy when you do it right. Just don't mistake it for tenderloin—that's far too small and lean to cook on a spit, or for any barbecue method, for that matter.

I prefer the bone-in version, as the bone helps the meat retain moisture and gives you bonus bones to gnaw on. If you want a more traditional barbecue flavor, use a dry rub and a vinegar-based mop; or if you want a pure pork flavor, season with salt, mop with white wine, and serve with lemon wedges and fleur de sel.

Rinse any blood off the pork and trim any large flaps of fat. Evenly coat the pork with the dry rub (see How to Apply Rub, page 97) or kosher salt. Let the roast sit for up to 1 hour before cooking.

About 1 hour or so before you begin your cook, start your feeder fire off to the side, ideally using a burn barrel (see page 33). Prepare a bed of coals below the spit and let them burn down until they're medium to medium-high (you should be able to hold your hand at spit level—30 inches above the ground—for 4 to 5 seconds). Make two parallel mounds of coal along the sides of the spit (3 to 4 shovelfuls a side) about a foot away from the center. Lay fresh wood on top of the coals.

Meanwhile, run the center rod through the middle of the loin meat. If using a bone-in loin roast, attach the forks to the rod and place them so the meaty side of the roast (away from the bone) rests against them. Secure the pork to the spit with 18-gauge wire. To do so, use a metal skewer to make a pilot hole through the meaty part of the roast, then thread wire through the eye of the roast and tie it onto the forks. If using boneless pork loin, insert the forks into the roast.

Check your coal bed and make sure you're getting a good amount of heat (about 4 to 5 seconds with the hand test) at spit level. If not, add a fresh shovelful of coals. Mop the roast with the Jack's Creek Sauce (see Mops, page 107) and rotate the spit an eighth-turn every 10 minutes, mopping the roast each time you rotate the spit.

After the loin has cooked for 30 minutes, use a shovel to pull the coals below the spit toward the sides, leaving a light layer of burning coals below the meat. Continue cooking the roast, rotating an eighth-turn and mopping every 10 minutes, until an instant-read thermometer inserted into the center of the roast reads 135°F, 2 to 2½ hours.

Transfer the roast to a cutting board and cut into chops. Serve with more barbecue sauce, if you used a rub, or with lemon wedges and a sprinkle of fleur de sel, if you salted the pork and mopped with wine.

6 to 10 servings

One 10-rib pork loin roast (10 to 13 pounds), chine bone removed, or one boneless pork loin roast (about 6 pounds)

1 cup Big Hoss Rub (page 96) or Diamond Crystal kosher salt

2 cups Jack's Creek Sauce (page 95) or cheap white wine, for mopping

Lemon wedges, for serving

Fleur de sel or other flaky salt, for serving

PIG
ON A SPIT

I f you want to have a true pig pickin' but don't want to invest the time it takes to cook a larger hog in a closed pit, this is the method for you. This pig will take anywhere from 8 to 12 hours to cook, which means you can start in the morning and be feasting before sunset. Just be sure to have a good supply of wood on hand; as with any spit barbecue, you'll be burning through wood more quickly than with an open or closed pit. I highly recommend using a burn barrel for this cook, or make a big enough feeder fire so you don't run out of fresh coals.

For spit barbecue, I use pigs in the 70- to 100-pound range, which are easier to source than larger hogs. I usually leave the head on when cooking whole pigs on a spit; not only does it look impressive to see a whole animal spinning over the fire, but removing the head causes the shoulders to cook more quickly, which in the open air means they can also dry out. It's also helpful to leave the hooves on, which makes it easier to move the pig around as you prepare it for the cook.

Clean and prepare the pig for barbecue (see West Tennessee Whole Hog, pages 173–76). Grab a buddy, as you'll need another set of hands to help you flip the pig and get it onto the spit.

About 1 hour or so before you begin your cook, start your feeder fire off to the side, ideally using a burn barrel (see page 33). Prepare a bed of coals below the spit and let them burn down until they're medium to medium-high (you should be able to hold your hand at spit level—30 inches above the ground—for 4 to 5 seconds). Lay fresh wood on top of the coals to form a rectangle around the area below the spit; although you're using a burn barrel for this cook, you'll still want the extra smoke that these logs produce, at least during the first half of your cook.

Meanwhile, mount the pig onto the spit: On a work surface, lay the pig on its back. With a cleaver or large, sturdy knife (one you don't mind messing up a bit, as you'll be cutting bones), separate the rib bones away from the spine, working down one side, then the other (see photos on page 127). Start at the top of the ribs, near the neck, and lay the tip of the knife near the first joint. Set your free hand on top of the knife and apply firm pressure, then run the knife down the side of the spine. It will take you 3 or 4 passes on each side to pop all of the rib bones free. Be careful not to cut through the skin. Season the cavity with a nice, even layer of the dry rub, saving about half for the skin side.

(recipe continues)

140 to 150 servings

One whole pig (70 to
    100 pounds off the hoof)

1 cup vegetable oil

3 cups Big Hoss Rub (page 96)

1½ gallons (6 recipes) Jack's
    Creek Sauce (page 95), for
    mopping

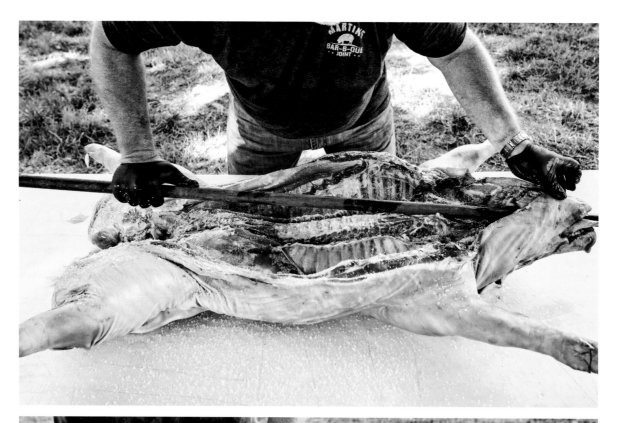

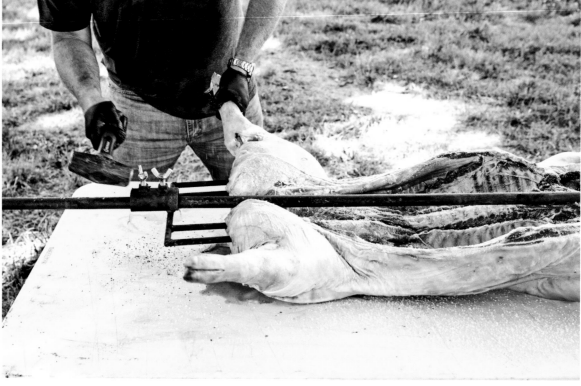

Insert the center rod through the pig's mouth and lay it on top of the spine so you have an equal amount of rod extending from either end of the pig. Hammer one of the spit forks deep into the shoulders through the muscle, and the other into the hams at the other end of the body. You want the pig to be as spread out as possible; its front and rear legs should be splayed out, with its hooves extending toward either end of the spit (see photo). Turn the pig on its side and use a metal skewer or tip of a knife to make two or three sets of holes down the spine on either side of the backbone, then thread some 18-gauge wire through the holes and twist them around the center rod to hold the pig in place. Now let me speak to you on this wire because the ends can be pretty dangerous. These bastards will cut the piss out of you if you're not paying attention. Make sure you use pliers to turn the ends back so they face the meat. And don't forget to take that wire out when the pig is finished.

Turn the pig over and use your hands to rub the skin down with the oil. Season the skin all over with the dry rub. Mount the pig to the spit, cavity-side down.

Check your coal bed and make sure you're getting a good amount of heat (4 to 5 seconds with the hand test) at spit level. If not, add a line of coals (two or three shovelfuls) down the center of the bed, directly below the pig.

Mop the sides and top of the pig. (You're going to use a LOT of mop when cooking a pig on a spit, as much of it will run off as the pig rotates.) After 15 minutes, rotate the pig an eighth-turn and mop again. Each time you move the pig (that is, every 15 minutes), scatter ½ to 1 shovelful of coals around the perimeter of the coal bed, adding fresh wood to the top of the coals as needed (your goal is to surround the pig with a constant and generous amount of smoke, so don't worry about adding too much). After every other turn (that is, every 30 minutes), scatter 1 to 2 shovelfuls of coals down the center of the coal bed as well.

(recipe continues)

Periodically check the temperature of your coal bed using the hand test (8 seconds at the level of the pig). If you can hear the pig's skin sizzling or quickly turning brown, your fire is too hot. To remedy this, you can rotate the pig more frequently (about every 10 minutes) until the fire cools off. If you continue to have an issue with the pig getting too hot, take your shovel and push your coals back 2 or 3 inches away from the pig. After the pig cools off a bit, you can push the coals back where they were.

Continue rotating the pig an eighth-turn every 15 minutes, mopping and replenishing the coal bed each time you move it. After the pig has completed 1 full turn (that is, 2 hours), use a shovel to push the majority of the coals below the pig to the perimeter of the coal bed, leaving a light smattering of lit coals under the pig. (If it's a particularly windy day, you may want to skip this step.) At this point, you should also start checking the temperature of the meat by inserting a thermometer into the thickest part of a ham. Once the internal temperature hits 120° to 130°F, you can stop adding fresh wood to the fire around the spit; the pig has absorbed all of the smoke it's going to absorb, and you're just cooking to doneness from here on out. (Of course, you'll still need to burn more wood in your burn barrel or feeder fire.)

Depending on the size of your pig (and many other factors), the pig will take anywhere from 8 to 12 hours to be finished. The pig is ready when the internal temperature of the hams reaches 180°F.

When the pig is done, put on a pair of heatproof gloves (and have your buddy do the same). Move the pig to a heatproof work surface, cavity-side up. (I use a picnic table with several layers of butcher paper on top.) Remove the spit forks, center bar, and wire.

You're ready to pick some pig! Get yourself some large containers, such as disposable aluminum pans or restaurant hotel pans, to hold the meat. I like to start with the shoulders and work my way down the pig. Shoulder meat has the perfect ratio of meat to fat, so I'll separate those from the carcass and begin pulling meat from those. As the shoulders are depleted, I'll serve a combination of fatty belly meat and lean ham, combining some of both for each serving. Serve with extra sauce on the side.

CHAPTER 4

THE
GOLDEI

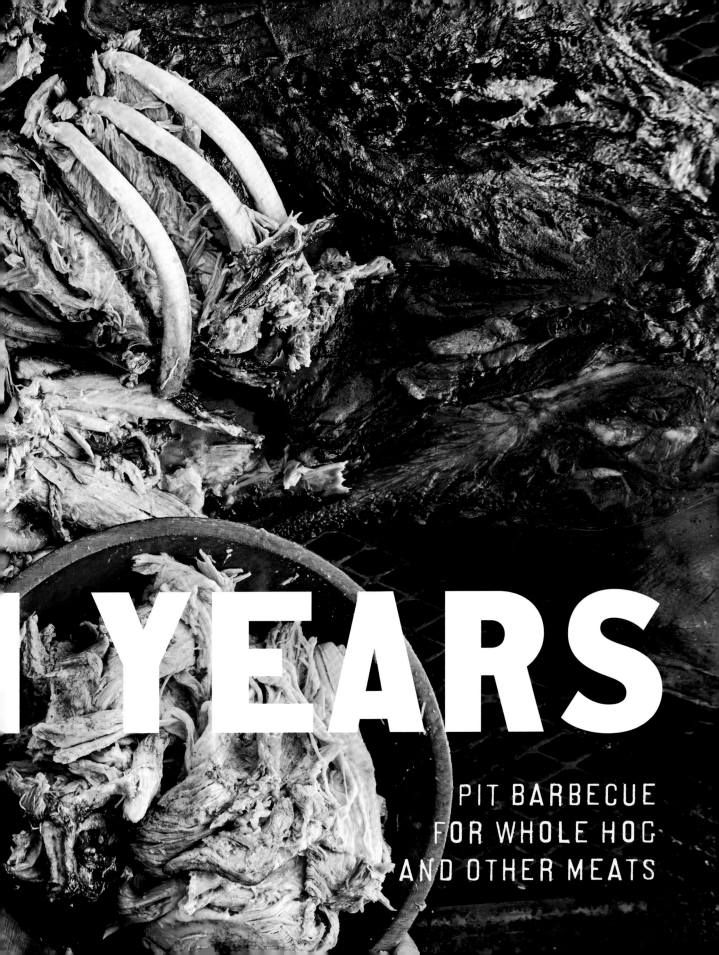

YEARS

PIT BARBECUE
FOR WHOLE HOG
AND OTHER MEATS

I LOVE A GOOD ROAD TRIP. If you asked me to jump in the truck and drive across the country tomorrow, I'd do it. If I want to go fishing down in the Florida Keys, I could just jump on a plane and be baiting my first line by midafternoon, but I'd rather take a couple of days to wind my way through the South, maybe grab a good meal in Atlanta; listen to lots of Ryan Bingham, R. L. Burnside, and Waylon Jennings; drink a Coke (always with a pack of salted peanuts dumped inside); and stop at every barbecue joint I pass along the way, just to see if it's a diamond in the rough (which is, sadly, getting more rare all the time). And if I've got a friend or two in the truck with me, like my buddy Steve Hutchinson, who loves the Keys more than life itself, even better.

For me, cooking a whole hog checks all the same boxes as a road trip, and many more. Not only is the journey a lot of fun—I get to spend quality time outdoors with my friends and family, sweat a bit, drink a bit, talk a bit—the destination is just as exciting: After 24 hours of that, *then* you get to have a party! And eat some amazing pork. When it's all over, you are worn out, but it was freaking fun and another life experience for the books. (Or, if you're us, you just get ready to do it all again tomorrow.)

On paper, cooking a whole hog for 24 hours is a pretty stupid idea. You'll invest at least a few hundred bucks in equipment and meat, spend hours sourcing and planning, and then run a two-day marathon of ass-breaking labor to cook the dadgum thing. And success, I hate to say, is far from guaranteed.

But I'm certainly not here to talk you *out* of cooking a whole hog. If the time commitment and financial investment don't scare you away, you're in the right place, and that investment will pay off—in the education you'll receive, the fun you'll have, and the satisfaction you'll feel when you start pulling that gorgeous meat out, then sharing it with your people.

If you've never attempted any form of barbecue before—not even a rack of ribs or chicken in your backyard—then you should probably not make an old-fashioned pit barbecue—or whole hog—your first foray. Go cook a few things on an open pit (see Chapter 3, page 82), then come back.

However, if you've dabbled in barbecue, have a basic understanding of how to cook with fire, and are ready to, well, go whole hog, let's dive into the deep end.

I'm building the procedure for pit barbecue around the process for cooking a whole hog. Even if you're not planning a whole hog, but rather shoulders, ribs, or other recipes in this chapter, read through the whole hog procedure first: There are many lessons layered into it that can be applied to whatever you cook in a pit.

Whether your first whole-hog endeavor ends in success or failure (or somewhere in between), you'll walk away baptized in *real*, old-school barbecue, with a fundamental understanding of how to cook any kind of meat over a bed of coals. You'll find yourself not leaning on recipes or outside guidance as much in the future, but on instinct. Then you can take this foundation and make it your own.

WHOLE HOG PREP TIMELINE

You don't have to follow this schedule to the letter, but it will help you plan ahead and stay organized for your cook.

➻ AT LEAST 1 MONTH BEFORE THE COOK
- ☐ Find a hog source (see Sourcing the Hog, page 148), and find out the lead time they'll need for you to order one.
- ☐ Have a metal shop make your grate and heat shield, if using (see Pit Materials, pages 159–60).
- ☐ Order the wood (see Selecting and Sourcing Wood page 27).

➻ AT LEAST 2 WEEKS (OR WHATEVER YOUR SOURCE TELLS YOU) BEFORE THE COOK
- ☐ Order the hog (see Sourcing Pigs and Hogs for Barbecue, pages 120–24)

➻ SOMETIME AHEAD OF THE COOK, A DAY OR A YEAR, DEPENDING ON WHO YOUR FRIENDS ARE
- ☐ Gather a crew of three or four to help you do this.

➻ 1 WEEK BEFORE THE COOK
- ☐ Prep your dry rub and sauces.

➻ 3 DAYS BEFORE THE COOK
- ☐ Order pit materials (see pages 159–60).

➻ 1 DAY BEFORE THE COOK
- ☐ Build the pit (see page 164) and prepare the burn barrel (see page 33) for the feeder fire.

➻ 3 TO 4 HOURS BEFORE THE COOK
- ☐ Load your burn barrel and light the feeder fire (see Starting the Fire, page 36).

➻ 2 TO 3 HOURS BEFORE THE COOK
- ☐ Fire the pit to burn off the ground.

➻ START OF THE COOK
- ☐ Load the hog, maintain a pit temperature of around 250°F.

➻ 4 HOURS INTO THE COOK
- ☐ Flip the hog, let the pit temperature come down to around 200°F.

➻ 20 HOURS INTO THE COOK
- ☐ Begin checking the hog for doneness.

➻ 24 HOURS (GIVE OR TAKE) INTO THE COOK
- ☐ The hog is ready. Let's eat!

PREPARATION

SOURCING
THE HOG

The best swine for West Tennessee-style whole-hog barbecue is a heritage breed hog that's 185 pounds "off the hoof" (that means after its guts have been removed), give or take 15 pounds. For comparison's sake, Carolina-style whole-hog barbecue typically involves slightly smaller hogs, around 150 pounds, and those are cooked at a higher temperature, around 250°F, compared to the 200°F we aim for in West Tennessee. (The difference in the final product is largely textural: In the Carolinas they chop their pork—along with its skin—and we pull our meat, leaving the skin behind to act as a "bowl" for holding everything in. The larger hog and the lower, slower smoking of West Tennessee barbecue makes the meat more tender and succulent.)

You may need to start your search a good while before you plan on your cook—a few weeks or even a month or more to be safe. See Sourcing Pigs and Hogs for Barbecue (pages 120–24) for more detail on what to look for and how to make sure you're getting the pig you need.

ORDERING WOOD

As I covered in Selecting and Sourcing Wood (page 27), you need three bundles of wood slats (preferably hickory or red oak, and preferably wood that's been sitting around for a couple months), or a full cord (4 × 4 × 8 feet) of firewood to cook a whole hog. You might not use all of it, but at least you won't run out of fuel. Do yourself a favor and have your wood delivered. You've got enough work to do. Remember to do this well in advance!

YOUR CREW

It's nearly impossible to cook a whole hog by yourself, so gather up a crew as large as you like—I usually enlist three or four friends. The cook is going to take a full 24 hours (plus another 6 or so hours of preparation), so put them on a schedule.

Cooking a whole hog is a marathon, not a sprint, but if you have a good crew, that marathon becomes a relay race. It's very important to identify who out of your crew is doing what. You may have twenty buddies there to "help," but you need to formally assign responsibilities to a few folks you can trust the most.

The first thing you should decide is who's taking the graveyard shift. Out of your group, which one is the

THE ESSENTIALS OF WEST TENNESSEE WHOLE HOG

Delicate heat, delicate treatment of the hog, delicate texture, delicate flavor

The skin must be kept intact so that the fat can pool and cook the "middlin" meat of the belly and ribs

The long strands of confit-like pork are sometimes referred to as "redneck spaghetti"

The meat is always pulled, never chopped

Lean ham is typically mixed with fatty belly; meat from the shoulder is kept separate

The skin is not chopped and mixed with the meat

The sauce is vinegar-based, and usually contains sugar

Sandwiches must always be topped with coleslaw.

WHOLE HOG

derelict who you know is going to drink too much and be too loud? You know who I'm talking about, we've all got that friend. Go ahead and get them wound up early during the day. That way they'll be in bed (at some point) and you won't have to deal with them all night, wanting everybody to do shots and all that mess. Relegate them to throwing wood in the burn barrel so they can't screw everything up. Now that you've got that person identified, you've got two important roles to fill.

Hopefully you have that buddy who's cool with not drinking and will sit up all night by himself to feed the burn barrel and watch over the pit as he appreciates the peacefulness and solitude of the overnight hours. Have this person come on around midnight and keep watch until about 7 a.m. That way, you can keep partying with your buddies until 1 a.m. and still get 6 hours of sleep. The next most important player is the one who shows up to relieve the graveyard guy in the morning. Choose your most responsible friend for this, because they have to show up right on time! Whoever's been watching

the pit all night will be tired and ready to take a nap. After supper and a couple of drinks, send your morning reliever to bed, not just so they are rested enough to show up at dawn, but so they arrive feeling good and will carry the load while y'all are dragging about waiting for the coffee to kick in. This handoff is really important, because the pit temperature has to be maintained.

Everyone else can just pitch in whenever and wherever you need them. Be sure to block out time for yourself to catch some sleep, or you'll be a worthless zombie by the time you're ready to serve the pork, and it's no fun to watch your guests enjoy themselves while you fall out in a chair. My personal advice to you, especially if you are going to have some drinks, is to call it a night no later than 1 a.m. As with a road trip, you've got to pace yourself so you aren't so worn out the next afternoon that you can't enjoy the end result. On a long road trip, you take your shift behind the wheel, then catch a snooze when you can, because you need to be ready to drive when it's your shift. You get me?

GEAR FOR YOURSELF

It's important to know *how* to cook a hog, of course, but it's just as important to understand that the process is long and arduous. I've seen so many people burn out during their first hog cook, and they're miserable by the time it's over. I want you to be able to enjoy this party you're doing all of this work for. I've been miserable at these things so many times, not just because I drank too much but because I'm underslept, my body aches, my feet hurt, and I didn't eat enough.

Here's an exhaustive, obsessive list of everything I use for a whole-hog cook, and I don't just mean shovels and mops. I mean to keep me and my crew going. Your needs and preferences may be different from mine, but read this through and think about whatever the equivalent would be for you. Just make the list and make sure you go by it, or you will hate running to the store during a cook as much as I do.

CLOTHING

CLOTHES YOU DON'T MIND RUINING. They should also be super comfortable and durable. Check the weather report and dress for the coldest temperature forecasted for the night, then pack an extra layer on top of that.

RAIN GEAR. If there's more than 0 percent chance of rain, bring rain gear to keep you dry in a downpour.

BROKEN-IN RUNNING SHOES OR SNEAKERS. You might think boots are the way to go, but your feet will be screaming at you on the second day, I promise you. I add work insoles to my sneakers for extra padding, and I suggest you do too. Unless you're a young kid, you really have to take care of your back and your feet.

FOOD AND DRINK

FOOD. Plan for three good meals a day (your hog will hopefully provide supper on the second day). It's vital to eat well when you're cooking a hog. At home, my mom will usually make us supper, or we'll grill up burgers or steaks out there by the fire. We usually send someone on a late-night run for tacos or pizza. For breakfast, we make sausage, eggs, and biscuits. Whatever you do, just make sure you eat.

GRILL GRATE. If you'll be doing any grilling on the side during the cook, bring a grill grate or a grill and a **LARGE CAST-IRON SKILLET**. The burn barrel is also a great place to cook some "Arsh" Potatoes (page 227).

COFFEE. Bring plenty of coffee and the means to brew it. I use a French press, but you can use whatever gadget you prefer. Come the second day of the cook, coffee is going to be your Lord and Savior, so don't cheap out: Buy the fancy beans and enjoy them.

DRINKING WATER. Factor 12 ounces per person per hour. Stay hydrated. I know I sound like a grandmother, but I'm serious: It'll be a game changer for how you feel.

STRAWS. When it's time to drink your water, you want to slam it as fast as possible before getting back to your beer or wine.

LIGHT BEER. If you plan to be drinking a lot, pack something that will give you a buzz but not blast you away. Domestic beer is the way to go here, pure and simple. A case of IPA is gonna cave your frickin' head in. I'm a Coors Light guy if I'm not drinking wine, but . . .

WINE. Most of the time, I'm going to treat myself and drink really good wine (see A Case for Wine, pages 155–56) and really enjoy it while my buddies are drinking their beer and getting bloated.

DRUGS

HEADACHE POWDERS. These are basically a mix of crushed-up aspirin and caffeine, and give me instant headache relief; my go-to brands are BC and Goody's. They are the quickest and best over-the-counter medicine. I'm not a doctor, so consult yours before taking.

VITAMIN B$_{12}$. I take a vitamin B$_{12}$ supplement for a few days before any long cook, which helps me combat hangovers and lack of good sleep.

PEDIALYTE. If you're drinking any amount of alcohol, chug some before you go to sleep. Trust me.

SHELTER

A GOOD LAWN CHAIR. Let me repeat: a GOOD CHAIR. Something you'll look forward to sitting in. You will be sitting down and standing up hundreds of times over the course of twenty-four hours, so make sure your chair is easy to get out of. At some point you'll want to recline, and perhaps sleep, so keep that in mind. I use a YETI Hondo Base Camp chair, partly because I'm a brand ambassador and they gave me a few, but more so because it's the most comfortable chair my ass has ever touched—ever!

SOMETHING TO PUT YOUR FEET UP ON. A 5-gallon bucket, cooler, cardboard box, whatever.

SOMEWHERE TO SLEEP. You (and your crew) are going to need some sleep at some point. Try to get at least six hours of sleep so you're not worthless. When I was younger, I used to sleep in my truck, but now I'm finding myself a proper bed. Wherever you do it, figure out ahead of time where you can rest, whether it's a tent, hotel room, or some other quiet spot away from the pit.

BOURBON. If you're going to drink bourbon or other liquor during the cook (which I do not recommend, see A Case for Wine, pages 155–56), splurge on one incredible bottle. Don't bring a handle of cheap whiskey for getting drunk. You'll be way more inclined to stop your buddy from drinking a three-finger pour topped with a spit of Coke, because you'll appreciate what you spent on a good bottle. I'm serious. Drink whatever you like in the end, but cooking a hog is an endurance sport, and getting yourself or your crew hammered is gonna make it real hard to get to the finish line.

EVERYONE (MYSELF INCLUDED) LIKES TO SAY THAT COOKING A WHOLE HOG IS A MARATHON, NOT A SPRINT, BUT IF YOU HAVE A GOOD CREW AROUND YOU, THAT MARATHON BECOMES A RELAY RACE.

GEAR FOR THE COOK

COOLERS. At least three large coolers—one just for ice, one filled with beverages, and one for holding the pork after it's been picked from the hog. If you're making other food during the cook, bring a fourth cooler for ingredients.

PREPPING TOOLS. A **HATCHET** (or heavy meat cleaver), a 2-pound **MALLET** or hammer, and a **SHARP KITCHEN KNIFE**, for prepping the hog.

TOWELS. Plenty of clean shop or kitchen towels, plus a couple rolls of paper towels as backup.

WATER COOLER WITH A SPIGOT. Fill it with hot water and use this as a handwashing station. You'll be amazed how much you'll find yourself rinsing your hands if you've got one.

FOLDING WORKTABLE. A sturdy table for prepping the hog before the cook, and eating or playing cards during the cook.

THERMOMETERS. If you'll be cooking your hog on a grate, buy 6 **OVEN THERMOMETERS**, the kind you can stand inside your oven. You'll place these around your pit to help you monitor the temperature. It doesn't hurt to also have a good **INSTANT-READ DIGITAL THERMOMETER** on hand, which you can use to check the internal temperature of the hog, as well as jam through the various parts of the lid to check the temperature of the pit.

FLASHLIGHTS AND HEADLAMPS. Bring backups because someone's going to lose theirs.

PANS. Have a few **BAKING DISHES**, **DISPOSABLE ALUMINUM PANS**, or deep **HOTEL PANS** for holding the barbecue, plus a big box of **PLASTIC WRAP** for covering the pans.

PORTABLE SPEAKER (AND EXTRA BATTERIES). For supplying your soundtrack. I always have Charlie Robertson, R. L. Burnside, Ryan Bingham, Waylon Jennings, and 1970s-era Jimmy Buffett on rotation.

A DECK OF CARDS. One of my favorite ways to pass the time with my buddies.

A GOOD BOOK. Half the fun of cooking barbecue is the social component, so I usually don't need any other entertainment, but if I volunteer for the graveyard shift, a good book comes in handy when I'm tending the pit in the middle of the night by myself. Just try not to stare at your dadgum phone for hours. As a matter of fact, just put the stupid thing up somewhere and enjoy the night without it, because you know you'll stare at it all night just like I would.

WHAT ABOUT BOURBON?

I love bourbon. But I never drink
it with barbecue. None of the old-
timers here were drinking whiskey
with their pork. Both bourbon and
barbecue are proud products of the
South, sure, but I think the two got
mashed together when Southern
food and American whiskey became
trendy at the same time, about
fifteen years ago. But have them
together and all you're gonna taste
is the bourbon. You might as well
be eating some steamed chicken
with it. Drink some bourbon while
you're cooking, if you want, and
save the rest for after the meal.

A CASE
FOR WINE

So, what are we gonna drink? In my part of the South, a lot of folks have something nonalcoholic with barbecue—sweet tea or a cold-ass Coke. For those who partake, it's almost always domestic light beer. But I want to sell you on wine as an equal, if not better, partner for barbecue. If you're not a wine drinker, I'm speaking directly to you; if you already "get it," feel free to flip the page.

Some of my friends who exclusively drink beer give me sideways looks when I bring a cooler full of wine to a cook. Down here in the Bible Belt, wine has never been part of our culture—unless it's the sweet, homemade variety we make with Muscadine grapes, which grow wild all over in West Tennessee and northern Mississippi. Here, alcohol was and is in itself polarizing—my dad's mom, Nonie, didn't even eat at my barbecue joint for close to a year because she was so put out that we served beer—but wine in particular has an extra problem of being seen as elitist, overpriced, and intimidating.

I was turned on to wine in my early twenties. I still remember the bottle that did it: a 1998 Duckhorn Merlot, served at a dinner when I was a junior trader in Charlotte. We went out to dinner one night with clients and one of the senior traders turned to me and said, "Patrick, you're not drinking beer tonight." He poured me a glass, and told me to think about the wine before I swallowed it. I dutifully followed his directive, and something clicked. I remember taking pause, almost confused, and thinking to myself, "Wow."

It was maybe the first time I understood that you can drink alcohol for something greater than catching a buzz. The way the flavors changed as I drank that glass, and how they changed the food I was eating—it was a whole new experience. And one, after I got into the restaurant business and started to really develop a passion for wine, I truly realized does not have to be relegated to fancy restaurants or special occasions.

One of the many great things about West Tennessee-style barbecue is its affinity for wine. Whole-hog barbecue is rich, succulent, and slightly smoky. We don't use a lot of intense rubs or sticky-sweet sauces that would overpower anything but the biggest, booziest reds. The subtle flavors of whole-hog barbecue go just as well with a bottle of bright, slightly tannic Carignan (one of my favorite red grapes) as they do with a dry Riesling or even some sparkling rosé—the combination of bubbles and acidity against fatty pork is just amazing.

When I'm smoking a shoulder, ribs, or other smaller cuts of pork on their own, I'll usually look toward red wines made with Gamay, Cabernet Franc, or Grenache—those three grapes can stand up to smokier, bolder-flavored barbecue, as will wines made with Nebbiolo or Nero D'Avola, which are dry and tannic but don't leave you with the taste of a leather belt in your mouth, like most Cabernet Sauvignon does for me. Dry Pinot Noir is a shot over the center field wall with pit-cooked ribs. These are all totally different wines, but they all work so well with barbecue pork.

Barbecue chicken and turkey are excellent with all sorts of whites: Chenin Blanc, Gruner Veltliner, dry Riesling and Sauvignon Blanc, as well as bubbly Champagne and cava. Most light-bodied, acidic reds are fair game as well.

I learned a lot of this because I've been blessed to find myself frequently cooking hogs with restaurant people and wine folks like the Mariani family at Scribe in Sonoma, Tuck Beckstoffer at Amulet Estate in St. Helena, and the Texas expat Paul Roberts at Colgin Cellars in Napa Valley, to name a few. These friends and others—especially my buddy Billy Durney, pitmaster and owner of Hometown BBQ in Brooklyn, New York, a king of brisket—have taught me loads about what to drink with barbecue.

So what wines should you drink? Honestly, that's not the point. My own tastes are continually changing. In the past few years I've found myself enjoying a lot of wines in the loosely defined "natural" category, which I like to refer to as "Jesus wine," because it's made using millennia-old techniques, without all the additives and stuff. These tend to be light-bodied, earthy reds; funky, oxidized-tasting whites; and stuff in between, like rosé and orange wines (white wine that's been made by letting pressed grapes sit in their juice). I also have a weak spot for good Champagne and sparkling rosé.

But that doesn't mean *you* need to like those things. What I'm getting at is that there is a whole universe of wine out there that will make any meal—from fine dining to barbecue to just a picnic with friends—better. Throw out all of the traditional "rules" about food and wine pairing—reds with red meat, whites with white meat, and so on. There are plenty of light, acidic reds that are awesome with poultry, and there's plenty of fuller-bodied whites that you'd love with some steak or a pork chop. And don't worry about whether you're making the "right" choice.

I just want you to try enough stuff to figure out what you like, then explore more wines from that grape, region, and style. Drink with friends and ask them what they like. Once you've got some awareness of your palate—that is, what tastes good to you—start branching out and trying new grapes, or similar wines from other regions. Over time you'll learn how to spot something you'll probably like, whether it's on a restaurant wine list or at the store. And if it tastes good to you, it's the right choice.

Whatever wine you decide to drink, please make sure it's the right temperature. No wine should be served at room temperature, unless you're in a cold-ass room. But your wines for the most part shouldn't be freezing cold, either, which makes it impossible to taste the wine at its best. Whites and rosé are best between 50°F to 60°F, which means you should take them out of the refrigerator and let them warm up for 10 minutes before you pour your first glass, then leave it out on the counter—their flavors will continue to evolve as the wine warms up. Reds should be drunk at 55°F to 65°F (lighter reds on the cooler side, fuller-bodied reds on the warmer side), so throw a room-temperature bottle into the fridge for an hour before you drink it. Only bubbles should be drunk ice cold, which maximizes how refreshing they are.

If I haven't convinced you to drink wine with live-fire foods by now, I hope you enjoy your tea, soda, beer, or whatever you choose to drink. I'll save a glass for you, just in case.

THE PIT

PIT MATERIALS

Do yourself a huge favor and buy as many of the materials for your pit from one store (for me, that's Home Depot or Lowe's) and have it all delivered for a reasonable fee.

CINDER BLOCKS. Aka concrete masonry units (or CMUs), these measure about 8 × 8 × 16 inches. You need exactly 93 cinder blocks to build your pit, but these are usually sold in 50-block pallets, so you'll need two pallets (100 blocks total).

SAND. For lining the bottom of your pit, you'll need four to six 50-pound bags of playground sand enough to give you a 2- to 3-inch-deep bed of sand. This is optional; it's to protect the surface you're cooking on if it's concrete or pavers you don't want ruined. If you're cooking on dirt or grass—the best surfaces for a pit—and don't mind the earth getting burnt up, you can skip the sand.

ANGLE IRON. To build the small door in your pit (for adding coals), you need a pair of 3 × 3 × 48-inch pieces of angle iron. You can also use steel "lintels" in a pinch, but those are usually curved and you want your cinder blocks to lie as flat as possible.

BARS. You need at least 5 but preferably 7 (plus an additional 3 or 4, if you're using a heat shield—see right) 60-inch steel rods of ⅝-inch thickness, which you can find at a building supply store. Bars that are ¾ inch thick are fine as well, but much thicker than that and your top row of blocks will start to have larger gaps where valuable heat will escape. If possible, get smooth steel bars instead of rebar, especially if you're using a grate. (If you can't find smooth rebar at the home supply store, your local metal shop will have it.) Rebar has little ridges on it, and when you're moving the hog around, the grate can catch on them and fall, causing your hog to slide off. This usually occurs during the flip, so if you're using ridged rebar, just be aware.

GRATE. While you can cook your hog directly on rebar, topping the bars with a grate makes the whole process easier. If you're new to whole-hog barbecue, or planning to cook multiple hogs in the next few years, I recommend hiring a metal shop to make you a grate (see diagram, below), as well as a heat shield.

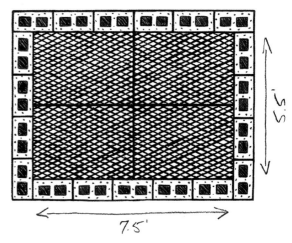

PIT OVERHEAD

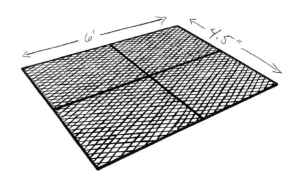

PIT GRATE

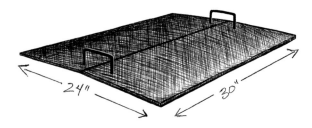

HEAT SHIELD. When you cook a hog too hot, its skin can blister and split, and fat can render and drip down onto your coals, putting you in danger of a pit fire (see Fire in the Pit!, page 180). When I teach new pit cooks how to cook a hog at my restaurants, I make them use a heat shield, which lies directly below the middle of the hog from the shoulders to the hams, to protect the cavity where a lot of the fat will render and collect. This is an insurance policy, blocking direct heat from the parts of the hog where the skin is more likely to blister and break. The only downside of using a heat shield is that it ain't real cool. It's kind of like using training wheels on a bike, and you'll never really learn how to manage a pit if you use a shield perpetually, just like you can never ride a bike fast if you keep the training wheels on it. So I make my guys use one for a few weeks to get acclimated with how we do things, because I don't want them wasting product if they mess up. After I'm confident in their skills, they cook without a shield, and that's when they really learn to cook by feel and instinct. I really encourage you to use a heat shield for your first few cooks, then take it away and become a real pitmaster.

If you want to add a heat shield to your grate, go to a metal shop and have them cut you a 24 × 30-inch piece of ⅛-inch flat sheet metal. Ask the metal shop to put a "break" down the center of the shield, so rendered fat will run down the gently sloped sides (see above illustration). This will prevent grease from pooling up in the center of the heat shield, which can result in a pit fire. Make sure it's not galvanized, because hot galvanized metal gives off poisonous fumes.

COVER. The pit cover serves a couple of functions. In addition to covering the pit for heat retention, it also regulates how the smoke escapes through small crevices where the cover meets the pit. You don't want an airtight seal on top of your pit—it'll get too hot, or if it gets too smoky inside, it could cut off the oxygen supply and choke out your fire. Smoke will naturally find its way out the top of your pit.

You have two options for cover materials: cardboard and metal. I prefer cardboard, as it's cheap, light, disposable, and insulates better than metal. I'll either use a couch box that I source from a furniture store, or a refrigerator box from an appliance store. You need a sheet of thick cardboard that's at least 6 × 5 feet, so grab two boxes if one isn't large enough.

However, if you're new to whole-hog barbecue, I'd start with a metal cover, because it's easier to gauge the temperature of your pit. Go to a building supply store and buy three 4 × 8-foot sheets of corrugated roofing panels, preferably "5V" panels if they stock them, which are flatter. Galvanized metal is fine here as well, as it won't get hot enough to release toxins. If you can only find corrugated metal, I recommend flattening the perimeter of your cover a bit by smashing it with a cinder block or sledgehammer; this will leave less room for smoke to escape around the edges of the cover.

GEAR FOR THE FIRE

BURN BARREL. I highly recommend making a burn barrel to use as your feeder fire for a whole-hog cook. See Feeder Fires for Pit Barbecue (page 32) for instructions for a burn barrel as well as alternative feeder fires.

STARTER AND BRIQUETTES. To get your feeder fire going, you'll need a charcoal chimney starter and a large bag of briquettes.

SHOVEL. For moving coals from your feeder fire to the pit, get a **SQUARE-POINT GRAVEL SHOVEL**, with as long a handle as possible. If you're planning to do a lot of barbecue, replace the handle with a 6-foot-long one. This will make it easier to fire the corners of the pit.

GLOVES. A couple pairs of **LONG-SLEEVE HEAT-PROOF GLOVES** is essential for whole-hog barbecue, as you'll need to handle the hog while it's hot, as well as move hot cinder blocks and the pit cover. I buy Schwer BBQ Grill gloves (see Resources, page 307), which can withstand heat up to 932°F, and have long sleeves for protecting your forearms. You'll need at least two pairs, so you can enlist some help removing the pit cover and flipping the hog. Also grab a box of **FOOD-SAFE NITRILE GLOVES** for prepping the hog and handling the meat.

READING THE COALS

Knowing how coals burn is an important skill when you're deciding when, and where, to fire a pit, and it helps to understand the life of a coal when you're grilling or doing open-pit barbecue as well. As wood burns down, it will start to break apart into coals. Depending on the type and dryness of the wood you're burning, these coals will be anywhere from the size of your fist down to small pebbles, and larger coals burn down more slowly than smaller ones. When those coals drop away from the log, they're as hot as they're going to get. They'll be glowing bright orange and pulsating, like a meteor burning through the atmosphere. As they burn down and cool off, the glowing parts of the coal pulsate more slowly and eventually turn to gray ash. Over time, as you both watch the evolution of the coals and feel for the temperature (or check the thermometers), you'll gain an instinct for when to add more coals based on how it all looks.

PIT CONSTRUCTION

Every time I do a whole hog, I make the exact same pit, and you can find the diagram for it on page 159. It might take you a while to get all the materials and to build the pit the first time, but after you do it once or twice, it should only take you about 20 minutes to put it together in the future.

Find a flat spot to build your pit, at least 7 × 9 feet (the pit will measure 5½ × 7½ feet). If possible, this location should be somewhat shielded from the wind, but more often than not you'll have to deal with wind. Dirt is the best base for a pit (Fig. 1). If it's a grassy area, you'll want to remove the grass with a shovel or just burn it off once the pit is built. Concrete is dangerous, because there's moisture trapped inside and it'll go off like a gun when it warms up. NEVER build a pit on asphalt, which gives off noxious chemicals when it burns. (I learned this the hard way.)

Position 19 cinder blocks in a rectangle: 6 blocks along one long side, 5 blocks along the other long side, and 4 blocks along the ends, all nice and tight. DO NOT use mortar. The beautiful thing about a "dry-stacked" block pit is how it "breathes" through the gaps between the blocks. Smokers, grills, or pits built with mortar are forced to draw oxygen in (usually from one intake), which creates hot zones inside the pit and makes it harder to manage consistent temperature. A dry-stack block pit intakes oxygen from all sides, and intakes it slowly, just enough to fuel your coal bed but not enough to get your heat racing. Now, there's nothing wrong with smokers and the like; the pits at my restaurants all have mortar because that's what building codes require. But in my opinion, no other pit cooks like a dry-stacked block pit.

Remove 2 blocks from the middle of one of the long sides, ideally the side facing away from the wind (where I live, this is facing east). This space is where you'll fire your pit. Take both cinder blocks that you've removed and bust off one half of each by holding a block on one side, then hit the other side with a hammer (or knock it against another block) until you have a neat half-block and probably some broken pieces (Fig. 2). Set the half-blocks and the busted pieces aside.

If you're using sand, fill the interior of the pit with 2 or 3 bags of playground sand and spread it evenly into a 3-inch-deep bed. Make sure the blocks are all level, adjusting them as needed by pushing some sand

FIG. 1

FIG. 2

underneath or scooping some dirt out from underneath, depending on the grade. Any uneven or wiggly spots will only create bigger problems as you continue building the pit. The interior dimensions of your pit should be 56 inches wide by 80 inches long.

Build a second "course," or layer, of cinder blocks on top of the first. You'll need to stagger these blocks so that they span the block gaps from the first layer; you don't want your blocks lined up as neat columns. Do this by looking at the layer of blocks on the ground and finding the long side that had 6 blocks; for this layer, that side will have 5 and the other will have 6. Another way to think of it is to start building this layer by laying the half-blocks down first, one on each side of the gap you made for firing the pit (Fig. 3). When you're finished with the second course, you'll have an opening that's 2 cinder blocks wide and 2 cinder blocks high (Fig. 4).

Place your pieces of angle iron—one facing inside the pit, one facing the outside of the pit—to support the blocks on top of the opening (Fig. 5).

FIG. 3

FIG. 4

FIG. 5

Repeat to make a third course of cinder blocks, staggered over the second, again making sure the gaps in the third course are offset from the second layer (Fig. 6).

If you're using a heat shield, at this point lay 3 or 4 lengths of bar spaced evenly over the middle of the pit, spacing them 12 to 15 inches apart. Lay the heat shield on top (Fig. 7 and 8).

You should now have a very stable, sturdy structure that is neatly built, with all the blocks fitting snugly together.

Add a fourth course of cinder blocks, staggered over the third. If you have a heat shield, the placement of the bars holding the heat shield will cause the fourth course of blocks to not fit as tightly as the first three courses, which is good because they'll allow for some airflow toward the top of the pit. Even though they'll be a little uneven, they will still hold the heat and smoke really tight—trust me. When you finish the fourth course, lay at least 5 (preferably 7) lengths of bar spaced evenly across the top of the pit, from one long side to the other (Fig. 9). If you're using a grate, set it on top of the bars (Fig. 10).

Finish the pit with a final, fifth course of cinder blocks. Because of the rebar or grate, these won't sit perfectly flush with the blocks either (Fig. 11). Just try to position them so they wobble as little as possible. Your pit is now ready to fire.

THE BEAUTIFUL THING ABOUT A "DRY-STACKED" BLOCK PIT IS HOW IT "BREATHES" THROUGH THE GAPS BETWEEN THE BLOCKS.

FIG. 6

FIG. 7

FIG. 8

FIG. 9

FIG. 10

FIG.11

PART OF THE REASON I TELL
YOU TO BUY A FULL CORD
OF WOOD IS SO YOU CAN KEEP
A VERY ACTIVE FIRE GOING
THROUGH THE FIRST LEG
OF THE COOK, BECAUSE THE
LAST THING YOU WANT IS
TO RUN OUT OF COALS AND
LOWER THE TEMPERATURE
OF YOUR PIT.

THE FIRE

PREPARE THE **FEEDER FIRE**

You'll need a lot of fuel to keep a hog cooking for 24 hours. I highly recommend making yourself a burn barrel (see page 33), which will be your source of coals throughout the cook. Set the burn barrel up close enough to the pit so you don't have to walk far every time you fire the pit. If you don't have a burn barrel, use the remaining blocks you have left to build an L-shaped cinder block wall (see page 33) and build your feeder fire inside of that. Plan on building your feeder fire 3 to 4 hours before you load the hog, assuming you're using green firewood. Do not miss this step, or it will put you behind!

Use a bag of charcoal to kickstart your feeder fire (see Starting the Fire, page 36). Once the charcoal is glowing red, start building up your supply of coals by feeding it with firewood. You're going use up a lot of your wood supply—around half—during the first 6 to 8 hours of the cook, as your pit will need less fuel as the cook progresses. Don't hold back on burning wood down in your feeder fire, and throw a couple pieces of fresh wood in there every 10 minutes or so for the first few hours. Part of the reason I tell you to buy a full cord of wood is so you can keep a very active fire going through the first leg of the cook, because the last thing you want is to run out of coals and lower the temperature of your pit.

FIRE **THE** PIT

Once your pit is ready and your feeder fire is going strong, you should have a good amount of coals ready. Two or three hours before you're ready to load the hog into the pit, fire the piss out of the ground inside. This will both dry out and warm up the sand and/or dirt below, which will help insulate the pit to stay warm during the cook. At the same time, you're filling the holes in your cinder blocks with hot air, which is a great insulator. If you're using new cinder blocks, they'll probably have a lot of moisture trapped inside of them, so this preheating step will get rid of that as well.

To fire the pit, scatter at least 8 to 10 shovelfuls of glowing coals evenly all over the inside of the pit. Place 2 or 3 cinder blocks (or some other piece of fireproof material) vertically in front of the opening of the pit—with the holes facing to the sides, of course—to cover that hole up. You want to get this closure as tight as you can. Cover the pit and walk away. Check it in about 15 minutes; the cover should feel so hot that you don't want to touch it. If it's not hot, then add a couple more shovelfuls of coals to the pit. As those coals burn down, the temperature inside of the pit will reach 400°F or higher, then start to come down to around 250°F.

Keep loading your feeder fire while you get ready to prep the hog. So long as you have a good amount of flames going, your fire is producing coals at a good clip. Once you've started this fire, you've got to keep feeding it for the duration of the cook, so make it your entire crew's job to pitch in to keep it going.

WEST TENNESSEE WHOLE HOG

Makes enough for 200 to 240 servings

YOU'LL NEED
1 whole hog off the hoof (175 to 190 pounds)
3 cups Big Hoss Rub (page 96) or your preferred rub
2 cups Diamond Crystal kosher salt
A few cups of vegetable oil

About 25 hours before you're planning on serving, take the hog out of the cooler. Lay your hog, skin-side up, on a clean worktable (lay some butcher paper or a tarp down first if you like) and give it a good sponge bath with water and a rag, wiping down the skin to remove any dried blood or other gunk.

Turn the hog over onto its back. Using a hatchet (or cleaver) and a mallet, split the breastbone down the middle, all the way through. Then rest the hatchet at the top of the spine, with the blade aiming down. Using the hammer, hit the blade a couple of times until it cuts all the way through the spine, splitting it in half, being careful not to cut any deeper, otherwise you risk cutting through the skin below (Fig. 1). I don't want to stress you out, but it's real important not to split the skin, because that can create major problems for you during the cook. (See Fire in the Pit!, page 180.)

Pull the blade out and repeat just below your first cut; this will give your hatchet a good place to begin splitting the rest of the spine. After the second cut, grab two buddies and ask each to stand at either side of the hog's shoulders and then press down on the shoulders, which will make splitting the spine easier (Fig. 2). Insert the hatchet into the cut you just made. Begin carefully hammering the back of the hatchet to split the spine in half, again making sure you don't cut any deeper than the spine, or you risk cutting through the skin on the back side. Your goal is to butterfly the spine from top to bottom, which allows the hog to lie as flat as possible. Although we're using some brutal tools, this is actually a delicate technique, because intact skin is so important to the outcome of the cook (Fig. 3 and 4).

FIG. 1

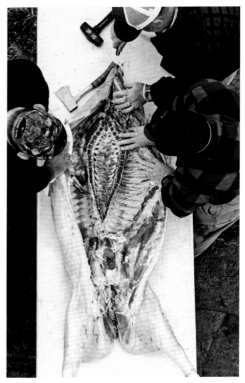

FIG. 2

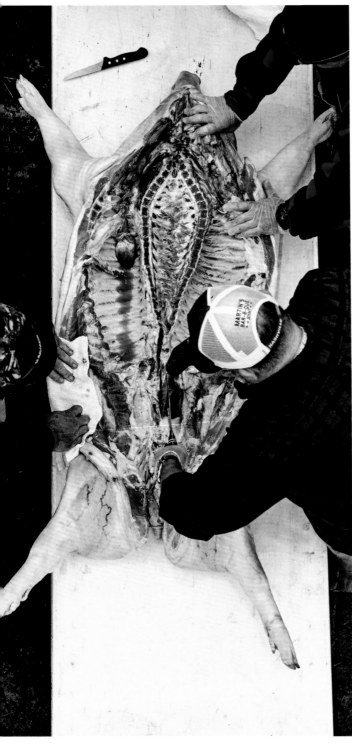

FIG. 3

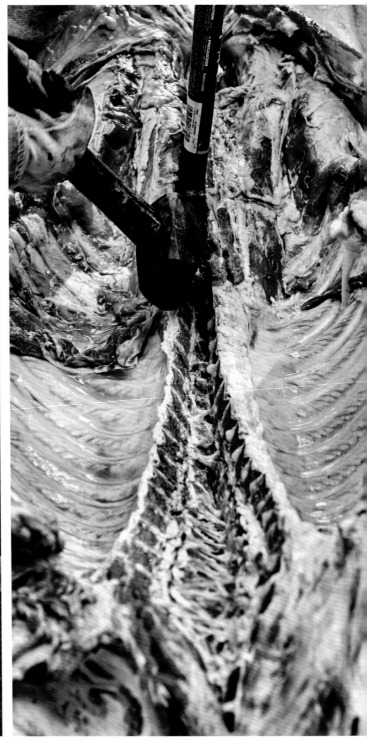

FIG. 4

FIG. 5

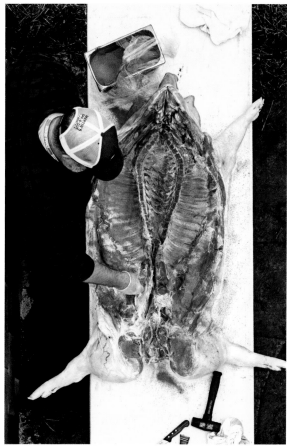

FIG. 6

Once you reach the hams, you can split the tailbone as well, especially if your hog is on the heavier side, as that will help it lie flatter.

Once the spine is butterflied from top to bottom, double-check the area around the neck and shoulders to make sure the lymph nodes (Fig. 5) were removed; if you see anything that resembles wet, shiny testicles, these are the lymph nodes and you'll want to cut them out with a knife (if left in, these can ruin the flavor of a whole hog during the cook, making it taste musty or funky).

Also trim away any dangling remnants of organs or anything else that looks like it should go. If it looks nasty, cut it out. Take some water (or beer) and wash off any slimy or bloody stuff. Use your common sense: If it looks gross, get rid of it.

Depending on its breed and diet, your hog's ribs might have a lot of leaf lard attached. Sometimes the meat processor will have already removed this, but if you see a couple inches or more of dense white fat attached to the ribs, especially near the hams, grab a knife and cut most of it out.

(You can render and cook with this fat. Or cure it in salt for a couple of weeks until it's nice and firm, then hang it up for a couple more weeks to equalize. You can even cold-smoke it for a couple of days. All are delicious ways to use it—just don't leave it in the hog because it's not going to do you any good and all that extra fat may cause flare-ups.)

Once the hog is butterflied (it should be lying pretty flat), grab your dry rub—you'll probably need between 2 and 3 cups total—and sprinkle any exposed meat with a fairly generous coating, spreading it evenly so you don't get any clumps or places where the rub can build up (Fig. 6).

LOAD
THE HOG

Before loading the hog, make sure your pit temperature is around 250°F. Place an oven thermometer on the grate to check. With your heatproof gloves on, remove the cinder blocks from the sides of the top layer of the pit, which will make it easier to load the hog inside. Set them out of the way so you don't trip over them when you're carrying the hog over (believe me, it happens, and it's no fun).

Soak a towel with vegetable oil and rub the bars or cooking grate down well, like you're seasoning a cast-iron skillet.

Grab a buddy or two and some paper towels. The hog's feet will be *sliiiick*—like deer guts on a doorknob—so you need something to help you grip them. Lay the hog on its side, then wrap a few layers of paper towels around each leg, just above the ankle; this will make it easier to grip the hog as you transfer it. Ask your buddy to grab both legs on one end of the hog as you grab the other. Lift the hog and walk it over to the pit. You'll want the hog centered on the grate or bars belly-side down. You might find it easiest to place the hog belly-up off to the side of the bars and then "roll" it over. Position the hog, belly-side down, and spread its legs; you want it to lie as flat as possible. The hog's belly area is floppy, so if you see any belly meat hanging out from below the skin, tuck it back under the body.

Grab your vegetable oil and give the hog's skin a good rubdown. You want to oil every bit of skin that you can see. You'll feel like you work at a Club Med spa.

Generously season the skin with kosher salt. Like *really* make it snow, coating it really well, then rub the salt into the skin. The salt will pool up in the skin's wrinkles and creases; this is good. Salt helps to tighten the skin, which will prevent it from splitting open after you flip it. Think of it this way: The hog's skin will be its baking dish after you flip the hog—for the final three-quarters of the cook—and, as I have stressed before, you don't want any holes in that baking dish, or the rendered fat that should be slowly cooking the meat (like a confit) will be lost to the fire, and will dry out the meat—or worse, start a pit fire (see Fire in the Pit!, page 180).

Take 6 oven thermometers and place them around the hog: 2 next to the shoulders, 2 next to the hips, 1 up by the neck or head, and 1 up against its crotch. Position them so you can quickly read them when you lift the cover to peek inside. If you're cooking directly over bars, you can secure the thermometers with wire. You hopefully won't have to check the thermometers often, but they'll be there when you need them, and they're a useful crutch when you're learning how to read the coal bed.

If you're not using a grate, you can jam probe thermometers straight through the cardboard cover, or drill small holes in a metal cover. Just make sure the tip of the thermometer is not touching metal when you're taking a reading, which will give a higher temp.

Cover the pit, then place a few logs and/or cinder block pieces around the edges of the cover to hold it in place, pushing down any spots on the lid that want to poke up.

If you're cooking in an area where there's a lot of wind, grab a tarp and hang it over the side(s) where the wind is hitting the pit. This will help regulate how much air is being pushed into the pit from the wind, and prevent it from getting too hot. If you don't have a tarp, park your truck on that side of the pit to block as much wind as you can.

THE HOG'S SKIN WILL BE ITS BAKING DISH AFTER YOU FLIP THE HOG—FOR THE FINAL THREE-QUARTERS OF THE COOK. YOU DON'T WANT ANY HOLES IN THAT BAKING DISH, OR THE RENDERED FAT THAT SHOULD BE SLOWLY COOKING THE MEAT (LIKE A CONFIT) WILL BE LOST TO THE FIRE, AND WILL DRY OUT THE MEAT—OR WORSE, START A PIT FIRE.

THE COOK

THE FRONT END

Most of the smoky flavor you're going to get into the meat will happen in the first few hours of the cook, when the hog is warming up. Once that hog warms up to around 140°F, it's not going to absorb any more smoke. This first leg of the cook is when you'll need to do the most work to ensure you keep as consistent a temperature in the pit as possible. You'll naturally have some spikes and dips in temperature, but you want the difference between the high and low temps to be as minimal as possible.

During the front end of the cook, keep your feeder fire going at a good clip, loading it with fresh wood as the previous load begins to break apart into coals. You'll go through a lot of fuel during this stretch, as much as half of it, but as long as you started with a cord of wood, you'll have plenty left for the back end.

After you load your hog and cover the pit, the cold meat is going to lower the temperature of the pit, so you'll need to bring your pit back up to around 250°F as quickly as possible. To do this, fire the pit with 4 shovelfuls of coal, wait 10 minutes, then see where that got you.

There is a bit of an art to placing coals inside the pit with a shovel, but it's pretty easy to learn. Scoop the coals from your feeder fire into your shovel, then walk it over to the pit. Kneel down and insert your shovel through the opening on the side if the pit, then slowly extend the shovel straight back until it hits the opposite wall of the pit. Holding the pit shovel flat, hold your front hand loosely around the handle, then use your back hand to gently rotate the shovel handle back and forth, about 45 degrees to each side. Each time you change directions, a few of the coals will fall to the side, right where you want them. As you empty the shovel you will need to rock it a little harder each time to get the remaining coals out. Begin by broadcasting coals along the back wall of the pit, then repeat to cover the middle and the side nearest you.

Now, a half shovelful of coals doesn't sound like enough to increase the temperature of a pit, and barbecue newbies tend to dump too many coals at once.

Consistency of temperature is vital to cooking a whole hog, and adding only a half to a full shovelful at a time gives you both tighter control over temperature and more accuracy of coal placement.

Once your pit's temperature levels out between 250° and 260°F, you'll begin feeding only a half shovelful of coals at a time. You'll need to do this about every 10 minutes to maintain that temperature. If a half shovelful isn't getting the pit hot enough, then add a full shovel of coals.

MONITORING
THE TEMPERATURE

During the front end of the cook, you want to monitor the temperature of the pit closely—not just in one spot, but all over. Mentally divide the pit into 6 sections, then check each section every 10 minutes by peeking through the opening at the base of the pit. If you're using thermometers, keep an eye on them for the overall temp; they can also help you see if one area of the pit is hotter than the others. If you see any spots where the smoke is rising more quickly, that's a sign that it's too hot, and you shouldn't add coals there the next time you fire the pit. If it still doesn't cool down after a firing or two, you can go to the opposite side of the pit and lift the cover up a few inches; this will help direct some of the airflow away from the hotspot. If it's still too hot, you just have to ride it out until the pit temp falls back down. Do not try to dig the coals out or move them around, especially after the hog has begun to render its fat, you can easily start a fire!

More important, while you're reading the coals (see Reading the Coals, page 163), look for any sections where the coals have stopped glowing; that's where you'll likely need to add some fresh coals the next time you fire the pit.

You should also monitor the temperature of the pit by feeling the cover with your hand. This is a learned skill, but you can develop it while using the oven thermometers I had you place around the hog. Place your hand on the cover, count how many seconds you can leave it there before you have to pull away, then lift the cover a few inches and peek at the thermometer below that spot (you'll probably need to shine a flashlight on it). With some practice, you'll be able to gauge the temperature of the pit without having to consult the thermometers. Now, this is way easier to do if you're using a metal cover—it conducts heat better than cardboard, obviously—but it's possible with a cardboard cover as well, with some practice.

If your entire pit is running too hot, you need to choke it down (while being careful to not choke it completely out). To do that, tightly cover the opening with cinder blocks and weight down any cracks around the perimeter of the cover with logs or cinder blocks. Wait about 15 minutes and check the temperature. Once it's back down to around 250°F, you can remove the block from the opening and any extra blocks you placed on the cover.

THIS FIRST LEG OF THE COOK IS WHEN YOU'LL NEED TO DO THE MOST WORK TO ENSURE YOU KEEP AS CONSISTENT A TEMPERATURE IN THE PIT AS POSSIBLE. YOU'LL NATURALLY HAVE SOME SPIKES AND DIPS IN TEMPERATURE, BUT YOU WANT THE DIFFERENCE BETWEEN THE HIGH AND LOW TEMPS TO BE AS MINIMAL AS POSSIBLE.

FIRE IN THE PIT!

Several years back, I was cooking a whole hog at a festival in Charleston, South Carolina. It was one of the hottest and most humid days I can remember, so my buddy Sam Jones and I were sitting in my rental truck with the air conditioning blasting while we waited for our friend Rodney Scott to arrive. I looked up and I noticed a lot of smoke racing out of the far side of the pit. I didn't do anything about it, figuring it would die down in a few minutes, but it kept going.

Now, you should always be watching the speed of the smoke exhaling from the pit. It should not be racing out, but just rising as if it had a gentle push. You should ALWAYS be glancing over at this as another way to keep tabs on the heat in the pit.

So after watching the smoke billowing out for a little while, I walked over to the pit and, despite having cooked hogs for twenty-five years, I pulled a huge dumbass rookie move (probably thanks to the Coors Light): I lifted the cover too high, and *whoosh*—it was like frickin' *Backdraft* in there. I'd let in a bunch of oxygen and the pit just went up in flames. I dropped the lid and immediately, and involuntarily, starting giggling. That's how hopeless the situation had become, in an instant. I mean this thing was *engulfed*. Sam took a video of the whole thing from his truck so he could bust my balls later. Luckily it happened on the very front end of the cook, so I was able to catch Rodney in time to have him to bring me another hog, and we started over. I got my soft ass out of the air conditioning and cooked the hog Rodney brought me, and no one ever knew the better.

My point is: Pit fires happen, no matter how long you've been cooking hogs. If you're accustomed to using an offset smoker, you might think that flames in the pit aren't a big deal, but they are. In an offset smoker, the fire is shielded from the meat. In a pit, the heat is direct, so fire is a huge problem.

If you have a flame-up in your pit, don't freak out; just get your shovel in there through the opening in your pit and smack the fire down with it until the flames are out. If you have a big log or something that's caught on fire, grab some tongs and pull it out.

You can get away with having a log igniting under the hog during the first 6 or so hours of the cook, because the hog hasn't fully rendered its fat yet. But after you flip the hog, if you see any flames, you need to stop that shit right away, because with all that grease that's dripping onto the coals it can suddenly light up like napalm. If this happens, you need to choke it out as quickly as possible by patting the fire down with the back side of a shovel.

If patting the flames with a shovel doesn't work, don't try to shovel out the fire, because it could catch other grease spots and make it worse. Instead, shovel some dirt or sand on top to choke them out completely. As long as the hog wasn't exposed to flames for more than a couple of minutes, you should be able to finish your cook and the meat will be just fine. But if the hog itself has caught fire, you might as well sit down, watch the flames, and laugh about it. There is nothing else you can do at this point.

Remember: Pit barbecue is cooking over burning coals, not flames.

THE FLIP

About 4 hours into the cook, you'll flip the hog over onto its back, where it will remain for the rest of the time. Up to this point, you've been cooking the exposed belly side over a higher temperature (around 250°F), but for the rest of the cook, you'll keep it at a lower temperature (around 200°F) to maximize tenderness. Now, most folks don't flip their hogs this early into the cook: Harold Thomas, who taught me how to cook a hog, flipped his midway through using wire, after about 12 hours, and some old-timers don't flip it at all. But when I opened my first Martin's, I would flip my hogs on the early side—by myself, like some professional wrestler getting ready to sweep up and pin his opponent—so I wouldn't have to drive back to the restaurant in the middle of the night. It worked great, and the flavor was the same, so I've done it this way ever since.

Flipping early helps prevent the hog from coming apart. As the hog cooks, its muscles and joints loosen up, and if you're not careful, you can end up tearing off a ham or shoulder during the flip. A hog that's only been cooking for 4 (and up to about 6) hours should stay intact when you flip it.

Another reason I like to flip early: Historically speaking, West Tennessee whole hog is just seasoned with salt, but I use a dry rub that has sugar in it. That sugar will be completely caramelized after 4 hours of cooking directly over the coals. Much longer and it will just burn.

FLIPPING ON A GRATE

How you flip the hog depends on if you're using a grate or cooking the hog directly on top of bars. If you're using a grate, grab your strongest helper and put your heatproof gloves on. Remove the pit cover, take a few cinder blocks down from the top row, and position them on the ground so they can support the grate. Remove the grate, hog and all, and set it on top of the cinder blocks. Stand on either side of the hog. Get in a low crouch and slide your hands below the hog and feel around the length of the animal for any spots where it's sticking to the grate. Be extra diligent around the middle of the hog, where the spine around the belly likes to stick. If you find any stuck spots, use your fingers to gently release the hog.

Once the hog is ready to flip, position yourselves at either end of the pig: one of you at the shoulder, and the other at the ham on the same side. No need for paper towels this time; the cook should have started to dry out the skin a bit already. With your heatproof gloves on, grab the hog just above the hoof with one hand, and slide your other hand and forearm deep under the leg—dang near all the way to your elbow. Your partner will do the same on the other side. Your fingertips should end up under the spine. Your arm below the hog will do most of the lifting, with your other hand holding the ankle for stability (don't pull too hard with your hoof hand, or you risk ripping the leg out).

Pull toward you and slide the hog toward one side of the grate until its spine is on top of the edge, and you're supporting the weight of half the hog. You are doing this to allow for enough free space on the grate so that when you flip the hog, its entire body will land safely back on the grate. Look your buddy in the eyes, do a three count, then, working swiftly and in sync, lift the hog a few inches above the grate (again, your hand supporting the shoulder or ham will bear most of the weight), and flip it over toward the center of the grate. It's vitally important that once you start your flip, you finish it. If you hesitate or stop midflip, you'll screw up the whole sync, meaning you might twist the hog and tear its skin. It's like the famous toilet bomb scene in *Lethal Weapon 2*: Once you and your buddy commit to the count, go on with it, and don't flinch! Try to keep the hog as flat as possible throughout the flip. You might hear a leg or rib cracking during the process; this is not a big deal, so long as you don't tear any skin or displace the prime sections (ham, belly, shoulder).

Once you've flipped the hog, reposition it into the center of the grate, if necessary, once again sliding your hand and forearm well under the big muscles to move it; don't just pull on the feet. If you feel like it, you can dump some vinegar-based barbecue sauce, a couple of beers, or even some water over the hog; this will make sure it stays nice and moist. Then load the grate back into the pit, replace the cinder blocks, and cover the pit. If, by chance, you mangled the hog some during the flip—maybe a ham or shoulder got torn out of socket, or a few ribs cracked—don't worry. Just push everything back together, and, if necessary, prop the skin around the belly up with a rock or a brick to keep its shape—you want the belly area to act like a "bowl" for collecting all of the fat as it renders.

FLIPPING ON BARS

If you're cooking the hog directly over bars, it's can be easier to do the flip by yourself—if you're stout enough. But if you're not sure you can handle the load, ask someone to help you. Uncover the pit and remove the blocks from the top row that you plan on flipping from. Slide your hands below the hog to check for any skin or meat sticking to the bars; because the animal's weight isn't evenly distributed, it's likely there will be some spots that need to be released. Do this all around the hog to release it. I can't stress this enough: It's *so* important to make sure the hog is completely unstuck. If it's not, and you begin your flip, it will pull and dislodge your bars off the blocks and that hog could slide off into the coals.

Once the hog is free of the bars, slide your left hand and forearm under the shoulder, and your right hand and forearm under the ham (or vice versa; if you've got a helper, one of you take the shoulder and the other the ham). Pull the hog toward you until its hooves reach the side of the pit. Count to three, bend your knees, and flip that bastard over and do it with no hesitation. Recenter it on the bars, if necessary, then replace the blocks and cover the pit.

I went to Montana a couple years back and cooked the shittiest hog I've ever cooked. The weather conditions were perfect: We set up our pit at this fancy farm, where the weather was a beautiful 72°F, no wind whatsoever. At night the sky was so clear we could watch the International Space Station pass overhead. I just knew this hog was going to be on point! But it wasn't: When we took the hog out of the pit the next day, it was dry as shit. I couldn't figure out what went wrong. The pit temperature had been right on the money the whole time. Later I figured out that I'd made not one, but two dumbass mistakes: The hogs we were given had been largely grass fed—virtually no corn in their diet whatsoever—so they had very little fat to keep the meat moist. The farmer was allowing them to be in small pasture. I should have made sure we were sourcing cornfed (or at least corn-finished) hogs, which is never an issue where I live, as all hogs eat a corn-heavy diet around me.

On top of that, we were cooking at a higher altitude, which affects your cook in a couple of ways. First, as altitude increases, atmospheric pressure lowers, as does the boiling point of water—about 1°F less for every 500-foot gain in elevation. The result is that moisture will evaporate from an animal more quickly, and at a lower temperature. Second, air gets drier as you go up in altitude. The muscles of a hog are mostly composed of water (around 75 percent), but that water content shoots up if the hog is leaner, as our grass-fed hog was. So by smoking a lean animal in a dry environment, we weren't barbecuing the animal so much as dehydrating it. What I should have done to remedy this—aside from sourcing a properly fatty hog—was to cook the thing at an even lower temperature (around 200°F the entire time) and mop the thing frequently to keep it moist. Lesson learned: Always adjust for the environment in which you're cooking, and make sure you start with the right kind of meat.

THE BACK END

By the time you flip the hog and replace the cover, the temperature inside the pit will likely have dropped significantly. Bring it back up by firing the pit with 2 or 3 shovelfuls of coals, distributing them evenly across the entire pit. (Yes, this is the one exception to the half-shovelful rule.) Re-cover the pit, wait 10 minutes, then check the pit temperature; you want to get it up between 200° and 210°F. It's okay if the pit is a bit hotter at this point.

Once the temperature has stabilized and drops down to 190°F, take a half shovelful of coals and sprinkle them around the inside edge of the pit; from here on out, you won't be adding any coals below the hog itself, just around the edges. I can't emphasize this enough: Don't fire below the hog any longer, or you risk burning through its skin.

Wait 10 or 15 minutes, then see how that small addition of coals affected the temperature of your pit. Every pit is a little different, and every climate is different, so it might have raised the temperature of your pit 5°F, 10°F, or had no effect at all. Use this knowledge to adjust how many coals you add the next time; if a half shovelful only raised the temperature a couple of degrees, try three-quarters of a shovelful the next time. If it jumped the temperature up 10°F, add a little less the next time.

Over the next few firings, you should be able to dial in the amount of coals you need to maintain a pit temperature of around 200°F, give or take 10°F. I'd actually rather you get the pit a little too hot at this point than to let it dip below 190°F. Depending on your pit and the ambient temperature, you might need to fire it every 15 minutes from here on out, or up to every hour. Either way, you'll be using up far less fuel during the back end of the cook, so you can feed your feeder fire more slowly—just be sure to keep it going. Now's a great time to use any surplus coals for grilling up a lunch, or bury some potatoes or other vegetables in the ashes (see Chapter 5, page 222) to eat with your hog.

In addition to checking the thermometers between firings, practice placing your hand on the cover and counting to see how long you can hold it there until it begins to hurt a little, then immediately look at the thermometer. By the end of the cook, you'll know what a 200°F pit feels like by just feeling the cover.

THE **END**

Around hour 20 of the cook, remove the pit cover and check the hog for doneness. You'll want to do this in a few spots. There should be a pool of rendered fat throughout the belly cavity, and the ribs will start popping out of their joints. The skin should have started separating from the meat around the hams and shoulders, and looking like a kid wearing his granddaddy's glove. This is a good indicator that you are almost home on it. Also, if you grab the shoulder blade (which will be poking through the base of the shoulder), it should feel loose enough to twist and pull out without a lot of effort (just don't actually pull it out). The hog probably won't be done cooking at this point because you'll still be waiting on your hams to finish. But you should have a good idea how close you are; replace the cover and check the hog again every hour. Don't forget to fire the pit every time you re-cover it, as the temperature inside will have dropped. You can stop loading wood into your feeder fire at this point, and you'll probably only need to fire the pit a few more times while your hams catch up to the rest of meat.

Around hour 23 or 24, the hams will be the last thing to get done. To test them for doneness, push the pad of your thumb into the ham ½ to 1 inch deep; if that indention stays when you remove your thumb, you're done firing the pit and the hog is pretty much ready. Just close the pit and let the remaining coals burn down; the remaining heat will take the hog over the finish line.

You can also check the hog's hams or shoulders with a thermometer: Insert it into the deepest part of the muscle, making sure it's not touching a bone. Your target is 185°F in the hams or 190°F in the shoulder; the temperature will continue to rise a few more degrees as the hog rests.

Let's eat!

THE **PIG PICKIN'**

Once your hog is ready to eat, gather your friends and family around and celebrate with a pig pickin'.

You might think of a pig pickin' as a line of folks serving themselves, buffet style, straight from the hog. You can certainly go this route, but if you've got a big crowd, you'll likely run out of pork before everyone has had their turn. People eat with their eyes, and usually take too much meat. By the time the back of the line reaches the hog, there ain't much left.

I prefer to do the pulling myself, then offer guests a sandwich (see Pulled Pork Sandwich, page 189) or a plate of pork. This way I can control the portion sizes and make sure each sandwich has balance. Balance meaning that it allows me to combine lean and fatty parts—which I call "marrying" the meat—so everyone can have the best experience.

HOLDING MEAT WARM

In a restaurant setting, we can't serve all of our meat straight off the pit, so we have to pick it into a pan and hold it for service. If you're cooking a whole hog and throwing a pig pickin', this won't be an issue—the pit will keep the hog warm. But if you're cooking some shoulders or ribs—either along with that hog or on their own—you might want to keep that meat warm and moist until you're ready to serve.

To do this, wrap the meat in the pan, good and tight, in a couple layers of plastic wrap. Wait about 10 minutes, then set it in a cooler and close the lid. If you're using a super-efficient cooler, like a YETI, leave the lid cracked a bit, because those things are so dang good at retaining heat that you'll continue cooking the meat inside if you don't leave room for some heat to escape.

If you're cooking multiple shoulders, it's okay to stack them in the cooler, but don't place more than one on top of another, or the extra weight will push all the fat and juice out of the bottom shoulder. Ribs are light enough that you can stack away.

I wouldn't recommend holding ribs for more than a couple hours (see page 134 for more on how to keep ribs warm), or they'll start to lose their bite. You can reheat ribs on a medium-hot grill, brushed with sauce if you like. Shoulders will stay warm in the cooler for hours and hours.

Before picking meat, I mentally divide the hog into thirds: shoulders, belly, and hams. The shoulder meat has a perfect ratio of meat to fat; the belly has an excess of fat to protein, and the hams have much more protein than fat. It's like Goldilocks: hams are too lean, belly meat is too fatty, shoulders are just right.

While picking the pork, I'll work down one side of the hog, then do the other. Put on your heatproof gloves. Remove one whole shoulder and transfer it to large disposable aluminum pan or stainless steel hotel pan. Scrape the fat off the skin that surrounded the shoulder and add that to the meat. Remove the bones from the shoulder, then lay the big chunks on a cutting board and gently punch it with one of your knuckles (see Punch and Fluff, page 188). Flip it, punch it again, and repeat a few times. Once it's broken up, use your fingers to pull it apart. Keep the meat loose and fluffy. Transfer all of the meat to the pan, then use cupped hands to scoop some of the rendered fat from the carcass into the pan. Cover the pan in plastic, and set it inside a cooler (see Holding Meat Warm, left).

Take your fingers and roll the loin out, which is the long muscle riding along the ribs, trying to get it out whole. You can serve the loin separately (folks who prefer lean pork like this), or you can break it into a few chunks, then punch and fluff it and marry it with the belly meat. I usually cut them into medallions to serve. Sometimes the loin comes out super dry; you can decide what you'd like to do with it.

If all of the coals in your pit have burned out, you can pull the belly and ham right on the hog. You'll want to create one big pile of lean ham and fat belly meat, all married together. Once that meat is all married, transfer it to a pan. Pull the rib meat off the bones. Discard any bones and ligaments as you go.

Around the belly, you'll find the middlin' meat, the long, stringy bacon meat at the base of the ribs. This and the jowls (if your hog has a head) are delicacies, so I like to set these aside for special requests (anyone who knows whole-hog barbecue is sure to ask for some).

Repeat on the other side, working from the shoulder first. You should end up with about 55 to 65 pounds of pulled pork, or enough to make about 200 to 240 sandwiches, or 120 to 240 plates of barbecue. When you are done there should be literally nothing left but the skin lying on the grate. Now you can see your "bowl" in all its glory.

PUNCH AND FLUFF

At my restaurants, we use an oxymoronic term, "punch and fluff," to describe the method we use to prepare pulled pork for a sandwich or plate of barbecue. The first step (the "punch") involves taking a large hunk of barbecue pork shoulder, setting it on a cutting board, then hitting it with a knuckle or two—I use the middle knuckle of my middle finger. It's really more of a light jab than a real punch; you just want to hit the meat hard enough to break it apart. Then I flip the meat over and punch it again, almost like I'm working some bread dough, and repeat until I've broken it into smaller chunks, then I gently pry the chunks apart with my fingers. This is better than grabbing and tearing shreds from the shoulder—which is how many folks pull pork—because it avoids squeezing the fat and juices out of the meat. The key is to be gentle and not squeeze the meat. Once I've got the pork in bite-size chunks, I'll gently lift it off the board and "fluff" it like a pile of feathers to create a loosely packed pile of pork that's ready to serve.

PULLED PORK
SANDWICHES

I'm very opinionated about pork sandwiches, so I have some rules that I feel like we should all live by. Like any great sandwich, the ideal pulled pork sandwich is balanced. That's the key. Too many barbecue sandwiches are too large; there's too much pork, and it throws off the equilibrium of meat to bun. I have the same issue with cheeseburgers—you shouldn't have to wrestle with it to eat it.

It's also possible to have too much bun: The best vessel for a pulled-pork sandwich is a potato roll, which is denser and springier than a white hamburger bun and a shade sweet. If you use a brioche roll or bun larger than 4 inches in diameter, you'll only taste the bread.

A pulled pork sandwich is also not a vehicle for enjoying your favorite barbecue sauce. There should be just enough sauce to help bring out the flavors of the smoky pork. The sauce should be thin and tart, so that the acid of it balances the fat from the pork. You can use my Jack's Creek Sauce (page 95) or another vinegar-based one. I add sauce to the top bun and let it soak in while I assemble the rest of my sandwich. Any thick, sweet, tomato-based sauce is only going to weigh the sandwich down, and you'll taste that sauce, not the meat. But if you must use one, then swap in a vinegar-based coleslaw instead of the one here.

Now, a lot of folks outside of the South will disagree with me on this, and some younger folks from the South may as well. But let me say it right here: A pulled pork sandwich gets topped with slaw. *Always.* I remember my first pulled pork sandwich as a young kid at Gridley's in Memphis, and slaw was on that sandwich, and every other one I've had since in West Tennessee. That's just how God meant for you to have it. If you don't like slaw, I implore you to give it a chance here. The crunch and acidity it brings to the sandwich will balance out the rich pork.

And you'll know you've hit the right balance of bread, meat, and slaw if some juices run through your fingers when you take a bite; if they run down your arms, your sandwich is too wet. I told you I had opinions!

Pour 1 tablespoon sauce on the top buns and let it soak into the buns while you build the rest of the sandwich.

Season the pulled pork with a pinch of salt. Place 4 to 5 ounces of pork on each bottom bun and divide the slaw among the sandwiches. Add the top bun and serve.

Makes 4 sandwiches

¼ cup Jack's Creek Sauce (page 95)
4 potato buns, toasted
1 to 1¼ pounds pulled pork
Kosher salt
1 cup Coleslaw (page 190)

LIKE ANY GREAT SANDWICH, THE IDEAL PULLED PORK SANDWICH IS BALANCED. THAT'S THE KEY. TOO MANY BARBECUE SANDWICHES ARE TOO LARGE; THERE'S TOO MUCH PORK, AND IT THROWS OFF THE EQUILIBRIUM OF MEAT TO BUN. I HAVE THE SAME ISSUE WITH CHEESEBURGERS—YOU SHOULDN'T HAVE TO WRESTLE WITH IT TO EAT IT.

COLESLAW

8 to 10 servings

2 cups half-and-half

½ cup apple cider vinegar

1 cup sugar

2 tablespoons mayonnaise

1 large garlic clove, finely chopped

1 small head green cabbage (about 1½ pounds)—halved, cored, and shredded (about 6 cups)

4 ounces shredded red cabbage (about 1 cup)

1 large or 2 medium carrots (about 4 ounces), coarsely grated

Like my barbecue sauces and rub, I developed this recipe back in my college dorm room, and it hasn't changed since. When I first set out to make this recipe, I couldn't decide between a mayonnaise- and a vinegar-based slaw, so I ended up combining both. I quickly discovered that mayo and vinegar don't mix well together, so I called my mom and asked her what to do. She told me to use half-and-half to bind it all together. The result is a very creamy slaw with a nice acidic punch. It's also noticeably sweet, but if I could travel back in time to 1991, I would have held back on the sugar some. If you feel like it's too sweet for you, start with half as much sugar and add to taste.

In a large bowl, combine the half-and-half, vinegar, sugar, mayonnaise, and garlic. Whisk until combined. Add the cabbages and carrots and toss to coat well. Refrigerate for at least 1 hour before serving. Toss to coat well just before serving.

A PULLED PORK SANDWICH GETS TOPPED WITH SLAW. ALWAYS. THAT'S JUST HOW GOD MEANT FOR YOU TO HAVE IT.

REDNECK
"TACOS"

T his is definitely NOT a taco, but an open-faced barbecue sandwich that you eat with a fork. When we were putting together the menu for my first Martin's location, my cook, Bo Collier, suggested that we honor the middle-Tennessee tradition of serving barbecue on hoecakes, which are essentially corn bread pancakes you cook in a skillet. I said fine, but it also needs slaw. Bo came up with the moniker, and it unfortunately stuck.

When you eat a redneck taco, your fork has to capture every bit of it: slaw, pork, hoecake. Don't eat the toppings, then eat the hoecake. That just breaks my heart, because the hoecake is what makes every bite so dadgum magical. And if you're going to put sugar in your hoecakes, just skip this dish and make something else.

Cook the hoecakes and transfer to a plate. Top each with 4 ounces (about ½ cup) pork. Drizzle each with 1 to 2 tablespoons of sauce and top with ¼ cup of slaw. Serve right away.

4 servings

4 Hoecakes (page 78)

1 pound Pit-Smoked Pork Shoulder (page 192), pulled

½ cup Jack's Creek Sauce (page 95)

1 cup Coleslaw (page 190)

PORK SHOULDER

*Makes about 10 pounds pulled
pork (enough for 30 to 40
sandwiches)*

⅓ cup Diamond Crystal
  kosher salt or Big Hoss Rub
  (page 96)
1 whole skin-on pork shoulder
  (18 to 20 pounds)
Vegetable oil, for the grates

If you're not ready to cook a whole hog, or just want to make some pulled pork sandwiches for a smaller crowd, barbecue pork shoulder is the way to go. If you've got a few more people coming over but don't want to do a whole hog, you may as well throw an extra shoulder, a few racks of ribs, or a couple chickens on there at the same time.

When buying meat for barbecuing a pork shoulder, you'll probably want to order it ahead of time to make sure you get the spec you want. First, make sure you get a whole shoulder, which is the Boston butt plus the shank. Make sure all of the skin is intact and covering the shank and the Boston butt (some meat plants and butchers will remove the skin from the butt end of the shoulder). Make sure the fat cap between the skin in the meat is good, clean, white fat, at least ¾ inch thick.

Be specific with your butcher about the size you want. Your shoulder should be at least 18 pounds; I usually buy 20-pound shoulders, which are the same size as the shoulders on a 185-pound whole hog, so I know how long they'll take to cook. A lot of shoulders sold at butcher shops and grocery stores come in the 16-pound and below range. These will work, but a 20-pound shoulder is better.

As always, inspect your pork before you pay for it. You want firm, white fat; if the fat is yellow or is soft and slimy, that indicates a shoulder that's got too much age on it and has probably been frozen and thawed a couple of times. A lot of pork you buy at a supermarket has been frozen, sometimes for more than a year (due to suppliers purchasing during favorable market conditions), so do a little homework to get yourself meat that was still walking around a week ago. Meat that's been frozen once is fine, but meat that's been repeatedly frozen and thawed becomes mushy, as the ice crystals that form with each freezing deteriorates the meat.

If possible, season the shoulder 1 day before you plan to cook it. Season it all over with a good, even coating of the salt. Transfer the pork to a wire rack set inside a sheet pan and refrigerate, uncovered, until ready to cook.

Build the pit, prepare the feeder fire, and fire the pit (pages 164–72). If you don't have a custom grate for your pit, lay a regular grill grate across 3 or 4 bars placed close together and let it heat up as well. Wipe the grate down with vegetable oil. Place the shoulder on the grate, skin-side up. Close the cover and fire the pit as needed to maintain a temperature of 250°F (see The Front End, page 178).

After 6 hours, open the pit to flip the shoulder. Using heatproof gloves, carefully loosen any parts stuck to the grate, then flip the shoulder in one clean go.

(recipe continues)

IF YOU'RE NOT
READY TO COOK A
WHOLE HOG, OR
JUST WANT TO MAKE
SOME PULLED PORK
SANDWICHES FOR
A SMALLER CROWD,
BARBECUE PORK
SHOULDER IS THE
WAY TO GO.

Cover the pit and continue cooking the shoulder, maintaining a pit temperature of about 220°F (see Monitoring the Temperature, page 179). The shoulder should take about 20 hours to cook (or about 1 hour per pound).

To check on the doneness, look for the blade bone (which will be sticking out of the butt end of the shoulder) and wiggle it; if it seems loose enough to pull out with little to no resistance, the shoulder is ready. Texture is a better indicator of doneness than temperature, but you can also insert a meat thermometer into the thickest part of the shoulder; the meat is ready when it's between 195° and 200°F—lower and it'll be tough, higher and it'll start to dry out.

Transfer the shoulder to a cutting board or clean work surface. You can pull the meat right away, but it's best to let it rest for 30 minutes to 1 hour.

To pull the meat, put on heatproof gloves and remove the skin from the shoulder. Pull out the bones. Scrape any unrendered fat from the underside of the skin onto the meat. Dig your fingers into the meat and separate it into smaller chunks, then combine the meat with the fat, as if you were tossing a salad. The meat will be so tender that it'll fall apart into large shreds between your fingers. Try not to pinch or squeeze the meat, as this will squeeze out juice and fat; just gently break it apart, or use the "punch and fluff" method (see page 188). As you pull the meat apart, you'll find a long, tenderloin-like muscle running through it. Competition barbecue folks call it the "dipstick" or "money muscle," because they usually slice and serve to judges alongside the shoulder. You can do the same or cut it into thirds and marry the meat with the rest of the shoulder.

Set the meat inside a baking dish or hotel pan and keep covered with plastic until you're ready to serve; if you're going to hold it for a while, place it in a cooler to keep warm (see Holding Meat Warm, page 187).

WHOLE HOG
IN THE GROUND

From a functional standpoint, cooking a hog in the ground is much harder than cooking in a pit. First, because you have to dig a huge hole and that's backbreaking work, unless you have access to some construction equipment. Second, cooking in the ground leaves so much to chance: Once that hog's inside the hole, it's harder to read the coals and control the cooking temperature. You also run a higher risk of a pit fire, which is why you'll NEVER place coals directly below the hog when cooking in the ground. And if a fire should happen (as it has for me), there's not much you can do about it—your hog is ruined.

But if you're set on cooking a hog in the ground, I don't want to talk you out of it at all. There is a romanticism about it, as it's the most old-school way to cook barbecue. Most of the folks who ask me how to do whole-hog barbecue want to do it in the ground, because that's the image in most people's heads when they think about it, or how their granddaddy did it. And nothing will teach you more about how to control a fire. If you can successfully cook a hog in the ground, then in my humble opinion you've reached the pinnacle of live-fire cooking, and you've earned your barbecue black belt. Even if you screw it up, you won't regret the fact that you tried. Even more, you'll be proud of the guts you had to take it on.

The process of cooking a hog in the ground mostly aligns with pit barbecue, and I highly recommend you read through my instructions for whole-hog closed pit barbecue (pages 146–88) first. But there are some differences. The entire smoking process takes a few hours less, and dirt is such an efficient insulator that you won't have to fire the pit as often, or with as many coals. But that's also part of the challenge—you'll have to take extra care to prevent overfiring your coal bed. You'll be cooking the hog on its back for the entire cook, so you won't need to flip it. And the finished pork is very similar to pit barbecue, though a hog cooked in the ground will be a bit lighter in color (more golden brown) and the smoky flavor won't be as pronounced, hence the lighter coloration.

SOURCING
THE HOG

Follow all of my advice for sourcing a hog for pit barbecue (see Sourcing Pigs and Hogs for Barbecue, pages 120–24), but buy a smaller hog, around 150 pounds off the hoof. Although the dimensions of your hole will be the same as the inside of a pit, the smaller hog leaves more room around the perimeter of the hole for your coal bed, which you don't want to extend to below the hog itself.

MATERIALS

For the hole, you'll need **FIVE LENGTHS OF BAR**, the same as you'd use on a closed pit: ⅝- to ¾-inch rebar, 60 inches long, preferably smooth. Oh, and a bunch of **FRIENDS** and **SHOVELS**. Or a **BACKHOE**, really, if you can get one.

For the cover, you need **THREE 4 × 8-FOOT SHEETS OF METAL**, either corrugated metal or "5V" roofing panels. I don't recommend using cardboard here, as it will be easy to catch it on fire when you're adding coals to the hole.

For the feeder fire, I still recommend sourcing **THREE BUNDLES OF WOOD SLATS** or a **FULL CORD OF FIREWOOD** (see Selecting and Sourcing Wood, page 27), which is more than you'll need, but better safe than sorry. You'll also need a **BURN BARREL** (see page 33) or some other means of maintaining the fire, plus **3 LARGE BAGS OF CHARCOAL BRIQUETTES** and **2 CHIMNEY STARTERS** for baking off the hole (see page 198).

> **IF YOU CAN SUCCESSFULLY COOK A HOG IN THE GROUND, THEN IN MY HUMBLE OPINION YOU'VE REACHED THE PINNACLE OF LIVE-FIRE COOKING, AND YOU'VE EARNED YOUR BARBECUE BLACK BELT.**

THE COOK

PREPARE THE HOLE

The day before your cook, gather up your buddies and shovels (or that backhoe). Dig a straight-sided hole that's the same dimensions as a cinder block pit: 56 inches wide by 80 inches long, and 32 inches deep. Once the hole is dug, dig a gentle slope (about 25 degrees steep) at one of the short ends—this is the opening you'll use to fire the hole.

Lay your bars across the top of the pit, positioning them so one bar will rest below the hog's shoulder, one below its hams, and the other three evenly spaced between. If possible, secure the bars in place using sod or garden stakes. Use wire to secure an oven thermometer to the bar nearest the sloped opening, making sure you'll be able to see it when you peek down into the hole.

Take some of the dirt from digging your hole and mound it around 3 sides of the hole (leaving the end with the sloped side open), creating a hill 8 to 12 inches high. Your cover will rest on this dirt mound, so pack it down well and make sure it's fairly even in height all the way around.

BAKE OFF THE HOLE

A few hours before you're ready to load your hog, you want to "bake off" the hole, which will both dry out its bottom and sides, and warm it up for the cook. Open one bag of charcoal, fill up 2 chimney starters, and light them. Once they're ready, scatter one chimney at either end of the hole. Divide the remaining charcoal from that bag over the lit coals, half at one end, half at the other. Once those coals are nice and red, pour the remaining 2 bags of charcoal over, then use a shovel to spread the coals evenly over the base of the hole. Cover the pit by laying two sheets of metal crosswise over the top—one should completely cover the sloped opening, and the other sheet should cover the opposite end—then overlap the

third sheet in the middle. Weight the perimeter of the cover down with logs or cinder blocks, then leave the hole alone for 3 or 4 hours.

START THE FEEDER FIRE

About 1 hour before you're ready to load the hog, get your feeder fire going following the instructions in Feeder Fires for Pit Barbecue, page 32.

PREPARE AND LOAD THE HOG

About 20 hours before you want to serve, take the hog out of the cooler. As with pit barbecue, you'll want to split the length of the hog's spine to help it lie flat (see West Tennessee Whole Hog, pages 173–76). Season the belly side of the pork with kosher salt. I don't use dry rub on hogs cooked in the ground, as some of the sugars won't caramelize (remember, the hog is on its back for the entire cook) and you end up with uncooked dry rub in the finished product. If you want to add dry rub, go for it, but use a light hand. You don't need to season the skin side of the hog, as salt will only dry the skin too much.

Uncover the hole and take a look inside. The dirt walls should be bone dry and the pit should be warm, sauna temperature or less, but not hot.

Grab a buddy and carry the hog over to the hole, then lay it down on the bars, skin-side down, with the backside of the hog facing the sloped opening.

IN-GROUND PIT

FIRE
THE PIT

Load a shovelful of coals from the feeder fire and scatter it along one of the long sides of the hole. Repeat with a shovelful on the opposite side. Grab a third shovelful of coals and scatter half along each of the ends of the hole (backside and frontside). VERY IMPORTANT: Make sure you keep the coal bed close to the sides of the hole, and don't scatter any coals directly below the hog itself. If you mess this up during the first couple hours of the cook, it probably won't matter much, but it's good practice, and once that hog's fat has starting rendering, you want to make double sure you're not adding any coals below the hog, or you could end up with a fire.

Cover the hole, then wait 10 or 15 minutes. Lift the cover over the sloped side and peek at your thermometer; you want the temperature inside the hole between 200° and 210°F—this is your target temperature for the entire cook. If the hole isn't warm enough, scatter a half shovelful of coals—no more—around the edges of the hole.

Once your hole is at the right temperature, feel around the cover with your bare hand; this is what a 200°F hole feels like, and you can use the hand test as often as you want to monitor its temperature going forward.

THE REST OF THE COOK

For the first few hours of the cook, you'll need to fire the hole frequently, about once every 15 or 20 minutes, because you've got 150 pounds of cold meat inside.

After a few hours, that hog has warmed up to around 140° to 150°F, and you can start to hear the sound of slow, steady drips sizzling as fat and moisture hit the coals and vaporizes. In addition to feeling the cover with your hand, you can listen for this sound to gauge the temperature of your hole going forward. If you don't hear anything at all, you probably need to fire the hole; if you hear a more steady or violent sizzling, ride it out until it subsides.

There's not much else to do during the rest of the cook except monitor the temperature of the pit and fire it as needed—always using just a half shovelful of coals, probably every 30 to 45 minutes. The ground is an excellent insulator, so that small amount of coals will go a long way, but you might need to fire it more or less frequently based on the composition of your soil and the ambient temperature and humidity. If your soil is full of clay, like it is where I come from, for instance, the ground holds the heat for a very long time.

If your friends will take on some of the pit-firing duties, make sure they don't add more than a half shovelful of coals at a time. I've lost hogs to drunken idiots or know-it-alls who get sloppy and add too many coals, or who add them directly below the hog. If you're going to delegate, make sure you educate. If you ever find yourself with a pit that's running cool, don't try to catch up by adding extra coals. Just be patient and know that it'll warm up.

I'VE LOST HOGS TO DRUNKEN IDIOTS OR KNOW-IT-ALLS WHO GET SLOPPY AND ADD TOO MANY COALS, OR WHO ADD THEM DIRECTLY BELOW THE HOG. IF YOU'RE GOING TO DELEGATE, MAKE SURE YOU EDUCATE.

THE END

The hog will take about 18 hours to cook, give or take an hour or two. To check the doneness of the hog, follow the instructions in The End (page 184). About 1 hour before it's done, stop firing the pit and let it start cooling off.

When the hog is ready, remove the entire cover. Get down on your knees alongside the hog (or push some coals aside and stand in the hole). Put on your heatproof gloves and remove both shoulders, placing them in a baking pan or hotel pan. Remove the belly meat and hams, and marry those meats together in another pan or two, then pull the shoulder meat and place it in another pan (see pulling instructions for the Pit-Cooked Pork Shoulder, page 192). Cover and keep everything warm in a cooler until you're ready to serve.

HAM

*Makes about 15 pounds of meat
(about 50 servings)*

1 skin-on ham (23 to 25 pounds)

⅓ cup Diamond Crystal
kosher salt or Big Hoss Rub
(page 96)

Vegetable oil, for grates

Pit-smoked ham is a style of barbecue you find more in East Tennessee, but its fans have found their way across the state, and I often have customers requesting smoked ham for events. The process for smoking a ham is nearly identical to a shoulder. Hams are considerably leaner than shoulder, so the meat will be more dense, and better sliced and served for barbecue plates or ham sandwiches.

If possible, season the ham 1 to 2 days before you plan to cook it. Season it all over with a good, even coating of the salt. Transfer the ham to a wire rack set inside a sheet pan and refrigerate, uncovered, until ready to cook.

Build a pit, prepare a feeder fire, and fire the pit (pages 164–72). If you don't have a custom grate for your pit, lay a regular grill grate across 3 or 4 bars placed close together and let it heat up as well. Wipe the grate down with vegetable oil. Place the ham on the grate, skin-side up. Close the cover and fire the pit as needed to maintain a temperature of 250°F.

After 6 hours, open the pit to flip the ham. Using heatproof gloves, carefully loosen the skin or any stuck parts from the grate as needed. Flip the ham in one smooth motion.

Cover the pit and continue cooking the ham, maintaining a pit temperature of about 220°F (see Monitoring the Temperature, page 179). The ham should take 20 to 22 hours to cook (or about 1 hour per pound).

Your ham is finished cooking when you can push your thumb into the meat and it doesn't spring back. Texture is a better indicator of doneness than temperature, but you can insert a meat thermometer into the thickest part of the ham; the meat is ready when it's between 180° and 185°F—lower and it'll be tough, higher and it'll start to dry out.

Transfer the ham to a cutting board or clean work surface. Let it rest for 30 minutes to 1 hour before removing the skin and cutting against the grain into slices. If you did good and the ham is tender and delicious, slice it the width of a pencil to show it off. If it's a little tough or dry, you can slice it a little thinner to help it along.

As you work through the ham you'll hit the femur bone; either carve around the bone or pull it out. You can also separate the ham into its large muscles, then slice those individually (always against the grain).

PITS FOR SMALLER CUTS

While I cook a whole hog, I'll often use the pit to simultaneously cook some shoulders, ribs, chickens, and whatever else I want to serve at the pig pickin', depending on extra room. But if you're not doing a whole hog, it will depend on what you're cooking. For shoulders, hams, or bellies—any of the larger primal cuts—I'd still use a full-size hog pit, or one that's smaller but the same height (5 cinder blocks high). But for ribs, chickens, and other much smaller cuts, you can either build a smaller pit that's just large enough to hold whatever you want to cook, or cook them on an open pit (see Open-Pit Barbecue, page 85). The assembly for a smaller pit is similar to a full-size pit, though you'll make it about half to two-thirds as big, and only 4 cinder blocks high. Place the bars or cooking grate on top of the third row of blocks, and the fourth row is the final row. As with a full-size pit, leave an opening on the side for shoveling in coals, and use cardboard or metal as your cover.

RIBS

8 to 10 servings

½ cup Big Hoss Rub (page 96) or Diamond Crystal kosher salt

4 slabs untrimmed spareribs (4 to 5 pounds each), St. Louis-style ribs (2½ to 3 pounds each), or baby back ribs (2¾ to 3 pounds each)

Vegetable oil, for grates

2 quarts (2 recipes) Jack's Creek Sauce (page 95)

Sweet Dixie BBQ Sauce (optional; page 100)

I USE MY EYES AND HANDS TO KNOW WHEN THE RIBS ARE DONE. THE MEAT WILL JUST BEGIN TO PULL BACK FROM THE BONES, AND I CAN PUT ON A PAIR OF GLOVES, PICK THE RACK UP IN THE MIDDLE, MEMBRANE-SIDE DOWN, AND THE ENDS WILL BOW DOWN SO THE RIBS RESEMBLE A FROWN.

These ribs will look and taste a lot like Open-Pit Spareribs (page 91), but they might take on a smokier flavor and darker color, due to the closed environment. As with open-pit ribs, I'd rather you source your meat from a good butcher shop or high-end grocery store. If you go to a supermarket, you're most likely going to get packer meat, which is leaner and not that great.

If possible, season the ribs the night before you plan to cook them. Season them all over with a good, even coating of the dry rub. Transfer the ribs to a wire rack set inside a sheet pan and refrigerate, uncovered, until ready to cook.

Build a pit, prepare a feeder fire, and fire the pit (pages 164–72). If you don't have a custom grate for your pit, lay a regular grill grate across 3 or 4 bars placed close together and let it heat up as well. Wipe the grate down with vegetable oil.

Place the ribs on the grate, meaty-side down. Close the cover and fire the pit as needed to maintain a temperature of 200° to 225°F (see Monitoring the Temperature, page 179). Unlike firing the pit for a whole hog, shoulders, or hams, where you should not have any coals directly under the hog after the first 4 hours, in the case of ribs, it's fine to keep some coals directly below them—unless they start getting too dark. In that case, only add coals around the perimeter of the meat.

After 1 hour, mop the ribs with the Jack's Creek Sauce, then turn them over and mop the other side. Keep cooking, mopping and flipping every hour, until the ribs are rosy red and cooked to your desired doneness, 6 to 7 hours total for untrimmed spareribs, or 4 to 5 hours total for St. Louis-style or baby backs.

I use my eyes and hands to know when the ribs are done. The meat will just begin to pull back from the bones, and I can put on a pair of gloves, pick the rack up in the middle, membrane-side down, and the ends will bow down so the ribs resemble a frown. The rack should be flexible enough that I can break it into two pieces by giving it a hard wiggle. You can also test for doneness by pressing your finger between two ribs; if you can push your finger into the meat, it's done. If you don't trust your other senses and want to use an instant-read thermometer, insert it into the meat between two ribs; they're finished when the thermometer reads between 185° and 190°F.

When the ribs are finished, transfer them to a cutting board and let them rest for about 10 minutes. If cooking untrimmed ribs, cut the flaps of brisket meat away from the ribs. You can snack on this bonus meat yourself or use it to make a Rib Meat Sandwich (page 99). Cut the racks into individual ribs. If desired, serve with the BBQ sauce or sprinkle with more of the dry rub.

BARBECUE
CHICKEN

Barbecue chicken is an unsung hero but can be as flavorful and enjoyable as any smoked pork. You can halve or quarter the chicken and eat it by itself, drizzled with Jack's Creek Sauce, or pull it and use it to make Pulled Chicken Sandwiches (page 210).

Using kitchen shears, split the chicken down the middle of the breast, cutting close to the breastbone and through the wishbone, and open the chicken up so that it will lie flat (see photo on page 108). Place a wire rack inside a sheet pan and set the chicken on top. Season the chicken generously with kosher salt and refrigerate, uncovered, for about 12 hours.

Build a pit, prepare a feeder fire, and fire the pit (pages 164–72). If you don't have a custom grate for your pit, lay a regular grill grate across 3 or 4 bars placed close together and let it heat up as well. Wipe the grate down with vegetable oil.

Season the chicken with the dry rub.

Place the chicken on the grate, skin-side up. Close the cover and fire the pit as needed to maintain a temperature of 200° to 225°F (see Monitoring the Temperature, page 179). It's fine to add coals directly below the meat.

After 1 hour, mop the chicken with Jack's Creek Sauce, turn it over and mop the other side, and then put the mop away. Keep cooking, until an instant-read thermometer inserted into the thickest part of the leg meat registers 160°F. If you don't have a thermometer, give the leg a tug; it's done when it feels like you can rip it off with very little effort. The chicken should take 4 to 5 hours total to cook.

Remove the chicken to a cutting board and cut it into leg, thigh, and breast pieces, if you'd like, and serve with Jack's Creek Sauce on the side.

2 to 4 servings

1 whole chicken (about 3½ pounds)

Kosher salt

2 tablespoons Big Hoss Rub (page 96)

Vegetable oil, for the grate

Jack's Creek Sauce (page 95), as needed for mopping and serving

PULLED CHICKEN
SANDWICHES

Makes 4 sandwiches

4 smoked chicken legs (thighs and drumsticks) or 1 whole chicken (page 209)

4 potato rolls, toasted, or 8 slices Texas toast

1 cup Coleslaw (page 190)

¼ cup Pat's Alabama White Sauce (page 113), at room temperature

When I first opened Martin's, there weren't a lot of joints serving pulled chicken. I wanted to give people a non-red meat option, so I originally sauced the chicken with Jack's Creek Sauce and served it with slaw, just like my pork sandwiches. As my Alabama white sauce, inspired by Big Bob Gibson's in Decatur, Alabama, got more popular, folks started asking for that with their chicken, and we made the switch. I'm a dark meat fan (and you should be too), so I make my sandwiches with dark meat. But you can certainly use smoked chicken breasts here as well.

Remove the chicken meat from the bones and tear it into small pieces, including some of the skin.

Divide the meat among the rolls and top with the coleslaw. Drizzle with the Alabama white sauce, close the sandwiches, and serve.

PIT-COOKED
TURKEY BREASTS

Smoked turkey breasts don't get the love that pork and other poultry receives, but they deserve it. A few slices of juicy, lightly smoky turkey are incredibly good on their own, and make a mean sandwich as well.

If possible, buy heritage-breed turkey breasts, which will have a deeper flavor, though they benefit from a dry brine for juiciness. If you buy non-heritage breed turkey, check the package to see if it's been "plumped" (injected with brine; if it has, skip the presalting step.

With smoked turkey breasts (and hams), I aim for slices that are as thick as a pencil (about ¼ inch); I think that shows off the texture of the meat best. You can usually gauge the quality of a barbecue joint by how they slice their meat. If you go someplace and they sell you anything—brisket, ham, turkey, whatever—thinly shaved, that's a good sign that they've overcooked their meat. And if they've shaved it AND mixed sauce into it? Turn around and walk away. That's barbecue heresy.

Place a wire rack inside a sheet pan and set the turkey breasts on top. Season the turkey breasts generously with kosher salt and refrigerate, uncovered, for 12 to 24 hours.

Build a pit, prepare a feeder fire, and fire the pit (pages 164–72). If you don't have a custom grate for your pit, lay a regular grill grate across 3 or 4 bars placed close together and let it heat up as well. Wipe the grate down with vegetable oil.

Season the turkey with a light coating of rub. Place the turkey on the grate, skin-side up. Close the cover and fire the pit as needed to maintain a temperature of 200° to 225°F (see Monitoring the Temperature, page 179). It's fine to add coals directly below the meat.

After 1 hour, mop the turkey breasts with the Jack's Creek Sauce, then turn them over and mop the other side. Keep cooking, mopping and flipping the turkey every hour, until an instant-read thermometer inserted into the center registers 160°F. The turkey should take 4 to 5 hours total to cook.

Transfer the turkey to a cutting board and let rest for 10 to 15 minutes. Before serving (or adding to turkey sandwiches, page 214), cut crosswise into ¼-inch-thick slices.

Makes enough for 20 sandwiches or 10 to 14 plates

2 boneless, skin-on turkey breasts (5 pounds each)

Kosher salt

Vegetable oil, for the grate

2 tablespoons Big Hoss Rub (page 96)

2 cups Jack's Creek Sauce (page 95)

YOU CAN USUALLY GAUGE THE QUALITY OF A BARBECUE JOINT BY HOW THEY SLICE THEIR MEAT. IF YOU GO SOMEPLACE AND THEY SELL YOU ANYTHING—BRISKET, HAM, TURKEY, WHATEVER—THINLY SHAVED, THAT'S A GOOD SIGN THAT THEY'VE OVERCOOKED THEIR MEAT. AND IF THEY'VE SHAVED IT AND MIXED SAUCE INTO IT? TURN AROUND AND WALK AWAY.

SMOKED
TURKEY SANDWICHES

Makes 4 sandwiches

1 pound Pit-Cooked Turkey
  Breast (page 213)

4 potato rolls, split and toasted

¼ cup Pat's Alabama White
  Sauce (page 113), at room
  temperature

This is a simple sandwich, but it's delicious without any extra adornment—not even slaw. I think the tart, mayo-based white sauce lends itself to turkey even better than chicken. They really are meant for each other.

Slice the turkey crosswise into ¼-inch-thick slices. Divide the slices among the rolls and top with the sauce. Close the sandwiches and serve.

PIT-COOKED
PORK BELLY

S moking a pork belly gives you super-tender, fatty meat that can be used in so many ways. Cuts of it are amazing for sandwiches. Sometimes I'll chill the portions, then heat them up in the deep fryer and make a sandwich out of that (if you go to the trouble, you won't regret it). Or I'll cut the belly into slices or smaller squares and use them as a succulent base for any number of porky dishes—they're incredible on top of a bowl of grits, for instance. (Just hold back on the butter, as the pork will add plenty of fat.)

Makes enough for 20 sandwiches

Vegetable oil, for the grate

1 pork belly (12 to 15 pounds), preferably with skin

2 tablespoons Big Hoss Rub (page 96)

2 cups Jack's Creek Sauce (page 95)

Build a pit, prepare a feeder fire, and fire the pit (pages 164–72). If you don't have a custom grate for your pit, lay a regular grill grate across 3 or 4 bars placed close together and let it heat up as well. Wipe the grate down with vegetable oil.

Season the pork belly with a light coating of the rub. Use a knife to score the meaty side, about ¼ inch deep in a crosshatch pattern, making the cuts either 2 inches apart (if you plan on serving the belly in squares or slices) or 4 inches apart (if you plan on making sandwiches). (See following page.) When you're finished, the top of the meat should look like a checkerboard. Important: Make sure you add the rub first, then score the meat; otherwise you'll end up with uncooked rub in the crevices.

Place the pork belly on the grate, skin-side down. Close the cover and fire the pit as needed to maintain a temperature of 200° to 225°F (see Monitoring the Temperature, page 179). As you fire the pit, spread the coals only around the perimeter of the grate, not directly under the meat, as with all that rendering fat it could possibly ignite, like with a whole hog. Cook, mopping the belly every hour or so with the Jack's Creek Sauce.

The belly should take about 8 hours to cook. You'll know it's ready when the meat is very tender, almost falling apart, and an instant-read thermometer inserted into the center registers 190°F.

If you're serving Pork Belly Sandwiches (page 218), cut the belly down to the skin, following the scores (like you're slicing a cake). Use a spatula to transfer individual servings to the buns. When all of the meat has been removed from the skin, you can discard the skin or use it to make cracklin's (see page 218).

If you're serving the pork on its own, simply slide the belly meat onto a cutting board, leaving the skin behind. (Yes, it should be that tender.) Slice the meat into 2- or 4-inch pieces and serve.

PORK BELLY
SANDWICHES

Makes 4 sandwiches

1 pound Pit-Cooked Pork Belly
(page 215), cut into 4 squares

8 slices Texas toast or 4 potato
rolls, split and toasted

½ cup Jack's Creek Sauce
(page 95)

Sliced pickles

Cracklin's (optional; see below)

This is like a pulled-pork sandwich, only twice as fatty and juicy. I'm begging you not to use a thick, tomato-based sauce on this sandwich. The thing that makes it so good is the soft belly fat, and you need a good amount of acidity to balance it out.

If you want to take this sandwich to the next level, use the leftover skin from your Pit-Cooked Pork Belly to make cracklin's and add some to the sandwich.

Divide the pork belly among the toast. Drizzle each piece of pork with the sauce (about 2 tablespoons per sandwich) and top with a few sliced pickles (be a little heavy-handed; you need some acid to cut through the fatty belly). Top with some cracklin's, if you want. Close the sandwiches and serve.

CRACKLIN'S

There's nothing like the crunch of smoked belly cracklin's. Unlike a roast pig, pit barbecue doesn't usually result in skin that's easy to eat. But drop it in a fryer and you'll be amazed at its crunch, and how it gleams like glass.

Scrape all of the excess fat away from the skin, then cut the skin into 4-inch squares. Refrigerate until cold.

Set up a big pot with a few inches of oil and at least a few inches of clearance to the top. Heat the oil over medium-high heat until it reaches 375°F. Add the skin, a piece or two at a time, and fry until the skin floats to the surface. Drain on paper towels. Serve the cracklin's in big pieces or chop them up and add them to the top of the sauced belly meat. Divine.

PIT-COOKED
BOLOGNA

There are bologna sandwiches all over the South. It's a cultish thing, and everyone knows which gas stations serve the best bologna. Barbecue bologna is a classic Memphis barbecue item, where it's usually topped with a spicy sauce.

When we first opened Martin's, I wanted to offer an off-menu item. If you're going to have a secret item, it better be frickin' impressive. Almost everyone serving bologna sandwiches cuts the meat into skinny slices, which cup up in the middle when you cook them on the griddle. So I figured I'd first smoke my bologna for added flavor, then slice it into obnoxiously thick pucks and deep-fry them. We serve them on a potato roll with yellow mustard, raw white onion slices, and sliced pickles. We gave these behemoths to regulars and anyone else who'd asked, and word quickly got around. Once we moved into our second location, the bologna sandwich became an official menu item, and has only grown in popularity since.

If you can't find a 10-pound roll of bologna at the grocery store, just ask: They almost always have them on hand at the deli counter.

20 servings

One 10-pound bologna
2 tablespoons Big Hoss Rub (page 96)

Build a pit, prepare a feeder fire, and fire the pit (pages 164–72). If you don't have a grate for your pit, lay a grill grate across two bars.

Lightly massage the rub all over the surface of the bologna.

Place the bologna on the grate. Close the cover and fire the pit as needed to maintain a temperature of 200° to 225°F (see Monitoring the Temperature, page 179). Never fire the pit directly below the bologna. Rotate the bologna a quarter turn every 2 hours; the bologna will take 8 hours total to cook.

To serve, slice the bologna crosswise into 1¼-inch-thick pieces, then transfer to wire rack set inside a sheet pan. Refrigerate until cold, about 2 hours. Set up a pot with at least 4 inches of oil and a few inches of clearance to the top. Heat over medium high heat until a thermometer reads 375°F, then fry a couple slices at a time for 3 minutes, until hot and nicely browned all over.

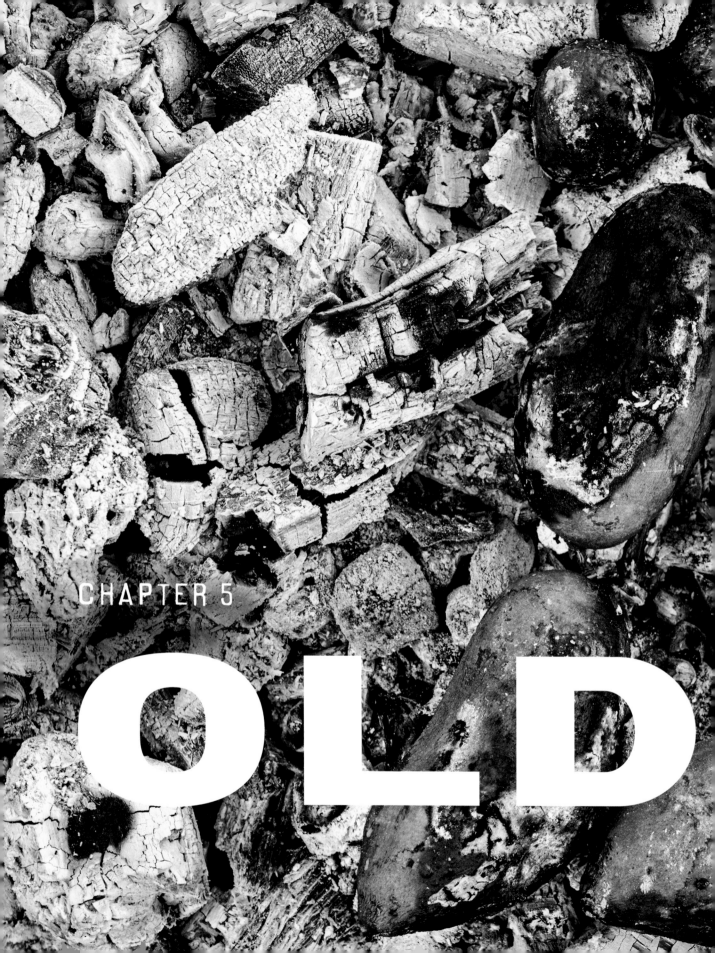

CHAPTER 5

OLD

AGE

COOKING IN ASHES AND EMBERS

ONCE YOUR FIRE HAS PRODUCED A HEAP OF SMOLDERING ASHES AND EMBERS, you have the opportunity to slowly cook a variety of vegetables directly in the gentle heat of the ashes. I love this technique not only because it imparts some smoke into the vegetables, but it also intensifies their flavors—giving you the combined results of both slow roasting and smoking. This is a great way to use the "shank" of a fire to prepare a side dish or two while you finish your meat.

Any dense vegetable with a good amount of internal moisture will work. When I'm cooking up a large meal over a live fire, I usually throw something in the ashes about an hour before I think the meat will be done. I typically use potatoes, sweet potatoes, or beets, but small winter squash and root vegetables like carrots, parsnips, turnips, and celery root work as well, and an ash-roasted onion is a thing to behold: Its insides will turn into a soft, sweet, custardy mess you can scoop out and add to sauces, soups, or mashed potatoes, or just eat by itself.

TECHNIQUE

There's not much to cooking in ashes and embers, but you want to find the right spot in your ashes to do it. Look for hot ashes that are still smoking but free of any coals that are still glowing red. You can usually find this near the perimeter of a coal bed, but not right at the edge. Tuck the vegetables into the ash and use a shovel to scoop just enough ash on top so you no longer see the vegetables—you don't want to bury them too deep or they'll burn; as long they're buried with about an inch of ash on top, you're good.

Check the ash pile occasionally, as you'll want to make sure that your heat doesn't completely die out. Add more hot ashes as needed to maintain the cooking process. You'll generally know when to do this by holding the back of your hand a couple inches away from where you have them buried. If you can withstand more than 5 or 6 seconds of heat, add a little more hot ash. Then all you have to do is wait.

Most vegetables will require about an hour, give or take, to cook through. Test them for doneness by sticking a knife or skewer into the center; you shouldn't feel any resistance. When they're finished, use tongs, a shovel, or barbecue gloves to remove the vegetables. No matter what you're cooking, this technique will create an encasement of hard, carbonized soot around the vegetable. Don't freak out about this shell; you're not going to eat this sacrificial layer, and it'll keep everything inside gloriously warm, moist, and flavorful.

When you're ready to serve, use a towel or spoon to scrape off most of the charred shell. Don't worry if you leave a little char behind; I like to leave a bit on to add flavor, especially when I'm making Ash-Roasted Mashed Potatoes (page 231).

TIMING

You'll need to think ahead a little bit: If you wait until your meat is finished cooking before burying your vegetables in the dying fire, your meat may end up cold by the time your ash-roasted food is ready. However, this timing challenge is easy to beat, and there are a couple of ways to make sure everything is ready at the same time. First, you can keep most barbecue warm for a couple of hours after it comes off the pit (see Holding Meat Warm, page 187). Better yet, you can simply start the ash-roasting process well before your meat is done—at least 1 hour, and up to 2 or 3. Unless you're doing some very quick grilling, your feeder fire will produce enough ashes and embers to cook in after about an hour after you light it. I like to create a roasting spot near my feeder fire that I can replenish as needed with ashes and embers (don't worry; your fire will produce plenty).

NO MATTER WHAT YOU'RE COOKING, THIS TECHNIQUE WILL CREATE AN ENCASEMENT OF HARD, CARBONIZED SOOT AROUND THE VEGETABLE. DON'T FREAK OUT ABOUT THIS SHELL; YOU'RE NOT GOING TO EAT THIS SACRIFICIAL LAYER, AND IT'LL KEEP EVERYTHING INSIDE GLORIOUSLY WARM, MOIST, AND FLAVORFUL.

"ARSH" POTATOES

My grandmother Nonie, who we called Maw-Maw, always called red potatoes "arsh potatoes." It wasn't until I was twenty that I realized that "arsh" potatoes weren't some specific variety, nor was she referring to cooking them in ashes—she was simply trying to say "Irish" potatoes. Anyway, potatoes are my favorite vegetable to cook in ashes because they can take an absolute beating. I prefer the creamy texture of red potatoes for this method; some potato varieties can come out chalky tasting when cooked in a dry environment. I usually use potatoes about the size of a lemon, as anything larger will take too long to cook. After they come off the fire, you'll break open the hard, charred shell to find a fluffy, creamy, slightly smoky, and extra potato-y treasure inside, like those bubblegum balls that had Nerds inside of them (I used to love those things as a kid). You can simply eat the potatoes by themselves with some butter and salt, use them to make mashed potatoes (see recipe, page 231), or smash and fry them in a well-oiled cast-iron skillet. I also like to cover smashed potatoes in cheddar cheese and let it melt and caramelize around the edges (see recipe, page 228), which is so dadgum good.

8 to 10 servings

10 to 12 medium red potatoes (about 4 ounces each), scrubbed

Vegetable oil

Kosher salt

Softened butter, for serving

Fleur de sel or other flaky salt, for serving

Build a fire and allow it to burn until it produces a bed of smoldering ashes and embers.

Lightly brush the potatoes with oil and season generously with kosher salt. Poke each potato a few times with a fork.

Using a shovel or long metal tongs, spread the ashes and coals to create a shallow well, making sure the ashes are smoking-hot, but without any burning red coals. Place the potatoes directly on the ashes in the well, bury in about 1 inch of ash, and cook. Check occasionally to see if the ashes are cooling down. (You will know they are if you can hold the back of your hand a few inches above the ash pile for more than 5 or 6 seconds.) Add more hot ashes as needed, and continue to cook until the potatoes are charred all over and tender when poked with a fork, 25 to 35 minutes. (Time will vary depending on the heat of the ashes and the size of the potatoes.)

Remove the potatoes from the coals with your tongs or shovel and let them cool slightly.

Put on heatproof barbecue gloves. Scrape and brush as much of the ash and char as possible from the skins of the potatoes. Let them cool slightly, then serve with softened butter and fleur de sel.

SMASHED POTATOES
WITH CRISPED CHEDDAR

6 servings

6 "Arsh" Potatoes (page 227)
2 cups grated cheddar cheese
1 tablespoon all-purpose flour
Vegetable oil
Kosher salt

At his Italian-influenced restaurant, City House, my friend Tandy Wilson likes to pair vegetables and potatoes with shards of frico, or skillet-fried cheese. When we grill around the pool at my house, I always make this dish for the kids. Crispy browned potatoes topped with crispy browned cheese . . . what kid's not gonna like that?

This recipe is a great way to use up leftover "Arsh" Potatoes and an excuse to build up the habit of throwing a few potatoes into your ashes after every grilling session, rather than walking away and leaving your fire to die a lonely death.

Refrigerate the potatoes until completely cold, about 2 hours. When ready to prepare, remove the potatoes from the refrigerator and set aside.

In a medium bowl, toss the cheddar and flour together. Set aside.

If cooking outdoors, prepare a hot fire and let it burn down to hot coals. Place a large cast-iron skillet directly on top of the coals. If cooking indoors, heat a cast-iron skillet over medium-high heat.

Add just enough oil to barely coat the bottom of the skillet. When the oil shimmers, place 2 potatoes in the skillet and gently mash with a spatula or the heel of your hand until it's flattened to about ½ inch or so. Season with salt and cook until golden brown on one side, 3 to 4 minutes.

Flip the potatoes, season with salt, and add two ⅓-cup portions of cheddar to the pan next to the potatoes, spreading the cheese to create an area about the same size as the flattened potato. Cook until the cheese has melted and is beginning to brown and crisp around the edges, 2 to 3 minutes. Flip the cheese onto the potatoes and continue to cook until the potatoes are browned on the bottom, 1 to 2 minutes longer. Transfer the potatoes to a platter, wipe the skillet clean, and repeat with the remaining potatoes and cheese. Serve.

ASH-ROASTED
MASHED POTATOES

The cooking procedure here is the same as for "Arsh" Potatoes (page 227), and you just smash the potatoes with butter and milk into a rich, smoky smash after removing the charred peel. How much peel you leave on is up to you: The more skin you leave on the potatoes, the less desirable the color will be. But if you don't care what your mash looks like, the charred skin is delicious. I leave enough on to have the little black specks throughout the mash.

6 servings

6 medium russet potatoes
(about 6 ounces each)

Vegetable oil

Kosher salt

1 stick (4 ounces) unsalted
butter, at room temperature

2 tablespoons whole milk, at
room temperature, plus more
as needed

Freshly ground black pepper

Build a fire and allow it to burn until it produces a bed of smoldering ashes and embers.

Lightly brush the potatoes with oil and season generously with kosher salt. Poke each potato a few times with a fork.

Using a shovel or long metal tongs, spread the ashes and coals to create a shallow well, making sure the ashes are smoking-hot, but without any burning red coals. Place the potatoes directly on the ashes in the well, cover with 1 inch of ashes, and cook. Check occasionally to see if the ashes are cooling down. (You will know they are if you can hold the back of your hand a few inches above the ash pile for more than 5 or 6 seconds.) Add more hot ashes as needed, and cook until the potatoes are charred all over and tender when poked with a fork, 1 hour 15 minutes to 1 hour 30 minutes. (Time will vary depending on the heat of the ashes and the size of the potatoes.)

Using your tongs or shovel, remove the potatoes from the coals and let them cool slightly.

Put on heatproof barbecue gloves. Brush as much of the ash as possible from the skins of the potatoes. Peel and discard about half of the potato skins, or more if desired.

Place the potatoes in a large bowl and mash with a potato masher until almost smooth. Add the butter and milk, season with kosher salt and pepper to taste, and mash to combine. If the potatoes are still too thick and pasty, add more milk, 1 tablespoon at a time, until they reach a light, whipped consistency. You are generally trying to avoid the texture of Play-Doh, if you know what I mean. Taste and adjust seasoning as needed. Serve.

ASH-ROASTED
SWEET POTATOES

6 to 8 servings

6 to 8 medium sweet potatoes
   (6 to 8 ounces each), scrubbed

Vegetable oil

Kosher salt

Softened butter, for serving

Fleur de sel or other flaky salt,
   for serving

Sorghum molasses, maple
   syrup, or dark honey, for
   serving

As a kid I loved loading up sweet potatoes with butter, brown sugar, and cinnamon—it was like I was sneaking in dessert during supper. Like ash-roasted white potatoes, sweet potatoes will intensify in flavor and absorb just the right amount of smokiness when roasted in ashes. The skin is thicker on sweet potatoes, so they're easier to peel after they roast, kind of like peeling a boiled egg. You can certainly eat these with little adornment, but I like to cut the cooked potatoes into large chunks, then gently smash them to create lots of nooks and crannies for soaking up melted butter and whatever sweetener I drizzle on top. For me, that's usually sorghum molasses or light brown sugar, but a dark maple syrup or honey is just as delicious.

Build a fire and allow it to burn until it produces a bed of smoldering ashes and embers.

Lightly brush the potatoes with oil and season generously with kosher salt. Poke each potato a few times with a fork.

Using a shovel or long metal tongs, spread the ashes and coals to create a shallow well, making sure the ashes are smoking-hot, but without any burning red coals. Place the potatoes directly on the ashes in the well, cover with about 1 inch of ash, and cook. Check occasionally to see if the ashes are cooling down. (You will know they are if you can hold the back of your hand a few inches above the ash pile for more than 5 or 6 seconds.) Add more hot ashes as needed, until the potatoes are charred all over and tender when poked with a fork, 1 hour 15 minutes to 1 hour 30 minutes. (Time will vary depending on the heat of the ashes and the size of the potatoes.)

Using your tongs or shovel, remove the potatoes from the coals and let them cool slightly.

Put on heatproof barbecue gloves. Scrape and brush as much of the ashy char as possible from the skins of the potatoes. Transfer the potatoes to a cutting board and let them cool slightly, then cut the potatoes into large chunks and gently smash them. Serve with softened butter and flaky salt, and drizzle with the sweetener of your choice.

If you've been reading along, you probably noticed that the method for ash-roasting vegetables has been pretty much been the same whether it's potatoes, sweet potatoes, or beets. Well, you don't have to stop there. Turnips, large carrots, and pretty much any root vegetable will be great cooked this way. Onions get transformed into a sweet custard. You can even try firmer, denser nonroot vegetables, like fennel, or certain fruits, like pineapple and watermelon. The only real rule is to make sure it's something that has a kind of round shape that you can easily peel after cooking. Ash-roasted broccoli florets? Maybe not. (But you could try the stems . . .)

ASH-ROASTED
BEETS

6 to 8 servings

10 to 12 medium beets, scrubbed
clean

Vegetable oil

Kosher salt

Fleur de sel or other flaky salt,
for serving

There's something about the earthy-sweet flavor of ash-roasted beets that makes them a great side for meat cooked over a fire. My wife loves beets, so she's always pumped when I cook them at home, as are my children: These beets are sweet enough that they make a great gateway vegetable for what I call "burger and chicken finger" kids. They're also savory enough to become the centerpiece of a meat-free main course: You can pair them with arugula or chicories in a salad, mix them into a grain bowl (I especially love barley with them), or dice them up and make some beet tacos.

Build a fire and allow it to burn until it produces a bed of smoldering ashes and embers.

Lightly brush the beets with oil and season generously with kosher salt. Poke each beet a few times with a fork.

Using a shovel or long metal tongs, spread the ashes and coals to create a shallow well, making sure the ashes are smoking-hot, but without any burning red coals. Place the beets directly on the ashes in the well and cover with 1 inch of ashes. Check occasionally to see if the ashes are cooling down. (You will know they are if you can hold the back of your hand a few inches above the ash pile for more than 5 or 6 seconds.) Add more hot ashes as needed, until the beets are charred all over and tender when poked with a fork, 45 minutes to 1 hour. (Time will vary depending on the heat of the ashes and the size of the beets.)

Using your tongs or shovel, remove the beets from the coals and let them cool slightly.

Put on heatproof barbecue gloves. Brush off as much ash as possible from the beets and peel.

Cut the beets into bite-size wedges, sprinkle with fleur de sel, and serve.

FOIL PACKS

An easy (and almost foolproof way) to cook a whole meal in ashes and embers is the classic Boy Scout-style foil pack, aka "hobo pack." You probably haven't made these since your youth, but they are so dadgum easy to assemble and you can put together endless combinations of ingredients. The foil keeps moisture inside, which helps reduce the chances of scorching and burning the food.

I was never a Boy Scout, but I started making these as a teenager when me and my buddies would camp out. Then, when my son Wyatt entered the Cub Scouts, it was like I was reintroduced to an old friend. Kids especially love foil packs because they can get involved in the process—choosing ingredients and assembling and folding them up—and they almost always eat the results.

You can cook pretty much anything in a foil pack that you'd bake in an oven, from fish and chicken to dense fruits to most vegetables. Because you can't do much to the food as it roasts and steams inside the foil, make sure you cut the ingredients to a size where they'll all be cooked in the same amount of time. I cut most ingredients into 1- to 1½-inch pieces, which usually means a cooking time of around 45 minutes in the ashes. To keep that cooking time consistent, I recommend making the recipes that follow as directed; if you want to scale up the portions, just make more packs of the same size, rather than making bigger packs.

Many foil pack recipes call for adding ingredients to a square of aluminum foil, then placing another sheet on top and folding up the edges to make a tight packet. This works fine, but I prefer to use a longer sheet of heavy-duty foil, placing the ingredients in the center and pulling the four corners up to meet in the center over the top of the food, creating a tent-like structure that resembles a wrapped Hershey's Kiss. This makes the packs easier to open for checking on doneness or adding additional ingredients during the cooking process.

As with roasting directly in ashes and embers, I usually use foil packs to cook my sides, or a snack, or a full-on meal while I'm grilling or smoking meat nearby. Likewise, you should plan ahead to make sure everything is ready to eat around the same time: Throw them on the ashes about an hour before you're ready to eat. If your hobo packs are done early, you can leave the packs closed and rewarm them on the ashes for a few minutes before serving.

You can also add foil packs to your charcoal grill once the coals have finished their main tasks. You don't even have to be outside to make them: During colder months, throw some into the fireplace off to the side of the logs; you'll need to rotate the packs a few times, but it's so easy.

YOU CAN COOK PRETTY MUCH ANYTHING IN A FOIL PACK THAT YOU'D BAKE IN AN OVEN, FROM FISH AND CHICKEN TO DENSE FRUITS TO MOST VEGETABLES.

SUGAR SNAP,
POTATO, AND BACON
FOIL PACK

2 servings

1 cup sugar snap peas, strings
    removed

2 medium red potatoes,
    scrubbed and cut into 1-inch
    chunks

1 medium white onion, cut into
    1-inch wedges

4 ounces bacon (preferably
    thick-cut), cut into 1-inch
    pieces

3 garlic cloves, smashed

2 lemon wedges

1 teaspoon vegetable oil

1 teaspoon red pepper flakes

Kosher salt

Jack's Creek Sauce (page 95) or
    sherry vinegar, for serving

I can eat snap peas by the bushel. Their sweet, green flavor goes great with potatoes and savory bacon; a splash of Jack's Creek Sauce or vinegar balances it out and keeps it light and savory.

Build a fire and allow it to burn until it produces a bed of smoldering ashes and embers.

In a large bowl, combine the snap peas, potatoes, onion, bacon, garlic, lemon wedges, and oil and toss until coated. Add the pepper flakes, season with kosher salt, and toss again.

Tear off one 18 × 18-inch piece of heavy-duty aluminum foil (if using regular foil, tear off 2 sheets 18 inches long and stack them to make a double-layered sheet).

Add the vegetable mixture to the foil, arranging it in a single layer in the center. Bring the four corners of the foil together to meet over the center of the pack, then twist the ends together to seal the pack; it should resemble a teepee.

Using a shovel, pull an area of coals back to expose the ground. Place the foil pack directly on the earth and cover completely with dying coals and ash, making sure to avoid any still-burning hot coals. Cook for about 45 minutes or until the potatoes are tender. Rotate the pack occasionally, and re-cover it with more hot ash whenever it gets cool enough to hold your hand a few inches away for more than 5 seconds.

Using tongs or heatproof gloves, remove the pack from the fire. Let it rest about 15 minutes, then carefully open the pack and drizzle with Jack's Creek Sauce. Serve.

OKRA, TOMATO, AND BROCCOLI
FOIL PACK

2 servings

8 okra pods, halved lengthwise

1 medium or 2 small heirloom tomatoes (I like Cherokee Purple), cut into 2-inch chunks

1 cup broccoli florets (1-inch pieces)

3 garlic cloves, smashed

1 tablespoon vegetable oil or peanut oil

Kosher salt

Jack's Creek Sauce (page 95), for serving

This is a dish I frequently cook in my Weber grill on weekday nights, when we want to eat outside but don't want to put on a big production. Okra and broccoli are two vegetables that I hated as a kid but now love as an adult. Okra can never go wrong when served with tomatoes in the summer (they sure don't like growing next to each other, though), and while broccoli isn't a common pairing for either ingredient, it gives the dish some texture and backbone. To keep things from getting too mushy, choose a tomato that's dense, meaty, and sweet.

Build a fire and allow it to burn until it produces a bed of smoldering ashes and embers.

In a large bowl, combine the okra, tomatoes, broccoli, garlic, and oil and toss until coated. Season with kosher salt to taste and toss again.

Tear off one 18 × 18-inch piece of heavy-duty aluminum foil (if using regular foil, tear off 2 sheets 18 inches long and stack them to make a double-layered sheet).

Add the okra mixture to the foil, arranging it in a single layer in the center. Bring the four corners of the foil together to meet over the center of the pack, then twist the ends together to seal the pack; it should resemble a teepee.

Using a shovel, pull an area of coals back to expose the ground. Place the foil pack directly on the earth and cover completely with dying coals and ash, making sure to avoid any still-burning hot coals. Cook for about 45 minutes or until the vegetables are tender. Rotate the pack occasionally, and re-cover it with more hot ash whenever it gets cool enough to hold your hand a few inches away for more than 5 seconds.

Using tongs or heatproof gloves, remove the pack from the fire. Let it rest about 15 minutes, then carefully open the pack, drizzle with Jack's Creek Sauce, and serve.

SUMMER SQUASH

FOIL PACK

At the beginning of every April, we begin planting our garden and raised beds. We always plant four or five rows of summer squash and zucchini, forgetting that we promised ourselves to only plant one or two, because squash put out like rabbits! They are one of the first vegetables to emerge from the garden, and after a couple weeks of harvesting squash, honestly, I get tired with dealing with so many of them. So we'll grill some (see Grilled Summer Squash, page 49), pickle some, or make Nonie Sue's Scrub (page 77). This foil pack is one more way I use up our squash bounty; the flavor of rosemary infuses the squash and the onion gets nice and sweet, creating a side dish you can assemble in a couple of minutes, or add to a bowl of cold noodles to make a quick pasta salad. Making this is a little bit of an act of desperation around here, but as long as you don't overplant your squash garden, you can just enjoy these packs as a delicious side dish.

2 servings

1 medium yellow summer squash, cut into 1½-inch chunks

1 medium zucchini, cut into 1½-inch chunks

1 medium Vidalia onion, cut into 1-inch wedges

2 lemon wedges

2 rosemary sprigs

1 tablespoon vegetable or peanut oil

¼ teaspoon dried marjoram

Kosher salt

Build a fire and allow it to burn until it produces a bed of smoldering ashes and embers.

In a large bowl, combine the yellow squash, zucchini, onion, lemon wedges, rosemary, and oil and toss until coated. Add the marjoram, season with kosher salt to taste, and toss again.

Tear off one 18 × 18-inch piece of heavy-duty aluminum foil (if using regular foil, tear off 2 sheets 18 inches long and stack them to make a double-layered sheet).

Add the vegetable mixture to the foil, arranging it in a single layer in the center. Bring the four corners of the foil together to meet over the center of the pack, then twist the ends together to seal the pack; it should resemble a teepee.

Using a shovel, pull an area of coals back to expose the ground. Place the foil pack directly on the earth and cover completely with dying coals and ash, making sure to avoid any still-burning hot coals. Cook for about 45 minutes or until the vegetables are tender. Rotate the pack occasionally, and re-cover it with more hot ash whenever it gets cool enough to hold your hand a few inches away for more than 5 seconds.

Using tongs or heatproof gloves, remove the pack from the fire. Let it rest about 15 minutes, then carefully open the pack and squeeze the lemon wedges over. Serve.

PEAR AND CHEESE
FOIL PACK

2 servings

2 firm-crisp pears, such as Bosc or Anjou

1 lemon, cut into 4 wedges

1 tablespoon vegetable oil or peanut oil

Kosher salt

2 ounces Manchego or similar semi-firm cheese, cut into ½-inch cubes

2 tablespoons sorghum molasses, pure cane syrup, or maple syrup

Fleur de sel or other flaky salt

This recipe always reminds me of late September, when the days are still warm, but the nights start to get really cool. Pears have always been one of those fruits that I could eat endlessly, and this combination of pears, chunks of melty cheese, and a drizzle of sweet syrup makes them a great way to finish a meal, hopefully with a really nice glass of Champagne or other dry sparkling wine.

Build a fire and allow it to burn until it produces a bed of smoldering ashes and embers.

Cut the pears in half lengthwise and scoop out the cores with a spoon or melon baller. In a bowl, toss the pears and lemon wedges with the vegetable oil and season with kosher salt.

Tear off one 18 × 18-inch piece of heavy-duty aluminum foil (if using regular foil, tear off 2 sheets 18 inches long and stack them to make a double-layered sheet). Arrange the pears, cut-side up, and lemons in a single layer in the center. Bring the four corners of the foil together to meet over the center of the pack, then twist the ends together to seal the pack; it should resemble a teepee.

Using a shovel, pull an area of coals back to expose the ground. Place the foil pack directly on the earth and cover completely with dying coals and ash, making sure to avoid any still-burning hot coals. Cook for 30 minutes, rotating the pack a few times and recovering the pack with more hot ash whenever it gets cool enough to hold your hand a few inches away for more than 5 seconds.

Using tongs or heatproof gloves, remove the pack from the fire and carefully open. Add the cheese (placing the cubes on top of the pears) and drizzle with the sorghum syrup. Reseal the packet and place on the ashes. Cook for 15 minutes, or until the cheese has melted. Carefully open the pack, squeeze the lemon over the pears, sprinkle on some flaky salt, and serve.

APPLE AND SQUASH
FOIL PACK

Apples and squash are one of my favorite flavor pairings. Almost any kind of squash will work here, from juicy summer squash to dense, sweet winter varieties. A splash of Jack's Creek Sauce adds some nice acidity and savory complexity. This pack makes a versatile side dish for barbecue; sometimes I add a splash of hot sauce, depending on my mood.

Build a fire and allow it to burn until it produces a bed of smoldering ashes and embers.

In a large bowl, combine the apples, squash, onion, pecans, oil, and Jack's Creek Sauce and toss until coated. Season with kosher salt to taste (and hot sauce if desired) and toss again.

Tear off one 18 × 18-inch piece of heavy-duty aluminum foil (if using regular foil, tear off 2 sheets 18 inches long and stack them to make a double-layered sheet).

Place the vegetable mixture in a single layer in the center of the foil. Bring the four corners of the foil together to meet over the center of the pack, then twist the ends together to seal the pack; it should resemble a teepee.

Using a shovel, pull an area of coals back to expose the ground. Place the foil pack directly on the earth and cover completely with dying coals and ash, making sure to avoid any still-burning hot coals. Cook for about 45 minutes or until the squash is tender. Rotate the pack occasionally, and re-cover with more hot ash whenever it gets cool enough to hold your hand a few inches away for more than 5 seconds.

Using tongs or heatproof gloves, remove the pack from the fire. Let it rest about 15 minutes, then carefully open the pack and serve.

2 servings

2 Granny Smith apples, cut into 1½-inch chunks

1 large or 2 medium winter squash, peeled and cut into 1½-inch chunks

1 small red onion, cut into 1-inch wedges

2 tablespoons roughly chopped pecans

1 tablespoon vegetable or peanut oil

1 tablespoon Jack's Creek Sauce (page 95)

Kosher salt

Hot sauce (optional)

CORN, POTATO, AND TOMATO
FOIL PACK

2 servings

2 ears sweet corn, shucked and cut crosswise into 2-inch pieces

10 Sun Gold or similar sweet cherry tomatoes, halved

2 medium red potatoes, cut into 1½-inch chunks

1 garlic clove, smashed

1 jalapeño pepper, halved lengthwise (remove the seeds if you want less heat)

2 lemon wedges

1 tablespoon vegetable oil or peanut oil

Kosher salt

I like to make this pack on the fringes of fresh tomato season, either late in the spring and in the earliest days of fall. Tomatoes are too dang good in the peak of summer to fuss with much, and tomatoes out of season just suck (there should be a law against serving fresh tomatoes out of season). So I'll make this dish when tomatoes are not quite at their best; roasting them brings out more flavor, which almost feels like cheating. The corn and jalapeño are a perfect pairing with tomatoes.

Build a fire and allow it to burn until it produces a bed of smoldering ashes and embers.

In a large bowl, combine the corn, tomatoes, potatoes, garlic, jalapeño, lemon wedges, and oil and toss until coated. Season with kosher salt to taste and toss again.

Tear off one 18 × 18-inch piece of heavy-duty aluminum foil (if using regular foil, tear off 2 sheets 18 inches long and stack them to make a double-layered sheet).

Add the corn mixture to the foil, arranging it in a single layer in the center. Bring the four corners of the foil together to meet over the center of each packet, then twist the ends together to seal the pack; it should resemble a teepee.

Using a shovel, pull an area of coals back to expose the ground. Place the foil pack directly on the earth and cover completely with dying coals and ash, making sure to avoid any still-burning hot coals. Cook for about 45 minutes or until the vegetables are tender. Rotate the pack occasionally, and re-cover it with more hot ash whenever it gets cool enough to hold your hand a few inches away for more than 5 seconds.

Using tongs or heatproof gloves, remove the pack from the fire. Let it rest about 15 minutes, then carefully open the pack and squeeze the lemon wedges over. Serve.

CHAPTER 6

COLD S

SMOKE

AND THE

WINTER FIRE

THE FIRE DIES AFTER THE LAST EMBERS TURN TO ASHES, but people have harnessed the powers of cold smoke for a long, long time.

The fall's first cold snap marks the unofficial end of outdoor barbecue season, and by the time Thanksgiving comes around, I've shifted my attention to using cold smoke to put up various cuts of pork—bacon, jowls, loins, sausages, and the almighty country hams—over the course of West Tennessee's (increasingly mild) winters. I do all my curing and smoking in a little shack in my backyard, which becomes a cold-weather clubhouse where me and my buddies sit and drink bourbon while a cloud of smoke hovers just above our heads, slowly flavoring the meat hanging in the rafters.

Cold-smoking meat isn't barbecue, of course, but the two practices share much in common, so those of us who love whole-hog barbecue often find ourselves keeping busy in the smokehouse in the off-season. Both transform pork into something smoky and sublime. And just as barbecuing a whole hog requires planning, preparation, and investment (plus a few trips to the hardware store), preserving pork and other meats demands the patience, attention to detail, and time commitment we too often trade for convenience. But as with barbecue, the process of curing and cold-smoking meat is part of the reward, and encourages fraternization, collaboration, and celebration.

IF YOU HAVE THE
SPACE AND ARE
COMFORTABLE WITH
BASIC TOOLS, YOU
CAN BUILD A SIMPLE
SMOKEHOUSE
OVER A WEEKEND—
ESPECIALLY IF YOU
CAN RECRUIT YOUR
BUDS TO HELP OUT.

BUILDING A SMOKEHOUSE

If the first step of whole-hog barbecue—constructing a pit—doesn't scare you off, then you're a good candidate for cold smoking, because this process begins with building a smokehouse. It sounds more expensive and complicated than it actually is, and you might have an existing structure—like a storage shed—that can be repurposed into a smokehouse. Even an old fridge would work, if you rigged a way to pipe smoke inside. (You can find a multitude of DIY smokehouse videos on YouTube, but basically you need some kind of fire box, such as a wood-burning stove, connected to your smoking vessel in a way that it's pumping in smoke without the extra heat.) But if you have the space and are comfortable with basic tools, you can build a simple smokehouse over a weekend—especially if you can recruit your buds to help out.

A basic smokehouse is a 10 × 10-foot wood-framed structure with a simple door, tin roof, dirt floor, and rough-cut lumber vertically wrapping the sides. The most important thing is that your smokehouse, like a barbecue pit, should breathe. The top half of the smokehouse should be pretty airtight, but the bottom half should have ample airflow; this will keep the smoke contained up in the rafters, around 7 feet off the ground, where the meat hangs. In my smokehouse, the vertical boards forming the walls of the structure shrink as they dry and age, which allows the perfect amount of airflow. This is why I highly recommend not insulating your smokehouse, nor using plywood for the walls. If your smokehouse is too airtight around the bottom, you can drill some holes in the walls to increase airflow. If you're worried about insects, you can add a framed door, seal the roof, and line the inside of the walls with porch screen. Beyond that, you'll need some butcher hooks for hanging the meat, and some chairs or a bench, because you and your friends will need someplace to sit.

Your smokehouse will also likely be where you do most of your curing, unless you live someplace that's especially warm or cold in the winter (more on this later). Mine has a small workbench for salting meat, a giant container full of my curing mix, and a steel water tank that I've repurposed as a smoking box (see My Smokehouse Fire, page 258).

CURING AND SMOKING MEAT

Humans have been salt-curing and smoking meat basically since we figured out fire, using it as a way to preserve the meat, and not much has changed in the methods we use today. The process begins by **CURING** the meat using salt alone or a mixture of salt, sugar, spices, nitrites, and/or nitrates (see Curing Salts, page 254). Salt draws out moisture—where microorganisms thrive—from the meat, and the more water you can pull out, the longer that meat will keep. Larger cuts of meat take longer to cure—I keep my hams packed in my cure for about 45 days—while smaller cuts, like jowls, take only a week or less.

Once the meat has been cured, it undergoes a process of **EQUALIZATION**, in which the salt continues to move throughout the interior of the meat as its surface continues to dry. (Smaller cuts of meat don't require a separate equalization step; this will happen simultaneously as the meat is smoked.)

After the meat is equalized, it's ready to be hung in the smokehouse for **COLD SMOKING**, which both further preserves the meat and adds flavor. (Smoke is acidic, which helps to thwart microorganism growth.) Once again, the amount of time you smoke the meat will vary based on the size of the cut, from 2 days for jowls and sock sausage, to up to 30 days for a big country ham.

Once the meat has finished its spell in the smokehouse, it's either ready to eat (if it's a smaller cut) or it needs to be hung, or aged, in an environment with ideal temperature and humidity levels (this is often a basement). How long you hang the meat depends on how you want it to taste. You can hang country hams for 12 months; this is a good guide for a minimum for great flavor. Some folks age theirs for 2 years or longer.

CURING SALTS

In the Middle Ages, someone figured out that adding potassium nitrate, or saltpeter, to cures helped prevent undesirable bacteria—specifically those that cause botulism—from developing, as well as preserving the meat's rosy hue. Then, around the turn of the twentieth century, some folks figured out that certain salt-tolerant bacteria turn nitrate into nitrite, which is the chemical doing the actual preservation. So they left the saltpeter to the gunpowder and fertilizer makers and started using smaller amounts of sodium nitrite in meat production. The most common nitrite for cured meats is called Prague Powder #1, aka pink salt or pink curing salt. This mixture comprises 6.25 percent sodium nitrite, and the rest common table salt, and a small amount of red food coloring to distinguish it from table salt (pink salt is harmful if consumed on its own).

There's also Prague Powder #2, which contains 6.25 percent sodium nitrite, 4 percent sodium nitrate, salt, and food coloring. The addition of sodium nitrate slows down the release of the blend's antimicrobial powers, so Prague #2 (sometimes labeled Insta Cure #2 or Slow Cure) is often used on meats that are dry-cured for longer stretches of time, including country ham.

I've done this enough over the years that I don't use any curing salt on my hams and other preserved meats—I'm confident that I cure them properly and snuff out any bacterial issues that arise—though I suggest you do as an extra safety measure, and I've included Prague Powder #1 in my cure recipe (see Kit King's Cure, page 266). If you decide to skip the pink salt, be doubly sure to check your hams every day as they cure.

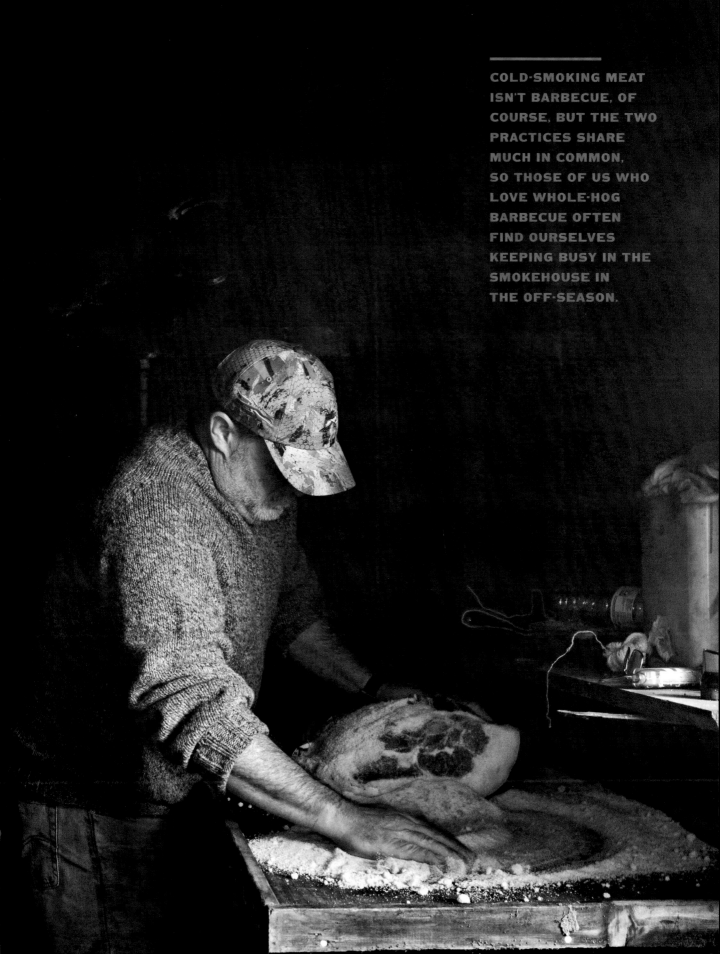

COLD-SMOKING MEAT
ISN'T BARBECUE, OF
COURSE, BUT THE TWO
PRACTICES SHARE
MUCH IN COMMON,
SO THOSE OF US WHO
LOVE WHOLE-HOG
BARBECUE OFTEN
FIND OURSELVES
KEEPING BUSY IN THE
SMOKEHOUSE IN
THE OFF-SEASON.

THE SMOKE- HOUSE FIRE

There are many ways to get smoke into your smokehouse. Many folks build a fire outside of the smokehouse and pipe the smoke in; this prevents the heat of the fire from making the smokehouse too hot. This is the most obvious difference between cold smoking and barbecue; you're not at all trying to cook the meat here. The esteemed Allen Benton, for example, has an old wood stove outside his smokehouse and runs the chimney inside. Other folks build a brick fire pit and pipe the smoke up through the floor of the smokehouse. These are fine methods, but they require frequent feeding of the fire, and an average Joe like me has to go to work. I prefer to build a slow-burning fire inside my smokehouse, using an old galvanized water tank that I pack with hickory sawdust and set alight. My method was inspired by the old smokehouses you'll find around my area—usually behind some old estate—where the traditional method was to build fires inside of poplar logs that have been dug out like a canoe. However you intend to get smoke into your smokehouse, do it in a fashion that doesn't raise the ambient temperature inside the smokehouse.

SMOKEHOUSE WITH VIEW INSIDE

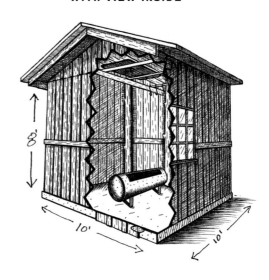

FIRE BOX WITH VIEW INSIDE

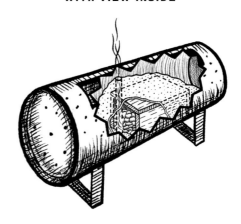

FIRE BOX INTERIOR SIDE VIEW

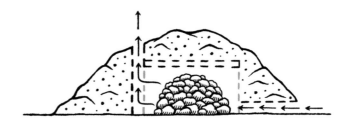

MANY FOLKS BUILD A FIRE OUTSIDE OF THE SMOKEHOUSE AND PIPE THE SMOKE IN; THIS PREVENTS THE HEAT OF THE FIRE FROM MAKING THE SMOKEHOUSE TOO HOT. THIS IS THE MOST OBVIOUS DIFFERENCE BETWEEN COLD SMOKING AND BARBECUE; YOU'RE NOT AT ALL TRYING TO COOK THE MEAT HERE.

MY SMOKEHOUSE FIRE

It's hard to describe in words how I build my smokehouse fire, but I'm going to do my best, and supplement the process with two diagrams and some photos. I took a metal water tank about 4 feet long and had a metal shop cut me a rectangular opening along one side, and also make me a steel frame for mounting the tank on its side. Inside the tank I pour a chimney full of burning hardwood charcoal and form it into a neat little pile about the size of a brick. Next I lay two hickory shims (each about 1 foot long and ¼ inch thick) on either side of the charcoal pile. I stand them up on their sides to form walls to "frame in" the coals. Then I pack the other side of those walls with moist hickory sawdust. I take a couple more shims and build a roof over the coals, then pack moist hickory sawdust all around the outside of the wood, making sure to leave a small hole on one end so the fire can draw air. Then I take a dowel and set it on the other end of the charcoal bed and pack more sawdust tightly around the dowel and over the hickory-enclosed coals. The sawdust needs to be pretty darn wet to burn slowly and so it can pack tight, so I spray it with water as I go until it's really damp in texture.

Once my little fire is completely encased with sawdust, I remove the dowel, twisting it carefully side to side while pulling it out, which leaves behind a small hole that acts like a chimney, allowing the smoke to escape. Finally, I make sure that the intake hole on the other end is free of any sawdust that may have collapsed in there. What's left is a slow-smoldering fire that has plenty of fuel, with just enough airflow to keep it going for up to 10 hours if it's breathing right. This provides enough smoke for the day, and I'll shovel out the ashes that evening and build a fresh fire to burn through the night, or if the previous fire has given me 8 to 10 hours of continuous smoke, I sometimes say "screw it" and skip the overnight fire. My goal is to get smoke on my meats for about 8 hours each day, because that's the way I like it, but if you can only get a couple of hours of smoke going each day, you'll be just fine.

I encourage you to try my method or tweak it as you see fit. Your goal is to build a small, slow-burning fire that won't heat up the smokehouse—you only want the smoke, not the heat—and that will burn for hours without needing to be maintained.

YOUR GOAL IS TO BUILD A SMALL, SLOW-BURNING FIRE THAT WON'T HEAT UP THE SMOKEHOUSE—YOU ONLY WANT THE SMOKE, NOT THE HEAT—AND THAT WILL BURN FOR HOURS WITHOUT NEEDING TO BE MAINTAINED.

COUNTRY HAM (AND A PRIMER FOR ALL THE REST)

If you're new to curing and cold smoking, I don't really recommend starting your education by actually making a country ham, but I *do* recommend reading through how to make a country ham first. It's the granddaddy of preserved pork, and I'll use it as a deep dive into each of the key steps to curing and smoking. But for practical reasons, I highly recommend starting with some smaller cuts—hog jowls, duck breasts, whole bellies, or sock sausage—to get yourself familiar with the process, before moving on to hams. Plus, ham will take you *at least a year* to make, more likely two or more, depending on how long you choose to age it. Starting with something like Cold-Smoked Hog Jowls (page 271) or bacon (see Cold-Smoked Pork Belly, page 273) is not only easier, but you'll get to enjoy it much sooner.

As with barbecue, when it comes to cured hams, you'll hear some pretty dogmatic opinions about who makes the "best." Spanish jamón serrano (and especially jamón Ibérico) and Italian prosciutto have long been considered the gold standard when it comes to cured hams, but I'll tell you right now that the country hams of the American South are every bit as good, if not better (yes, I'm going there) than any ham on the planet.

Other folks agree with me, but this is a relatively new position. It's really only been in the past decade or two that chefs outside of the South have included our style of cured ham in the global conversation. In the early 2000s, chefs around the country, especially those in New York City, started showcasing country hams on their menus, selling hams from Mr. Bob Woods of The Hamery in Murfreesboro, Tennessee; Col. Bill Newsom in Princeton, Kentucky; or Mr. Allen Benton of Benton's Smoky Mountains Country Hams in Madisonville, Tennessee. These producers—and several more—scattered through the South are putting out hams that taste so freaking good they make your eyes roll back in your head.

Many of these ham producers—and folks like me who make ham for the fun of it—are located in the "upper" South, the mountains and plateau regions that include Tennessee, Kentucky, and Virginia. Cured ham has deep roots in our regional culture, but primarily because of this region's historical climate.

I use the word "historical" because that's exactly what that climate is: history. Global warming is real, folks! Don't believe me? Look no further than the country ham. When my grandparents were young, they slaughtered hogs and hung hams from December till dang near April with nothing aiding them because the winters here—albeit mild compared to Northern climates—were still *winters*! Now our winters are somewhat warmer and consistently inconsistent. You just can't safely cure in open ambient temperatures that jump into the 60s in mid-January. Where I am, February is about the only month that's now consistently cold enough to risk it, and even then you can only safely bet

on curing bellies, sock sausage, and other smaller cuts, because there's simply not enough time left in the season to get a ham to the point of aging. A 30-pound ham takes 3 to 4 months to cure, rest, and smoke. My gosh, by then you're in mid-March and spring is well on its way. So, yeah, global warming is real and it's screwing up our winter tradition of curing, smoking, and hanging meat outside. It sucks.

But I'm going to teach you how to make a country ham anyway, with the hopes that you live somewhere where the winter is still cold enough, for long enough. Once you understand what goes into the method, you'll be able to use it to cure and cold-smoke just about any cut of meat.

SELECTING AND PREPARING A HAM

My country ham process begins in October, when I go in search of hams from a good hog that's around 300 pounds. Here in the South these were traditionally nicknamed "sausage hogs," because they were too big for the family's cook to want to mess with, and they were raised to be cured and "put up" for winter meals. A sausage hog will provide two hams that are around 30 pounds each.

You'll want to get your ham from a local butcher shop, the kind where the folks who process the meat know the farmer who raised it (preferably a farmer who is raising heritage-breed pork). Heritage-breed pigs taste better and flat out make a better country ham, and there are several to consider. The more readily available choices are Berkshire, Duroc, and Yorkshire—or some cross thereof. Swallow-belly breeds, such as Mangalitsa, have an amazing flavor because they have so much fat, but because of the amount of the fat, the hams themselves are surprisingly small, so for country ham I prefer a big Berkshire or Berkshire-cross (meaning a blend of Berkshire with another breed) sausage hog.

Ask your butcher for a "whole hind leg" and tell him or her what you intend to do with it. Before you commit to purchasing the ham, give it a good inspection. You don't want any dark bruises, which are more likely to spoil. Pigs are violent! When they go to slaughter, they're often placed in a holding pen, where they'll bite and walk all over one another, which can lead to bruising—so really look out for this. (But don't confuse a USDA stamp with a bruise.) You also want

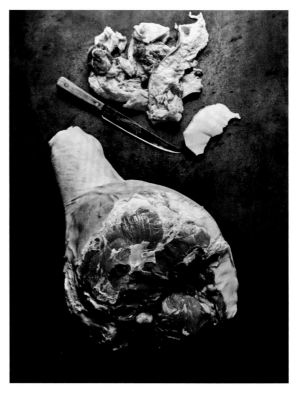

meat that's dense and tight, with no visible separation of the muscles at the seams, which happens when hams have been sitting around for weeks after they've been butchered. Also look for well-marbled meat, which means more flavor later on. Simply put: If the ham looks old or beat up, ask for another.

Your butcher should ask you if you want the aitch bone removed. You do. This H-shaped pelvic bone attaches the hind quarters to the femur, and there's a lot of blood around it, which increases the chance of spoilage. Removing the bone also allows the cure to penetrate the meat more quickly, greatly reducing the chance of bad bacteria getting into the ham and ruining it or, god forbid, making someone sick. Traditionally, we don't cut the aitch bone out—and you're welcome to leave it in—but if you do, be prepared to baby that ham and check it every day (which I recommend doing anyway) as it cures. Tell the butcher you also want the hoof removed.

When you get your ham home, rinse it thoroughly with water, cheap white wine, or distilled vinegar, then rinse it again with water. Trim away any egg yolk-colored fat, leaving the good, hard white fat intact. Cut any loose-hanging skin off the ham. Basically, if it doesn't look desirable, cut it off. Rinse the ham again with water and pat it dry. It's now ready to cure.

TOOLS
AND GEAR

To cure your ham, you'll need a **TUB** large enough to hold the ham (or hams); I use large (26 × 18 × 15-inch or similar) Lexan or Cambro food storage tubs that I buy from a restaurant supply store. You'll also need a **FEW DOWELS**—at least four, each about 12 inches long and 1 to 2 inches thick—for supporting your ham over the base of the tub, so they don't sit in their own liquid. I buy unstained oak curtain rods and cut them to fit my tub, and I wash them with bleach before every use.

CURING
THE HAM

In many ways, curing is the most important step in making country ham. Do the cure right, and you're less likely to encounter any problems down the road. Usually, around Thanksgiving weekend I mix up a big batch of my cure (see Kit King's Cure, page 266): around 20 pounds (or 50 cups) of it, which will be plenty for one ham. I keep mine in a tub on the floor of my smokehouse so I can grab a handful or two whenever I need it. You'll find various opinions out there on how much salt you'll need for the cure, or a specific ratio of salt to ham, but I don't really pay attention when I'm curing a big-ass, dense ham, because I'll be checking on that thing daily throughout the process to make sure it stays well-salted. I put my hams on cure around December 1, and look after my hams like a dadgum helicopter parent. For me it's a welcome chore—like stoking a fire or maintaining a pit.

Set the ham inside the tub and start rubbing it with cure, making sure to work the salt mixture into all of the pockets, crevices, and seams, especially anywhere where muscles are exposed to the air. You want to cover that ham with as much cure as you can; you'll end up using around 2 to 3 cups per ham for the first rub. The cure won't stick as well to the parts covered with skin, but rub as much into the skin as you can.

Pick up the ham and lay the dowels across the bottom of the tub, then set the ham on top, skin-side up. Grab something flat and heavy to lay on top of the ham. I use a 35-pound weight plate (like you would use for weightlifting) for one ham; a smooth paver, cinder block, or piece of limestone also work (wrap them in butcher paper or plastic first). If I'm curing two hams in the same tub, I'll either place one ham on top of the other, or lay the 35-pound plate across the top of both hams. The extra weight will help push the moisture from the ham as it cures.

If you have room in your refrigerator, set the tub inside. If not, find a place with an ambient temperature between 30° and 40°F, such as a garage, three-season porch, or your smokehouse. (The salt lowers the freezing temperature to 28°F, so don't worry about freezing the meat if it gets down to 30°F.)

Check your ham 24 to 36 hours later. Remove the ham from the tub and pour out any liquid that's accumulated on the bottom. Inspect the ham all over; if you notice any slimy spots, scrub them off with a vinegar-soaked towel. Give it a sniff; at this point the ham shouldn't give off much of an aroma. If you smell anything funny, like a sulfur smell, clean that spot out well with vinegar or cheap white wine, then salt it really well. Don't be shocked if you find a few of these spots during the first week or two of the curing process—this does not mean your ham has gone sour, it happens all the time. If you notice something happening in the same spot over and over, that's a sign that the ham is bruised or there's something amiss inside the muscles. If you see any meat change from pink to gray, trim that spot away and wash it well. Don't freak out; just keep scrubbing and salting that spot well and check it frequently.

After inspecting the ham, apply a fresh layer of cure all over, making sure, once again, to get plenty of cure into any crevices and wherever meat is exposed. You'll need less cure this time around, probably ¾ to 1 cup. Lay the dowels back in the tub and set the ham on top, flipping it over from its previous orientation. If you're curing two hams on top of each other, flip and rotate them top to bottom. Replace the weight, give your ham a kiss, and tuck it into bed.

Repeat this process for the duration of the cure: Empty the liquid, inspect the ham, deal with any problem spots, salt the sucker well, flip, and press. I cure my hams for 1½ days for every pound of weight, so a 30-pound ham will be cured for 45 days.

EQUALIZATION

If you start your cure on December 1, that step will be wrapped up around mid-January. You're ready to equalize the ham, which means allowing the salt to finish moving throughout the meat. At the same time, the surface of the ham—both exposed meat and skin—will start to dry out.

Remove the ham from the tub and wash it well, making sure to rinse any cure from the surface, and from inside any pockets or crevices. I'll use the sprayer on my kitchen sink, and have even used a pressure washer on a low setting. You want it really clean and free of cure. Pat the ham dry, set it back inside the tub on top of the dowels, and replace the weight. Return the tub to the refrigerator or a cold place, again between 30° and 40°F, and check it every day or two. Pour out any liquid that accumulates on the bottom of the tub,

inspect the ham, then flip it and replace the weight. You're less likely to notice any problem spots at this point, but if you do, scrub them down with vinegar or wine and keep going. Do this for another 30 days.

SMOKING

Once your ham is equalized, you're ready to smoke it. Again wash and dry the ham. Grab some butcher twine and tie a slip knot around the shank, then tie the ham up in the smokehouse. I tie mine around the rafters or a sturdy nail, about head high, and away from my fire.

The length of time you'll smoke your ham depends on how long you want to age it. The longer you plan to age it, the longer you should smoke it. I like to age my hams for at least 12 months and I prefer around 1½ years, which gives them a richer, more complex flavor. I smoke them for 30 straight days before aging. If you're planning on aging yours for less time, say a year or as little as 6 months (I wouldn't recommend any less than 6 months of aging), smoke your ham for about 2 weeks.

I like to fire up the smokehouse first thing in the morning, when the hams are at their coldest temperature (as with barbecue, the colder the meat, the more smoke it will absorb), then again at night before I go to bed, though skipping a night here and there isn't a big deal. Just try to give your hams 8 to 10 hours of smoke each day.

During the smoking process, keep your eye on the weather. Your ideal temperature inside the smokehouse is between 32° and 40°F. If the temperature is going to dip below 25°F, take your ham inside and put it in the fridge or another cold spot. If you're in the northern climes, where it's often below 25°F, you can heat the smokehouse with a space heater. Likewise, if the temperature goes above 50°F for more than 4 or 5 hours during the day, bring the ham inside and refrigerate it for a day to thoroughly chill it before returning it to the smokehouse.

AGING

By the time spring arrives in mid-March, I'm done smoking and I'm ready to age my hams. I usually leave mine hanging in the smokehouse for another month or so, or until the temperature outside is frequently above 50°F.

Once it's time to bring your ham inside for aging, find a cool, dark spot that doesn't get too cold in the

BAD HAM

I'm not going to pretend that curing never goes wrong. Despite your best efforts, sometimes your meat will develop bad bacteria and spoil. Though it's not common, it happens, and has happened to me. It's important to recognize when it does. When a ham (or other cured meat) goes bad, you'll notice a slick, gooey film developing on the outside—like a wound that won't heal—and then it will start to smell funky. If you notice this happening during the curing process, you can clean off the nasty parts and scrub it well with vinegar or white wine, then pack the area with a lot of fresh salt. This will often do the trick. This is why I check the meat every day when it's curing, especially during the first 3 weeks of the cure, and make sure it's completely covered in salt. If you do a good job curing your ham, you're probably in the clear for the rest of the smoking and aging process. But if bad bacteria take over a ham while it ages and keep reappearing after you've scrubbed it away, it's done. Throw it away and try again. It's a real bummer, but way better to waste a piece of meat and some time than have to live with getting someone sick.

winter, or too hot in the summer. For most of us, this is a basement, screen porch, or garage. The ideal temperature range for aging ham is generous, between 45° and 85°F, so you might start it inside the porch and move it to the basement come late spring. I want my ham to go through the seasonal phases it needs to make a really great ham. Humidity and air ventilation are also important; you don't want to age your ham in a very damp basement—an average relative humidity of 70 to 75 percent is ideal—and you want some decent airflow. You can counteract an especially humid spot by circulating the air with a fan.

To prep your ham for aging, wash and dry it well. Coat it with 1 tablespoon each of black peppercorns and red pepper flakes (both are great natural bug repellents, and won't affect the finished ham's flavor). Wrap the ham in three layers of ham socks (also called stockinettes, or ham bags; see Resources, page 307) and tie them tightly around the shank at the top to prevent any bugs from sneaking in. Then hang 'em up.

As the ham ages, it's going to swell up and continue pushing out moisture (especially as it gets into the heat of the summer), so you might want to place something below it to catch any drips. This is a good thing, as it's also pushing out excess sodium. Check your ham every couple of days. Inspect the socks for tiny holes. If you see any, take it down and check it carefully; this could be a worm that has bored into the meat. If you catch it soon enough you can cut that out and hang it back up. Also give the ham a sniff; if it doesn't smell like smoky pork, something's not right. If this happens, remove the socks and inspect the ham. If anything looks moldy or slimy, trim that part off and wash it off with white vinegar, pack the spot with peppercorns or red pepper flakes, then rewrap and hang. As it ages, you'll notice white mold growing over parts of the ham; this is just fine, and you don't need to remove it. Other colors of mold should be removed.

Even if everything seems fine, take your ham down once a month, remove the ham socks, and give it a good inspection. Wrap it in a triple layer of new socks and hang it again. Repeat this inspection monthly until your ham is aged to your liking. As I said, I like to age mine for 1½ years, and I've gone as far as 3 years, but you won't notice much change in flavor from 2 years on.

STORING AND SERVING

You've just invested countless hours in making a beautifully preserved hunk of pork, and you should celebrate your efforts by eating the ham.

A country ham is usually about half to two-thirds of its original weight. Factoring in the weight of the bones and skin, you're left with 10 to 15 pounds of meat.

Before digging in, give your ham a final bath. Wash it well, using white wine or vinegar. There will likely be some white mold on the ham; wipe that off. Inspect the crevices, trimming out anything that's green, brown, black, or red. You can leave the skin and any tough external meat intact; you'll trim that away as you consume the ham.

Country ham will keep indefinitely, but you'll probably use yours up pretty quickly. I typically eat country ham one of two ways: thinly sliced lengthwise as charcuterie or cut crosswise into thicker slices and fried up in a skillet for breakfast. If you're going to eat off your ham every day, leave it on the counter and keep it covered with a clean towel, then trim and slice as you go. You might even treat yourself to one of those fancy ham stands. If you want to save some ham for later, slice the ham crosswise into ¼-inch-thick pieces, then vacuum-seal and refrigerate or freeze. You can also bring your ham to your butcher and ask them to slice it for you.

COOKING COUNTRY HAM

If you didn't grow up cooking country ham for breakfast, you probably don't know the proper way to do it. Here's how: Cut the ham crosswise into thick slices, between ¼ and ⅜ inch thick. Heat a cast-iron skillet over medium heat. While the skillet is heating up, make a few 1-inch cuts around the perimeter of the ham (perpendicular to the edge): This will prevent the ham from "cupping up" while it cooks, allowing it to brown evenly. If the slice is pretty wide, then cut it in half so it can brown well. Cook the ham until the bottom is evenly browned, 4 to 5 minutes, then flip and cook the other side for about 3 minutes.

KIT KING'S CURE

Makes about 50 cups (about 26 pounds; enough for 1 country ham)

13 pounds 12 ounces Diamond Crystal kosher salt

6 pounds 14 ounces granulated sugar

3 pounds 2 ounces dry molasses powder or light brown sugar

1 pound 14 ounces Prague Powder #1

3 tablespoons plus 1 teaspoon red pepper flakes

There's nothing super unique about my family's cure recipe, but it is one of my most beloved heirlooms. My granddaddy Kit King grew up with this recipe and had used it for years, but he'd forgotten it by the time I was getting into barbecue and tried to remember it so he could give it to me. Like something out of a novel, it came back to him a week before he died, and he rushed to write it down. So it's very special to me. I've made two tweaks to the original: I swap out brown sugar for dry molasses powder, which has a bold molasses flavor but isn't as sweet (you can order the stuff online or find it in some grocery stores around the South). I personally quit using pink curing salt (aka Prague Powder #1), but I've added it to this recipe for the sake of added food safety, so your ass doesn't get sick.

In a very large container with an airtight lid, mix the ingredients well. Keep covered until ready to use.

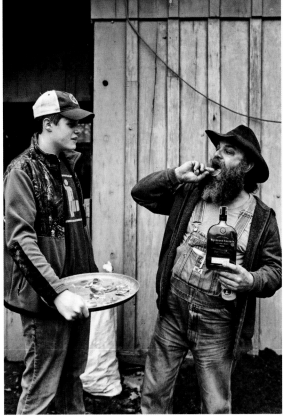

DUCK BREASTS

I don't know what it is that makes someone want to wade out in frozen water to freeze his or her balls off, trying to coax some ducks into a pond so they can shoot them, but my buddies and I do just that. I love to cook duck like anyone else, but after preparing a few meals with fresh meat, I put the rest of my catch on cure, knowing that I'll have some delicious smoked duck "ham" a week later.

The wild ducks we hunt are very different from the farm-raised duck you buy. They're a bit smaller and much leaner, and I'm too lazy to pluck all of the feathers, so I just remove the skin when I prep the breasts for curing. There is not a lot of fat under a wild duck's skin, so I don't miss much when I remove it. I'm going to assume you'll be purchasing plump duck breasts from the meat case, so my recipe is based around that, but I've added instructions for you hunters as well.

The final product is tender, smoky, and pleasantly gamy. I treat smoked duck breast much like ham, thinly slicing it, then laying the slices over crackers spread with cream cheese—or, better yet, cooking it like bacon and eating it for breakfast.

8 servings (farm-raised),
4 servings (wild)

4 duck breasts (about
1½ pounds each if farm-
raised, or 5 to 6 ounces
each if wild)
1 cup Kit King's Cure (page 266)

PREPARE

If using farm-raised duck, leave the fat and skin on. Trim any flappy parts and sinew with a sharp knife. If using a wild duck, remove the skin and sinew.

CURE

Rub each breast with 2 teaspoons of the Kit King's Cure (1 tablespoon per farm-raised breast or 2 teaspoons per wild breast) and place on a wire rack set inside a sheet pan. Refrigerate, uncovered, for 5 days (for farm-raised) or 2 days (for wild). Drain any liquid a couple of times daily and re-season each breast with Kit King's Cure as needed each day. After curing is complete, rinse thoroughly with cold water and pat dry.

EQUALIZE

Place the breasts on a wire rack set inside a sheet pan and refrigerate for 2 days, flipping them over after the first day.

SMOKE

Pat the duck breasts dry. Place them on a wire rack in the smokehouse, high enough where they'll be exposed to the smoke. Build the fire (see My Smokehouse Fire, page 258) and smoke for 1 day, with 8 to 10 hours of smoke. Make sure the temperature in the smokehouse is between 30° and 40°F while the duck is smoking; stop and refrigerate the breasts if it gets warmer. Return the duck to the smokehouse when the temperature comes back down and the meat is well chilled.

SERVE AND STORE

To serve, thinly slice the breasts across the grain and serve. To store, wrap the breasts in plastic and refrigerate for up to 30 days.

COLD-SMOKED BONELESS
PORK LOIN

8 to 10 servings

1 boneless pork loin (3 to 4 pounds)

3 to 4 tablespoons Kit King's Cure (page 266), plus more as needed

Somewhere along the way, Martha developed a real liking for Canadian bacon, which she eats for breakfast, or on toast with mayonnaise as a quick lunch. Unlike bacon, which is made from pork belly, Canadian bacon is essentially smoked pork loin. As my father-in-law and I got our smokehouse going, Martha asked me to make her some, so now every winter I cure and smoke her a loin or two. I treat it like a lean bacon, frying slices up in a skillet or on the grill. Also, this is a pretty prime lunch sandwich: Top it with lettuce, onion, mayo, and a dash of Tabasco. My kids love it.

PREPARE

Trim the pork loin of excess fat and sinew. Rinse with cold water and pat dry.

CURE

Rub the pork loin with 1 tablespoon of the Kit King's Cure per pound of meat and place on a wire rack set inside a sheet pan. Refrigerate, uncovered, for 2 days *per pound*. Drain the liquid twice daily and re-season with a light coating of cure each day.

After curing is complete, rinse thoroughly with cold water and pat dry.

EQUALIZE

Place the pork on a wire rack set inside a sheet pan and refrigerate for 1 day per pound of meat.

SMOKE

Pat the pork dry. Place the loin on a wire rack in the smokehouse, high enough where it will be exposed to the smoke. Build the fire (see My Smokehouse Fire, page 258) and smoke for 1 day per pound, with 8 to 10 hours of smoke per day. Make sure the temperature in the smokehouse is between 30° and 40°F while the meat is smoking; stop and refrigerate the meat if it gets warmer. Return the meat to the smokehouse when the temperature comes back down and the meat is well chilled.

SERVE AND STORE

To serve, slice the loin against the grain into ½-inch-thick slices and sear in a medium-hot skillet or over a medium-hot grill until well browned, 1 to 2 minutes per side. To store, wrap the meat in plastic and refrigerate for up to 30 days.

HOG JOWLS

H og jowls are a great way to get your feet wet with curing and cold smoking. The time commitment is short—less than 2 weeks start to finish—and jowls are one of the tastiest parts of a pig, like a fattier, more intensely flavored, miniature ham. I treat mine like bacon and cook up thick slices for breakfast.

Makes 4 jowls

4 hog jowls (about 2 pounds each)

About 1 cup Kit King's Cure (page 266)

PREPARE

Trim the jowls, removing the skin (if any), sinew, and any jagged or flimsy pieces. Wash and pat dry with paper towels.

CURE

Rub each jowl with 2 teaspoons of the Kit King's Cure and place on a wire rack set inside a sheet pan. Refrigerate, uncovered, for 5 days. Drain any liquid a couple of times daily and re-season each jowl with about 2 teaspoons cure each day.

After curing is complete, rinse thoroughly with cold water and pat dry.

EQUALIZE

Place the jowl on a wire rack set inside a sheet pan and refrigerate for 4 days, turning them over each day.

SMOKE

Pat the jowls dry. Place them on a wire rack in the smokehouse, high enough where they'll be exposed to the smoke. Build the fire (see My Smokehouse Fire, page 258) and smoke for 1 to 2 days, with 8 to 10 hours of smoke per day. (If any day the temperature in the smokehouse is above 40°F while the meat is smoking, remove the jowls from the smokehouse and refrigerate the jowls until the temp falls back below 40°F before returning to the smokehouse.)

SERVE AND STORE

To serve, slice the jowls against the grain into ¼-inch-thick slices and cook in a skillet over medium heat until browned, flipping frequently. You can store whole cured, smoked jowls wrapped in plastic and refrigerated indefinitely.

COLD-SMOKED
PORK BELLY (BACON)

I really don't like most store-bought bacon; it tends to be wet, mushy, and not smoky enough. Making your own bacon allows you to control how smoky you want it, and you can play around with the cure recipe as well. Most commercial bacon is injected with brine rather than cured, so the depth of flavor you get from a true cured bacon is on a whole other level. Plus, it just feels good to fry up a delicious breakfast knowing you made it yourself.

I call for skin-on pork belly, but if you only find skinless, don't worry. The skin mostly helps the meat hold its shape while it cures, but there won't be too much of a difference in the result. If you plan to make lots of bacon, I recommend buying an 8- to 10-prong meat hook (see Resources, page 307) and mounting it up high in your smokehouse. You can also use the hanger for jowls, duck breasts, and loins, or for tying up hams and sock sausage.

Makes 10 to 15 pounds

1 pork belly, preferably with skin (15 to 20 pounds)

6 cups Kit King's Cure (page 266), or as needed

PREPARE

Trim the pork belly to square up the sides, removing any dangling bits of meat. You should end up with a nice, even rectangle.

CURE

Rub the pork belly with about 1 cup of the Kit King's Cure, making sure to coat it well. Place the pork belly on a wire rack set inside a sheet pan or plastic container large enough for it to lie flat. Refrigerate, uncovered, for 1 day *per pound*. Drain the liquid twice daily and re-season with a light coating of cure (about ¼ cup) each day.

After curing is complete, rinse thoroughly with cold water and pat dry.

EQUALIZE AND SMOKE

The bacon will equalize while smoking. Pat the belly dry. If you have meat hooks, skewer the belly through the skin and meat on one of the short ends, and hang in the smokehouse where it will be exposed to smoke. You can also lay the belly flat on a wire rack if you can balance it well lying across the rafters. Build the fire (see My Smokehouse Fire, page 258) and smoke for 1 to 2 weeks, depending on your desired flavor, with 8 to 10 hours of smoke per day. Bellies will take on a light brown, golden hue over this time. To check the flavor to see if you want more smoke, cut a small strip off of the side, cook it, and decide if you want to keep smoking.

Make sure the temperature in the smokehouse is between 30° and 40°F while the meat is smoking; stop and refrigerate the meat if it gets warmer. Return the meat to the smokehouse when the temperature comes back down and the meat is well chilled.

SERVE AND STORE

If your belly has any skin on it, remove it before cooking. Slice the belly against the grain into your desired thickness. Fry in a cast-iron skillet over medium heat until cooked through (or until crispy if desired). To store, wrap the belly in plastic and refrigerate for up to 2 weeks, or cut the belly into quarters or slabs, wrap tightly in plastic, and freeze for up to 6 months.

SOCK SAUSAGE

To the uninitiated, sock sausage (some call it "sack sausage" or "sage sausage") is a blend of ground pork, sage, pepper flakes, and other seasonings that's been cured and (often, but not always) cold-smoked. Along with bacon, it was always on my family's breakfast table, but I didn't start making it myself until 2008, when my father-in-law, Buzzy, and I turned an old feed shed into a smokehouse. Around the same time, I—along with my chef friends Tandy Wilson, Tyler Brown, and our journalist friend, the late John Egerton—got really obsessive about sock sausage (especially John and Tyler). We used my smokehouse as a lab for experimenting and sharing.

I've tinkered with my recipe over the years, but Tandy turned me on to the idea of adding finely diced pork skin to the mix. The skin adds a sublime, otherworldly texture—"sticky" is the best word I can find to describe it—that makes it so dadgum addictive that I can't stop eating it and you won't be able to either. Allowing this sausage to hang in the "heat" of a warmer winter day allows it to ferment a little, which gives it a bit of a sour zing that is just so tasty. You gotta be careful, when cooking it, though: The skin can pop and splatter you with grease, so make sure you finely dice the skin and put a splatter screen over your skillet, just to be safe. You can usually buy pork skin, which has been removed from bellies, from your butcher.

Sock sausage has since become my absolute favorite thing to smoke, and I'll make a big batch in the winter. After I take it off cure, I like to let it hang for a day when the daytime temperatures are between 40° and 50°F. Getting those few hours of warmth lets it ferment a little, giving it that zing that all great sock sausages have.

GATHER EQUIPMENT

You'll need a meat grinder with a #8 die and six 2-pound white or red stitch cloth sausage bags (see Resources, page 307). If you have a sausage stuffer and want to use that, go ahead, but I just do it by hand with a spoon.

PREPARE

Make sure all the meat is cold and firm; you can place it in the freezer for 15 to 20 minutes if needed. In a large bowl, combine all the ingredients and use your hands to mix, making sure all of the pork pieces are well coated in the seasonings. Fit a meat grinder with a #8 die and pass the mixture through. Take a sausage bag and roll it down about halfway. Using a spoon, stuff the sausage mixture into the sausage bag, packing it firmly and unrolling the bag as you fill it, leaving enough space at the top so you can tie it off (the sausage bag comes with a drawstring at the top). Repeat to fill all the bags.

(recipe continues)

---

6 sausages (about 20 patties per sausage)

10 pounds pork butt, cut into 1-inch cubes

1½ pounds pork back fat, cut into 1-inch cubes

1½ pounds pork skin, cut into ⅛-inch dice (or smaller) with a heavy knife or cleaver

6 tablespoons Diamond Crystal kosher salt

1 tablespoon Prague Powder #1

1 tablespoon red pepper flakes

1 tablespoon ground sage

1 teaspoon ground ginger

CURE AND EQUALIZE

Hang the sausages in the refrigerator over a drip pan, or place on a wire rack set inside a sheet pan, for 1 week. The sausage will equalize as it cures, so no need to add in more time.

HANG

If desired, after curing, hang the sausages in your smokehouse (or somewhere else that's between 40° and 50°F) for 1 day. The sausage will begin to ferment, which adds more flavor at the end. If it's too cold out, you can also let the sausage sit at room temperature in the house for 6 to 8 hours, but know that your local health department won't suggest you do that.

SMOKE

Build the fire (see My Smokehouse Fire, page 258) and hang the sock sausages in the smokehouse where they will be exposed to the smoke for at least 2 days, and up to 1 week, with as much smoke as you want to put on them. I like to get at least 4 hours of smoke per day, depending how smoky you want them. The sausages are ready when they are dry to the touch and start to dimple in spots, and the rest is just about how much smoke flavor you want to add. For my taste, I personally don't think you can get them too smoky; I'm more concerned with not getting enough smoke on them.

If you want to check the flavor, you can cut into one, cook and taste it, and bring it back to the smokehouse if you want. The longer the sausages hang, the drier they'll get, and they might begin to develop a "rind" on the outside. (This is not the end of the world by any means whatsoever. You are going to enjoy it either way.)

Make sure the temperature in the smokehouse is between 30° and 40°F while the meat is smoking; stop and refrigerate the meat if it gets warmer. Return the meat to the smokehouse when the temperature comes back down and the meat is well chilled.

SERVE AND STORE

Unwrap the sausage and slice crosswise into ½-inch-thick patties. If any hard rind has formed on the outside, trim those bits off before cooking.

Cook the patties in a cast-iron skillet over medium-low heat until browned on both sides. A splatter screen will help keep things a little neater and safer. Do not press on the meat; if the sausage begins to curl around the edges, reduce the heat. Wrap any extra sausage in parchment paper and refrigerate until ready to use, up to a 1 week. The sausages can also be frozen whole (wrap the sock in plastic) for up to 6 months; thaw overnight in the refrigerator.

CHAPTER 7

AFTER THE F

IRE

DESSERTS

I'VE LONG KNOWN that I wanted to write a book about what I know about barbecue, and I knew that it wasn't going to be about novelties like grilled pies or smoked ice cream. But if you're having a few dozen of your friends over for a pig pickin' or a pile of ribs, you'll probably want to have some killer desserts to serve afterward.

So we come to the place where, for the most part, I'm gonna exit stage left and let the women in my life—especially my mom, Pam—take over. We all have that mom, aunt, or grandmother who was the star cook of the family. Well, I grew up really spoiled because I had all of them, and they were all incredible cooks. My dad's mother, "Maw-Maw" Nonie Martin, was truly a legendary cook in and around Northeast Mississippi. She was known throughout the county, as was her sister, my aunt Jewel.

Back in the day, the church denominations would put together little spiral cookbooks and all the women in the community would add a recipe to it for them to sell and raise money for their congregations. The Methodists, Baptists, Church of Christ, and so on all had their own recipe books, and you had to be part of their denomination to be included. We all belonged to the Church of Christ, and of course we had our books. But Maw-Maw and Aunt Jewel were so popular in and around Alcorn County, Mississippi, that, from time to time, other denominations would include them in their books too. As popular as their local fame was though, my mom's mother, Nadine (we called her Mi-Mi) was equally good, as was my Aunt B. My Aunt Cathy and my mom learned everything from them, and she's passed her knowledge along to Martha and my baby sister, Mary. And now I'm watching those skill sets trickle down to my daughter, Daisy.

Those family recipes, and the small-but-essential details that come with them, warm my heart. Watching my mom in the kitchen with Daisy always makes me take pause; it's so special to me. So these are my favorite recipes from the women who've shaped my life.

Speaking of small details, you'll see that my family is as dogmatic and passionate about homemade ice cream as I am about pit barbecue.

The Martin's

MAW-MAW MARTIN'S
PECAN PIE

Most pecan pies are almost always too sweet. But this version—which comes from my mother-in-law, Nonie—has just the right amount of sweetness and really features the flavor of the pecans. Nonie always called for chopped pecans because she didn't like it when your fork would hit a whole pecan, smash the slice, and ruin it. She wanted it to look pretty while you were eating it.
—PAM MARTIN

8 to 10 servings

4 tablespoons (½ stick) salted butter

1 cup sugar

1 cup light corn syrup

3 extra-large eggs, beaten

1 teaspoon pure vanilla extract

1½ cups coarsely chopped pecans

All-purpose flour, for dusting

Pie Crust (page 291), unbaked

Position a rack in the center of the oven and preheat the oven to 300°F.

In a saucepan, warm the butter over medium-high heat until just melted. Remove from the heat and mix in the sugar until thoroughly combined. Let cool slightly.

In a medium bowl, whisk together the corn syrup, eggs, and vanilla to combine. Slowly add the melted butter/sugar mixture, whisking constantly. Add the pecans and stir to combine.

Make the pie dough, roll it out, and line a standard 9-inch pie pan as directed. Pour the mixture into the pie shell.

Bake until the center of the pie reaches 200°F on an instant-read thermometer and a skewer inserted into the center of the pie comes out clean, 50 to 55 minutes.

Let cool completely (about 3 hours) before slicing and serving.

MARTHA'S
FUDGE PIE

8 to 10 servings

2 sticks (8 ounces) salted butter, plus more for the pan

1¼ cups sugar

¼ cup all-purpose flour, plus more for dusting

¼ cup Hershey's unsweetened cocoa powder

3 large eggs, beaten

½ teaspoon pure pure vanilla extract

Pie Crust (page 291), unbaked

My daughter-in-law Martha's fudge pie is heavy on chocolate and butter, with a creamy, airy texture that's akin to a soft fudge. Martha's recipe, which was passed down from her mother, uses a pantry staple found throughout the South: Hershey's cocoa powder. This has been a favorite at Patrick's restaurants since the beginning. **—PAM MARTIN**

Preheat the oven to 300°F. Butter a 9-inch round glass pie plate.

In a medium saucepan, combine the butter and sugar and whisk together over low heat until the sugar is melted into the butter and the mixture resembles a yellow paste. Set aside and allow to cool slightly.

In a medium bowl, combine the flour, cocoa powder, eggs, and vanilla and whisk until combined. Add the melted butter/sugar mixture and whisk together.

Make the pie dough, roll it out, and line the buttered pie plate as directed. Pour the filling into the prepared pie shell.

Bake until the pie is set and the top appears dry, 45 to 50 minutes.

Let cool completely before slicing and serving.

STRAWBERRY CAKE

This is one of Patrick's favorite desserts and I would usually make one every year for his birthday in March, which always got me excited for the fresh strawberry season to come. But since these light, airy cakes are made with frozen strawberries (which usually taste far better than rock-hard fresh ones out of season from the supermarket), you can enjoy it year-round—whatever your birthday. **—PAM MARTIN**

MAKE THE CAKE

Position a rack in the center of the oven and preheat the oven to 350°F. Mist a 9 × 13-inch cake pan with cooking spray and lightly flour, then tap out the excess.

In a large bowl, with an electric mixer, beat together the cake mix, strawberries, gelatin, vegetable oil, and eggs until just combined. Evenly spread the batter in the prepared pan.

Bake until a toothpick inserted into the center comes out clean, 30 to 35 minutes. Place the pan on a cooling rack and let cool completely.

MAKE THE ICING

In a large bowl, with an electric mixer, combine the melted butter, strawberries (the larger amount for a thinner icing), and salt and beat until combined. Add the powdered sugar, a little at a time, and beat until incorporated.

Once the cake has cooled completely, spread with icing and serve. Store at room temperature in an airtight container for up to 5 days.

Makes one 9 × 13-inch cake (20 to 24 servings)

FOR THE CAKE

Cooking spray and all-purpose flour, for the pan

One 15- to 16-ounce box white cake mix plus ½ cup

1 cup thawed frozen strawberries with juice

One 3-ounce box strawberry-flavored gelatin powder

½ cup vegetable oil

3 large eggs, beaten

FOR THE ICING

1 stick (4 ounces) unsalted butter, melted

¼ to ⅓ cup thawed frozen strawberries with juice

½ teaspoon kosher salt

1 pound (3½ cups) powdered sugar

STRAWBERRY PIE

The first time I ever had this pie was when Danny (my husband) and I were dating, and I went to his house for supper for the first time. Mrs. Martin made this recipe because she loved the strawberry pie at Shoney's so much, but the closest location was over in Memphis, some sixty-five miles away. The combination of two whole pints of fresh strawberries held together in a cold Jell-O mixture is almost like eating a frozen dessert, and so refreshing on a hot summer night. She gave me the recipe and I'd make it for Danny back at Mississippi State when we would go out on dates—I'd eat one piece and Danny would eat the rest of the pie! **—PAM MARTIN**

8 to 10 servings

1 cup sugar

2 tablespoons strawberry-flavored gelatin powder

3 tablespoons cornstarch

1 cup water

2 pints strawberries, hulled and cut into ½-inch pieces

Pie Crust (page 291), fully baked

Sweetened whipped cream, for serving

In a small saucepan, combine the sugar, gelatin powder, and cornstarch and whisk until mixed. Add the water and stir to combine. Set the pan over medium-high heat and bring to a boil, stirring constantly. Cook until the liquid is mostly clear and has slightly thickened, 2 to 3 minutes (do not overcook). Remove from the heat.

Set aside the gelatin mixture to cool to room temperature, stirring occasionally to prevent a film from forming on the top. Add the strawberries and stir to combine. Transfer to the baked pie crust and refrigerate until set, about 6 hours.

To serve, cut the pie into slices and top each with a large dollop of whipped cream.

MI-MI KING'S
SWEET POTATO PIE

8 to 10 servings

FOR THE FILLING

2 medium sweet potatoes
(about 1¼ pounds)—peeled,
quartered, and sliced into
¼-inch cubes

6 tablespoons unsalted butter, at
room temperature

1 cup sugar

2 large egg yolks

½ teaspoon pure pure vanilla
extract

½ teaspoon orange extract

½ teaspoon coconut extract

½ teaspoon lemon extract

¼ teaspoon almond extract

1 Pie Crust (recipe follows),
unbaked

FOR THE MERINGUE

3 egg whites, at room
temperature

6 tablespoons sugar

½ teaspoon pure pure vanilla
extract

Pinch of kosher salt

My momma and daddy loved sweet potato pie and they were very specific on when to make the best ones. My granny Kink (my daddy's mother) always told us to make the pies in the late summer or early fall, right after the sweet potatoes were dug up from the ground because that's when they were the sweetest. Her sweet potato pie is light and airy—not the dense texture you find in a lot of sweet potato pies—and not too sweet, and the combination of five flavor extracts gives it a slightly tropical flavor. Momma would make several of them and take them to friends in the community or to church. **—PAM MARTIN**

MAKE THE FILLING

In a small saucepan, combine the sweet potatoes with water to cover and bring to a boil over medium heat. Cook until tender, about 20 minutes.

Preheat the oven to 350°F.

Drain the potatoes and transfer to a large bowl. Beat with an electric hand mixer until smooth and let cool slightly. Add the butter and beat until incorporated. Gradually add the sugar and beat to combine. Add the egg yolks, one a time, and beat until incorporated. Add the vanilla, orange, coconut, lemon, and almond extracts and beat until combined.

Prepare the pie dough, roll out, and line a 9-inch pie pan as directed. Pour the mixture into the pie shell and spread it out evenly.

Bake until the filling is set and a toothpick inserted into the filling comes out clean, about 50 minutes. Let cool to room temperature.

MAKE THE MERINGUE

In a stand mixer fitted with the whisk (or in a bowl with a handheld electric mixer), beat the egg whites until stiff. With the machine on, add the sugar gradually and beat until dissolved. Beat in the vanilla and salt.

When the pie is fully cooled to room temperature, spread the meringue over the top of the pie. Cut the pie into slices and serve.

PIE CRUST

Makes one 9-inch pie crust

1 cup all-purpose flour, plus more for rolling

1 teaspoon sugar

⅛ teaspoon kosher salt

⅓ cup plus 1 tablespoon shortening

2½ to 3 tablespoons ice-cold water

In a medium bowl, whisk together the flour, sugar, and salt. Add the shortening and work it into the flour using a fork or a pastry blender until the mixture resembles small peas. Add 2½ tablespoons of the cold water and work it into the mixture until it forms a ball of dough, adding small splashes of additional water if the dough is too dry to come together. Flatten the dough ball into a disk, then wrap in plastic and refrigerate until ready to use, at least 1 hour (and up to 3 days).

LINE A PIE PAN

Place the ball of dough on a lightly floured surface and pat into a disk. Roll out the dough into a round about 11 inches in diameter. Transfer the dough to a 9-inch standard pie pan, press it into the sides and bottom of the pan, and fold the edge over onto itself and crimp it all the way around. Prick the bottom of the pie shell all over with the tines of a fork.

TO PARBAKE THE CRUST

Preheat the oven to 400°F. Lay a piece of parchment down over the pie shell and fill with pie weights or dried beans in a single layer to prevent the dough from rising. Place the crust in the oven and bake for 5 to 10 minutes or until lightly browned.

TO FULLY BAKE THE CRUST

Follow the directions for parbaking, then remove the parchment and pie weights and continue baking until the crust is golden brown and cooked through, 15 to 20 minutes.

YOU MAY BE TEMPTED TO EAT THEM HOT OUT OF THE FRYER, BUT IN MY OPINION THEY'RE BETTER SERVED AT ROOM TEMPERATURE, AFTER THEY'VE SAT OUT ON THE COUNTER FOR AWHILE.

BLACKBERRY
FRIED PIES

My daddy loved fried pies about as much as anything. They had apple trees and would dry the slices of apples in the sun so they'd keep during the winter. Momma would cook these down for us and make fried pies with them. Patrick always preferred blackberry or peach pies, and that's what he serves at the restaurants, so that's the recipe I've included here. You may be tempted to eat them hot out of the fryer, but in my opinion they're better served at room temperature, after they've sat out on the counter for a while. (In fact, most restaurants around the South that sell them serve them wrapped in plastic wrap by the cash register for folks to grab.) This is how most of us around here are used to eating them, and personally, I think they're better this way because the filling and the crust have some time to combine a bit, and the whole thing is a soft, delicious bite. **—PAM MARTIN**

MAKE THE CRUST

In a large bowl, combine the flour, sugar, and salt and whisk to mix. Using your fingers or a pastry cutter, work the shortening into the flour until the mixture resembles coarse crumbs, with no pieces larger than a pea. Add the milk 2 to 3 tablespoons at a time and work into the flour mixture using a spatula, stirring just until a dough comes together. Form the dough into a ball, wrap in plastic, and refrigerate for 1 hour.

MAKE THE FILLING

In a medium saucepan, combine the blackberries, sugar, lemon juice, and pectin. Bring to a simmer over medium heat and cook, stirring constantly, until the berries begin to break down, about 10 minutes. Remove the mixture from the heat and let cool completely.

TO ASSEMBLE

Lightly flour a surface and roll the dough out into a ¼-inch thickness. Using a 4-inch round pastry cutter, cut out as many rounds as you can. Set aside. Gather the scraps and repeat once. Discard any remaining scraps.

Spoon 2 tablespoons of filling into the center of each round, leaving ¼ inch of space around the edges. Brush the edges with the egg wash, fold the dough over the filling, and seal the edges by pressing them together with the tines of a fork. Repeat until all the dough rounds have been used. Refrigerate the pies while you heat the oil.

Pour 1 to 2 inches of oil into a large saucepan or Dutch oven and set over high heat. Bring the oil to 360°F. Line a wire rack with paper towels and set the rack inside a sheet pan.

Using a slotted spoon, carefully place 2 pies at a time into the oil and fry until golden brown, 3 to 5 minutes. Transfer to the lined rack to drain. Let cool completely before serving.

Makes 10 to 12 pies

FOR THE CRUST

2 cups all-purpose flour

2 teaspoons sugar

1 teaspoon Diamond Crystal kosher salt

½ cup chilled shortening, cut into small pieces

½ cup cold whole milk, or as needed

FOR THE FILLING

16 ounces blackberries (about 3 cups)

1 cup sugar

Juice of ½ lemon

Half of a 1.75-ounce packet light pectin

FOR ASSEMBLY

All-purpose flour, for rolling

Egg wash: 1 egg beaten with 1 teaspoon water

Peanut oil, for frying

COCONUT CAKE

Makes one 9 × 13-inch cake
(20 to 24 servings)

FOR THE CAKE

Cooking spray and flour, for
 the pan

One 15- to 16-ounce box white
 cake mix plus ½ cup

3 large egg whites

1⅓ cups water

½ cup vegetable oil

½ teaspoon almond extract

FOR THE TOPPING

14 ounces sweetened condensed
 milk, preferably Eagle brand

7.5 ounces (half a can)
 sweetened cream of coconut,
 preferably Coco López

8 ounces frozen whipped
 topping (preferably Cool
 Whip), thawed

Two 6-ounce bags Bird's Eye
 frozen coconut flakes, thawed

When Patrick was a little boy and we'd come home to Corinth, Mississippi, he loved his grandmother's coconut cakes. They are the traditional round three-layered cakes that most women in the area typically made. I eventually started making mine as a sheet cake, and when Patrick opened Martin's, I wouldn't let him serve it because I was afraid he wouldn't make it right. So I would bake ten coconut sheet cakes and Danny and I would drive them up from Memphis each Saturday for him to serve. They would sell out before supper on most Saturdays, and it got to a point where folks would put in orders days ahead for a whole cake. After a while I just couldn't keep up, so I let Pat and Bo start making them at the restaurant, and they turn out just fine. —**PAM MARTIN**

MAKE THE CAKE

Position a rack in the center of the oven and preheat the oven to 300°F. Mist a 9 × 13-inch cake pan with cooking spray and lightly flour, then tap out the excess.

In a large bowl, with an electric mixer, beat the cake mix, egg whites, water, vegetable oil, and almond extract until just combined. Evenly spread the mixture into the cake pan.

Bake until a toothpick inserted comes out clean, about 30 minutes.

MEANWHILE, MAKE THE TOPPING

In a small bowl, combine the condensed milk and cream of coconut.

While the cake is still hot, poke holes over the entire cake with a fork. Evenly pour the milk mixture over the top and allow it to sink into the cake.

Once the cake is cooled and saturated with the milk mixture, spread the whipped topping evenly over the cake. Sprinkle evenly with the coconut flakes. Slice and serve.

TANDY'S WATERMELON
WITH MINT AND PEPPER FLAKES

At every family gathering, we always had slices of watermelon on the table, and we always seasoned the watermelon with salt (which is a common thing around the Mississippi/Tennessee border). A few years ago, my buddy Tandy Wilson served me a watermelon dish with mint on it at his Nashville restaurant, City House, and I loved that combination, especially with a little heat from red pepper flakes.

Arrange the watermelon on a serving platter. Sprinkle with the salt, mint, and pepper flakes and serve.

4 servings

4 large watermelon wedges (about ½ inch thick)

1 teaspoon fleur de sel or other flaky salt

¼ cup chopped fresh mint

2 teaspoons red pepper flakes

BUTTERMILK BISCUITS
[AND STRAWBERRY SHORTCAKE]

12 to 14 biscuits

FOR THE BISCUITS

2 cups self-rising flour, plus more for kneading

¼ cup plus 1 tablespoon shortening

¾ cup buttermilk, preferably whole (see Note)

Vegetable oil, for the skillet

Melted butter or vegetable shortening, for brushing the biscuits

FOR SERVING AS STRAWBERRY SHORTCAKES

Fresh strawberries (¼ cup per person)

Sugar

Heavy cream, whipped (a big dollop per person)

NOTE If you can't find whole buttermilk, add a splash of heavy cream to low-fat (1%) or light (1.5%) buttermilk.

At my mom's house (and Maw-Maw's before her), there are always fresh buttermilk biscuits on the table at breakfast time. My Uncle Mike likes crusty biscuits, so Maw-Maw would make him drop biscuits, which have more crunch. I've included instructions for this technique below, as well as classic biscuits made with a cutter (or, in my mom's case, a tomato paste can). Most pastry chefs will tell you to punch biscuit dough straight, instead of turning and twisting. I disagree. Twisting as you punch out the rounds makes a taller, fluffier biscuit in my experience.

She would also whip these up and serve them as strawberry shortcakes—you slice up as many fresh strawberries as you want, toss them with sugar, and serve it all with whipped cream.

MAKE THE BISCUITS

Pour the flour into a bowl. Add the shortening and use a pastry cutter or two knives to cut the shortening into the flour until it's the size of small pebbles. Add the buttermilk and stir until blended. Turn the dough onto a lightly floured surface and knead several times, until smooth. Bake the biscuits until golden brown, about 10 minutes. Serve warm.

TO MAKE DROP BISCUITS

Preheat the oven to 475°F. Grease a large cast-iron skillet with oil. Use the middle three fingers of your hand (or a ⅓-cup measuring cup) to scoop 12 portions of dough onto the prepared skillet, spacing them about ½ inch apart. Brush the tops with melted butter or shortening. Don't crowd the pan; bake in batches if necessary.

TO MAKE SHAPED BISCUITS

Preheat the oven to 475°F. With a rolling pin, roll the dough out to make a round about ½ inch thick. Using a 2-inch biscuit cutter or can, punch the dough into rounds, twisting the cutter as you go. Re-roll the scraps and repeat. Arrange the biscuits in the skillet, leaving about ½ inch of space between them, again baking in batches rather than crowding them if necessary. Brush the tops with melted butter or shortening. Bake the biscuits until golden brown, about 10 minutes. Serve warm.

FOR STRAWBERRY SHORTCAKES

You can do this all by eye and to taste, but hull and slice up the strawberries and place in a bowl. Add sugar to taste—I like 3 tablespoons per pound of berries—and let it sit until the natural syrup comes out, at least 10 minutes.

Whip the cream until it's at the fluffiness you like.

Split a biscuit open, top with ¼ cup strawberries and some of its syrup, and top with a dollop of whipped cream. Repeat as much as you want.

HAND-CRANKED
VANILLA ICE CREAM

Hand-cranked ice cream used to be a common thing to make in the South, but over time folks began using the new machines with electric motors. These things suck! Most of them have a clutch in the motor that will shut it down too soon, which means they never get the ice cream hard enough. Instead, you are left with this soupy mixture that is already half melted before you get set to eat it, or you have to pack it and stick it in the freezer for a day before you get to enjoy it. In my opinion, that's why most people don't make ice cream at home anymore.

My family still makes it the old way . . . but we take it to another level. The recipe for the ice cream base is uncooked, and exceptionally easy. It's the rest of it that's a team effort. Making ice cream is a tradition we repeat every summer, and it involves every member of the family: My mom, my daughter, Daisy, and Aunt Cathy make the ice cream base, then bring it out to our carport, where my sons, uncles, and dad have set up our old 4-quart White Mountain hand-crank ice cream maker (which are harder and harder to find; if you see one, buy it!). Once the bucket is tightly packed with ice, the fun begins.

The youngest kid in the family (these days my son Walker) gets the first turn on the crank, when the ice cream base is at its loosest. When his arm tires out, he tags off to the next oldest (Wyatt, my older son), and so on up through the family ranks. As the ice cream freezes, the cranking becomes more labored, and by the time I get my turn, about 30 minutes into the process, I'm using every ounce of my strength to move the handle, even sitting on the machine to get more leverage. But the payoff is so worth it: Where most electric-cranked ice cream is soft and soupy, ours is as hard as a carton you'd pull out of the supermarket freezer. After the final turn of the crank, we dig into our thick, icy reward, topping our bowls with sugared peaches or strawberries.

Our secret lies in three things: how you handle the ice, the salt we use, and the fact that we crank it until none of us can crank the bastard anymore. The traditional method for making hand-cranked ice cream is to fill the bucket with ice cubes and rock salt, which leaves large air pockets around the ice cream cannister and never gets it cold enough to completely freeze. Our method calls for using loads of crushed ice. We freeze water in half-gallon milk or orange juice cartons, then carefully smack the frozen blocks against the pavement until they're crushed into tiny shards. We pack layers of ice into the bucket along with a liberal amount of iodized table salt, creating a solid cylinder of ice that completely encases the canister. I credit this approach to Pa-Pa, my paternal grandfather, who was an insanely talented man and had an exceptional engineering mind. You can certainly make the same base and freeze it in an electric ice cream maker, but it won't ever be as good as hand-cranked.

(recipe continues)

Makes about 1 gallon

2¾ cups granulated sugar

1 tablespoon all-purpose flour

¼ teaspoon kosher salt

6 large eggs

12 ounces evaporated milk

1 tablespoon pure vanilla extract

1 quart whole milk

2½ cups iodized table salt

Sugared Fruit (recipe follows), for serving

A day or two before you make the ice cream, prepare the ice: Fill 5 clean half-gallon milk or orange juice cartons with water, fold the tops closed, and place them on the lowest (coldest) part of your freezer until they're frozen solid.

To make the ice cream base, in a large bowl, whisk together the sugar, flour, and salt. Add the eggs and use an electric mixer to beat until well combined. Add the evaporated milk and vanilla and stir to combine. If you're not making ice cream right away, refrigerate the base until ready to use.

Remove the ice from the freezer and hold one carton sideways over a concrete surface. Smack one side of the carton firmly on the concrete, then rotate it a quarter-turn and smack the next side. Repeat until you've smacked each side twice, or until you can hear that all of the ice block has been shattered into small, powdery shards.

Pour the ice cream base into the canister of a hand-crank ice cream maker and add whole milk until the liquid reaches about 3 inches from the top; you may not end up using the whole quart. Insert the dasher (the blades that do the churning), attach the top, and insert the crank. Add one carton of crushed ice to the bucket, then sprinkle about ½ cup of the table salt on top of the ice. Repeat, packing each layer of ice down as you go, until you've filled the bucket tightly with ice and it's slightly mounded over the brim; this should take 4 to 5 cartons of ice.

Drape a couple of kitchen towels over the top of the bucket; this will both insulate the ice below and provide a bit of cushion for your behind—if you, like us, end up sitting on the thing to get it to crank in the end. Churn the ice cream, slowly and steadily, packing in more ice and salt as needed to keep the bucket full. After 15 minutes or so, the ice cream will be semi-frozen and the cranking will get more difficult. Continue cranking until the ice cream is so firm that you can barely move the crank. In my family, this takes about 30 minutes total, and in my family, it takes the power of two boys and a few grown men.

Remove the top of the ice cream maker and check the ice cream's texture. It should be firm and compact, similar to commercial ice cream pulled straight from the freezer.

Serve the ice cream with sugared fruit and immediately freeze any leftovers in an airtight storage container.

(recipe continues)

SUGARED FRUIT

4 to 6 servings

1 pound strawberries,
  blackberries, or peaches
3 tablespoons sugar
Finely grated zest and juice of
  1 lemon

If using strawberries, hull and slice them. If using peaches, peel and thinly slice them.

In a medium bowl, combine the fruit, sugar, lemon zest, and lemon juice and toss to combine well. Cover and set aside at room temperature for at least 30 minutes. Toss occasionally.

Serve with the ice cream.

RESOURCES

BURN BARREL (GRAINGER.COM): If possible, buy a new 55-gallon steel drum for making your burn barrel. You can buy these from building supply stores or industrial supply companies such as W. W. Grainger.

CHIMNEY STARTER (WEBER.COM): I love the durability of the Weber Rapidfire Chimney Starter, but whatever chimney starter you use, make sure it has ventilation holes on the side of the chimney, which will help the coals light quickly and burn evenly.

COOLERS AND COMFY CHAIRS (YETI.COM): Yes, I'm a brand ambassador, but only because they make the best. I also love their insulated wine glasses for drinking around the pit.

HAM STOCKINETTES (SAUSAGEMAKER .COM): Also called ham bags or ham socks, I use a triple layer of 36-inch socks. These usually come ten to a package, but they're cheap, so buy extra just in case.

HOGS (USDA.GOV): The USDA website can direct you to pork-processing plants in your area.

ICE CREAM MAKERS: To make ice cream like my family does, you need a 4-quart hand-cranked ice cream maker (the electric versions won't cut it). We use an old White Mountain model (whitemountainproducts.com), but they've stopped making hand-cranked machines, so if you can't find one, look for one made by Immergood (myimmergood.com).

MARTIN'S BAR·B·QUE RUBS AND SAUCES (MARTINSBBQJOINT.COM): If you don't want to make your own, you can order all of my prepared rubs and sauces online.

MEAT HOOKS (SAUSAGEMAKER.COM): I use a variety of meat hooks in my smokehouse and for aging cold-smoked meats.

PIT AND GRILLING GLOVES (AMAZON.COM): For working around the pit and grill, I use neoprene Schwer BBQ Grill gloves, which are waterproof and heatproof up to 932°F.

SAUSAGE BAGS (BUTCHERSUPPLYCOMPANY .COM): For making sock sausage, I use 2-pound white or red stitch cloth bags.

ACKNOWLEDGMENTS

Dadgum, this may be the easiest and the hardest part about putting this book together. I really don't know how to condense my feelings and gratitude to those who have made such an impact on my life and my story. So I'm just going to sling it all up at the wall.

First, I'm thankful to God for blessing me with the skill set that He's given me, and the opportunity to experience what this life has to offer. I don't deserve it.

Mom and Dad, I don't have the space here to list all that I'd like to. Mom, your love for me will always be a cornerstone in my life, a deep-down comfort that I know is always there, no matter what. Dad, your example of how you carry yourself as a man is what I love about you the most. Your integrity, character, and hard work will always be what shapes me. I wanted to be you, in every way, when I was a kid, but you showed how to be myself and follow my own path. I gave you both so many reasons to give up on me, but you didn't. You believed in me and my potential, many times when virtually no one else did. You taught me to never quit and always believe in possibility, no matter how big the dream or how difficult the solution to a problem is. Because of that, I've never worried about "can it happen" and instead focus on how to solve the puzzle. Without the two of you and your love, guidance, and support, I really don't know where I would be in life.

Martha, you are such a rock. As with Mom and Dad, you also believed in me when I didn't even believe in myself. You were the one person who truly pushed me to pursue this crazy barbecue dream of mine. You've taken such great care of me and supported me. I truly can't think of a better mother to our children, which has enabled me to work and build this life, and for that I am forever grateful to you. I can't thank you enough for being the wife that you are. I love you.

Wyatt, Daisy, and Walker: You will never understand how much your lives mean to me. You will never know how much I love you—ever. I don't know why God chose to bless Martha and me with each of you, but I know at least for me that I didn't deserve you. I'm so thankful for each of you, so blessed to have you, and so excited about your futures. Stay strong in your faith and your dreams and never let anyone or anything distract you from them! Thank you for loving me and letting me be your dad.

Buzzy and Sharon, thanks for being great in-laws. You've been such a help to Martha and our home life, which in turn has been a big help for me to operate our restaurants. Buzzy, thanks for fixing up that old shed years ago and fashioning our smokehouse. I appreciate all the winter mornings you fired it for me very much.

Mr. Harold Thomas, I wish you were here to read this. Without you I wouldn't be typing this right now. Thank you from the bottom of my heart for teaching me how to cook *real* pit barbecue. You were so kind and gentle, and so giving of your time. Thank you for letting me hang around Thomas & Webb BBQ, and for answering all of my questions. I wish I had come to see you before you passed and for that I am so sorry. My favorite sandwich has been, and always will be, the whole hog sandwiches that you used to make me.

Bryan (Ball), John, and Michael: It's been a heck of a ride from that first hog we cooked in Kossuth back in 1991. Whether it was that hog or when you worked for free on weekends to help me open Martin's Bar-B-Que Joint, you boys have always been there for me.

Shannon Sewell, thanks for stealing and hauling those bricks from the new Freed-Hardeman gym site. Without you we wouldn't have had a pit with which to cook our first hog, and for that I'm appreciative.

Jim Chandler, thanks for letting me build a pit at your house. More important, thanks for taking me in when Freed kicked me out of school. I miss you.

John Willingham, thank you for letting me in your world for a year or so in the late '90s and letting me learn your perspectives. Memphis in 1998 was an unforgettable year for me.

Bo Collier, I'll always be indebted to you for helping me open Martin's. Brother, you are a walking enigma and I love you for it. I still have an alarm on my phone at 4:50 p.m. so you can hit your pipe, and so we can get through service without me wanting to hit you in the head with a pit shovel. Thanks man, I love you.

Marteen Garcia Pimentel, my kid brother, you've been with me way before opening Martin's. We've laid a lot of sod and cooked a lot of meat together. You've never asked me for anything other than my friendship, and you'll always have it. *Gracias por tu lealtad Camarino!*

Ward Boone, gosh man, thanks for manning the cash register so I could get on the line, and for being a spiritual friend and mentor. Thanks for being a living testimony to your faith and walking your walk.

Cho-Cho, you were there to load meat or prep no matter how early or late it was, and you are still one of the best line cooks I've ever seen. Thanks, *hermano*!

Roberto, you've been with me since 2007 and you're still here. I'm so grateful for you.

Brad Nelson, I was so broke I couldn't pay attention and you gave me a line of credit when you probably shouldn't have. You are not just my banker, but my friend.

Mike Bodnar, if Harold Thomas showed me how to cook pit barbecue, you showed me how to run not just a restaurant, but a *business.* That day you walked in my little kitchen (uninvited) to ask me how I cut my French fries almost got you thrown out, but I'm so glad you did it. Your mentorship and instruction on how to operate a restaurant the way one *should* be operated will always be the guiding map on how I run any business I'm involved in. The attention to daily operational details is truly the single most important ingredient in the recipe of being successful. Everything from you coming over on a Sunday in 2010 to work the fry station to get us out of the weeds, to us walking miles in Iowa chasing pheasants and bobwhites . . . I cherish those memories and lessons.

Kizer, what can I say? Thanks for getting my back and working so hard. I'm sorry for being mean to you in the dorms at Freed (even though I have no recollection of that). But if I was, your ass shouldn't have been up so late keeping me and everybody else on the floor up with all your mischief.

John Haire, thank you for being an incredible wingman. Thank you even more for your character and example.

To the rest of the Martin's staff, I don't know how to begin here. Andrew, Kelsey, Blake, Grace, Hal, my general managers, management, longtime staff, and so many more: You've all been such an integral part of our success in your own way, whether it was the restaurants, events, this book, or beyond. I'll always owe y'all way more than 0.143 percent of the rest of that bottle of pét-nat, and way more of my thanks!

To all of the Martin's guests who've spent their hard-earned money to eat my food, thank you so much for your support; you'll really never know what a big deal it is to us.

To Nolensville: You'll always be our roots.

To all of my guests through the years who have supported Martins Bar-B-Que Joint and Hugh-Baby's BBQ & Burger Shop, you will never comprehend how much it has meant to me and my family. Thank you for all your support. I owe you all a debt I can never repay.

Jim Myers and Bill Ramsey, I'm so glad the two of you drove way out to Nolensville to eat with me that day way back in 2007. Jim, your fingerprints will always be on this book, and Bill, thanks for keeping me right with the law.

Francis, first, thank you for your friendship over the years. Second, I don't know why you believed in me for this project, but thank you so much for doing so, and thank you for all of your patience, man. I hope I've made you proud!

Nick, I know you've wanted to pull your hair out at times while writing this thing with me, but thanks for being my wingman.

Andy, your photographs spoke to my story like no one else could have.

Randi Anglin, thanks for all your pics in the early days of this journey. I'll always be indebted to you. Lerma, thanks for all of the barbecue lifestyle shots you've taken for me over the years; you are one gifted S.O.B.!

Blake Morgan, thank you so much for taking the crazy design ideas in my head and putting them to paper! The illustrations you provided for this book are incredible!

Tamie Renay, you are like a sister to me, thanks for taking the time to work on my recipes.

David Black, you are the best. So many conversations we've had were about life and family, not the business of the book. Thanks for being so genuine.

Mackey, Cedrick, Keith Jones, and Steve Wilbanks: Thanks so much for all your help shooting this book—it was much greater than y'all will probably ever realize.

Trevor, you are an inspiration and one of the most gifted chefs I've ever met; thank you for cooking in our family pasture.

Team YETI and Leigh Ann Bakunis, I can't thank you enough for your support over the years. You are and will always be the very best in the game!

Tandy, Tyler, Jason: That 2006 to 2007 stretch, when we all opened our spots and TB took the helm at Capitol, seems like yesterday. Man, we were young.

Thanks for letting an overgrown, immature, and complicated barbecue guy not just be your friend, but a close family friend. Through all of the meals we've cooked, all the meals we've shared, and all of the laughs with our wives and families, you boys have always supported me, and it means a lot to me.

John Egerton, thanks for the smokehouse memories, the talks over whole-hog sandwiches, and for being an example of what we should strive to be as folks from the South. I can see your loving smile right now.

Thank you to the barbecue community, starting with my roots: Zach and Daryl. Thanks for keeping the West Tennessee whole-hog barbecue flame alive. I'm proud to be a part of this thing we have, and I cherish our friendship. And then there are my fellow pitmasters around the country. I look up to so many of you, and you aren't even aware of it. Whether it's at the Big Apple BBQ, Southern Smoke, Memphis in May, South Beach Food & Wine, or all the other events we do each year, we are so fortunate to spend time with one another like we do, and you've given me some of my favorite memories. Mike Mills, thank you for the example you set for all of us pitmasters, and

for teaching us that no matter our success, we are to always remain humble.

My buddies: Thanks for being there, fellas. Your laughs and ball-busting have worked like WD-40 in my life, making the good times great and the bad times smoother. Ball, John, Michael, Tracy Jarrell, Bill the Greek, Sam Jones, Mackey, Ced, Hutch, Billy Durney, Piller, Hal, Toddy, JJ, Teddy . . . gosh, I know I'm missing a few. The next round is on me, boys.

Tuck, Stephen, and Kipp, thank you so much for all the bottles and all the fires together. I love you boys. Andrew, Kelly, and Adam, y'all are like extended family to me. Thank you so much for all of the meals and wine at Scribe, and a special thanks for letting me shoot part of this book there—what a magical place.

Coach Clark and Bobby Bush, you believed in me, for what reason I don't know.

To all the teachers, principals, coaches, deans, cops, and judges whom I've infuriated over the years: I'm really sorry (well, kinda). Thanks for being a part of my story; you were the sandpaper that helped round me out.

My baby sister, Mary: I love you and will always be here for you.

INDEX

Copyright © 2022 by Pat Martin
Photographs © 2022 by Andrew Thomas Lee

Published in the United States by Clarkson Potter/
Publishers, an imprint of Random House,
a division of Penguin Random House LLC,
New York. clarksonpotter.com

CLARKSON POTTER is a trademark
and **POTTER** with colophon is a registered
trademark of Penguin Random House LLC.

Library of Congress
Cataloging-in-Publication Data
Names: Martin, Pat, 1972- author. | Fauchald,
Nick, author.
Title: Life of fire : mastering the arts of
pit-cooked barbecue, the grill, and the
smokehouse / Pat Martin and Nick Fauchald,
Andrew Thomas Lee (photographer).
Description: New York, New York : Clarkson
Potter/Publishers, 2022. | Includes index.
Identifiers: LCCN 2021029082 (print) | LCCN
2021029083 (ebook) | ISBN 9781984826121 (hardcover) |
ISBN 9781984826138 (ebook)
Subjects: LCSH: Barbecuing. | Roasting (Cooking) |
LCGFT: Cookbooks.
Classification: LCC TX840.B3 M37 2022 (print) | LCC
TX840.B3 (ebook) | DDC 641.5/784—dc23
LC record available at lccn.loc.gov/2021029082
LC ebook record available at lccn.loc.gov/2021029083

ISBN 978-1-9848-2612-1
Ebook ISBN 978-1-9848-2613-8

Printed in China

Photographer: Andrew Thomas Lee
Illustrator: Blake Morgan
Editor: Francis Lam
Editorial assistants: Lydia O'Brien and Darian Keels
Designer: Mia Johnson
Production editor: Abby Oladipo
Compositors: Hannah Hunt and Nick Patton
Copy editor: Kate Slate
Indexer: Elizabeth Parson
Marketer: Samantha Simon
Publicist: Kristin Casemore

10 9 8 7 6 5 4 3 2 1
First Edition

"Cinder blocks, pits, split logs, and hot coals are the roots of barbecue and the lifeblood of Pat Martin. He's a true friend with an old-school soul and has barbecue knowledge second to none. Do you have a pit big enough to handle his barbecue inspiration? You soon will."

—CHRIS LILLY

"Pat Martin has delivered the most important book on cooking over live fire in decades. *Life of Fire* illuminates it all, from coal beds to home-built pits (in minutes!) to simple, delicious recipes, and enough whole hog know-how to impress the weekend warriors without intimidating newcomers."

—ANDREW ZIMMERN

"*Life of Fire* is quite simply the most practical and profound barbecue bible to date. As Pat Martin walks us through the differences between spit, block pit, smokehouse, hog-in-the-ground, and open-pit preparations, the connection between West Tennessee barbecue joints and our earliest ancestors who controlled fire seasons the journey."

—ALICE RANDALL

"*Life of Fire* will change how you feel about barbecue forever. I can smell and taste the history on these pages and can't wait to fire up the spits and dig even deeper into this love letter to proper barbecue."

—MICHAEL SYMON

"When true legends share their lives with us you stop, listen, and tend to the fire and coals like God is watching. Pat Martin is my higher power for hog cookery."

—MATTY MATHESON

"I've eaten at as many barbecue joints as anyone across the nation, and I can get down with anybody when it comes to cookin' meat low and slow, hot and fast, you name it. But DDD O.G. Pat Martin is an old-school pitmaster whose West Tennessee style is at the very foundation of what it means to cook over coals. *Life of Fire* is about as close as most of us will get to the true soul and tradition of pit barbecue."

—GUY FIERI

"Pat Martin's passion for his craft and the legend he has become in the barbecue world is inspiring. He's a magician who can coax flavor out of the simplest ingredients."

—MANEET CHAUHAN